Opinions on the book *Communities Dominate Brands:*

Already into its second printing, the global bestseller is being tranlsated into four languages: Korean, Japanese, German and Finnish; with more to come

"This is a great book with a key message for our business about engagement. Consumers want a relationship with companies and they want - indeed expect - to be treated with care and respect. This book has changed the way we look at our business and our relationship with our customers. Good research, background and case study examples including where it can all go wrong. Very Good Book."
Rob Castle, Managing Director, Korg UK

"This book provides a comprehensive understanding as to why business, media and customers will never be the same again; where interrupting audiences and one-way flows of marketing communications are things of the past."
Rishad Tobaccowala, Chief Innovation Officer, Publicis Groupe Media USA

"This book clearly identifies the significant issues facing the audio-visual industry and the impact these have on commercial broadcasting."
John Ranelagh - Vice President TV2 Norway, former Commissioner of the ITC

"While the new media do offer companies new opportunities to communicate with their customers, their principal effect is to provide customers with many more ways of communicating with each other. This book is invaluable in predicting how the power to make and break brands will soon reside far more with ordinary people than with company budget holders."
Rory Sutherland, Vice Chairman & Creative Director, OgilvyOne UK

"The authors understand how living in a converging mobile world introduces threats to your business model from a wide range of competitors, and then the book gives concrete examples of how to survive, which is why I recommend you read this book."
Kazutomo Robert Hori, CEO, Cybird Japan

"Wake up. Get inspired. Understand the change that's happening in the world of marketing. And the change in consumer behaviour. Marketing communications today and in the future should not be interruptive, it should be creative, engaging, entertaining, conversational and personal, be it in mass media or in the mobile device in someone's jeans pocket. Showing respect to the consumers is your first step towards success, the consumer now truly holds the power.Read this book."
Ami Hasan, Chairman and Chief Creative Officer, hasan & partners Finland

"The authors vividly illustrate the rapidly growing power of digital communities with examples of real cases where companies have achieved considerable business success by being creative and engaging customers."
Harry Drnec, Managing Director Red Bull UK

Communities Dominate Brands

Business and Marketing Challenges for the 21st Century

By
Tomi T Ahonen and Alan Moore

website www.futuretext.com

Copyright 2005 futuretext Limited
Issue Date 20 March 2005
second printing November 2005
Published by
futuretext
36 St George Street
Mayfair 
London
W1S 2FW
UK
Email: info@futuretext.com
www.futuretext.com

ISBN: 0-9544327-3-8

Contents

Chapter 3 – Business entities transforming **29**
From dinosaur to puma
TV, music, airlines, sports, newspapers, telecoms

        Tomi T Ahonen & Alan Moore

Contents

Chapter 6 – Delivery channels splintering   81
Battle of the channels
Newsagents, department stores, video rental, internet, TV

Contents

Chapter 9 – Generation-C

The Connected Community

Text messaging, fashion, gaming, politics, dating, telecoms

            Tomi T Ahonen & Alan Moore

Chapter 10 – Advertising in crisis   155
If we say it just one more time
Television, advertising, music, movies

Chapter 13 – Communities dominate brands   207
Companies from Mars, Customers from Venus
Newsmedia, automobiles, tourist guides, IT, wineries

Tomi T Ahonen & Alan Moore

Contents

Foreword

A few weeks ago I was visiting The Harvard Business School as a guest lecturer and during a break was sitting in Spangler Hall reviewing *Tomi Ahonen's* and *Alan Moore's* powerful new book, Communities Dominate Brands, when I looked up at the dozens of groups chatting away and wondered: "What the hell are these students going to do with this insight and opportunity? Should I even share it with them at the risk of blowing their finely tuned minds? Or maybe they'll dive into their first post-grad job determined to implement such bold directions." So I shared some of Moore and Ahonen's thoughts later in the lecture hall. There wasn't one student who didn't believe that they were not a member of a virtual connected community. Soon we'll see what they do with it as leaders.

Five years ago, in January 2000, I became Chief Marketing Officer of The Coca-Cola Company – at the height of the dot-com craze and fresh out of Japan where I had lived and worked for the previous six years. When I arrived in Japan there wasn't a cell phone to be found but a year later DoCoMo introduced them for the price of one yen (and a hefty monthly fee) and a few months later they had 60% penetration. Months later the Georgia Coffee team and DoCoMo introduced the 'ring tone down load' concept using the famous Georgia Coffee jingle that took the country by storm. At about the same time internet use soared from a few after hours office workers to a national phenomenon. We played outside the traditional marketing box with some entry level internet marketing promotions which unintentionally started a dialogue with six million consumers! Wireless cellular technology and the internet forever changed the consumer and our approach to marketing in Japan. And it reshaped my own mental model of how to engage in a relationship with consumers.

As the new CMO facing an unprecedented period of change, I asked Anne Chambers – our resident enthusiast – to search for best-in-class examples of how the others were engaging in what I had experienced in Japan, and surprisingly we found them either unaware or so fearful that they would lose control of the brand message that many had actually banned the use of the internet as a marketing tool. Only a few were experimenting but they were operating in the world of wireless technology. I had read some of Alan's material and found a sense of excitement that validated my own intuition that the virtual community I saw developing in Japan couldn't be stopped; mustn't be stopped. One of my closest advisors, Nick Donatiello, CEO of Odyssey, who was an early pioneer of internet research and a brilliant strategist, gave the best advice possible. "Just jump into the dialogue. Let's see where it takes us."

It is difficult to put a lens on a developing social trend moving as fast as 'connected communities' but Alan and Tomi have done that. Together they have made a rare and important breakthrough insight, have developed a credible hypothesis and backed it up with validated supporting points. This is not radical misinformed extremist hype. This work is an accurate description of the issue, the opportunity and the crisis confronting marketers if they don't cut loose the shackles of the traditional advertising agency and TV network model and explore the world of possibilities recommended by this book.

Move quickly but act thoughtfully, even slowly. You want to implement this without sending your organisation into a tailspin. The traditional marketing company that wastes its investments solely on TV advertising is underpinned by bureaucratic values of safety, efficiency and control. The marketing group that embraces these insights and moves forward to implement them is underpinned by interdependent values of sharing, listening, equity rights, global harmony and synergy. That's a big leap. Tomi and Alan are not proposing a process tweak but a mindset shift, one that requires an evolution of values and a transfusion of talent. Their thinking is visionary. To succeed with this model you need to line up your organisation's vision with the prerequisite values and talent. Do it. But do it thoughtfully so that everyone understands and believes the plot first. You'll succeed with lightning speed if you do. You risk crashing and burning if you don't.

I am a believer in Alan and Tomi's insight and forecast. The consumer and their connected communities, selecting the products and brands that are engaged in the most relevant dialogue with them, is the centre of any modern and sustainable marketing model. Wireless technology has enabled the consumer to review and reject much of the one-way messaging they receive and re-sort the dialogue that's relevant to fit the way they live. Experiencing a Coke or interacting with an enthusiastic Coke employee online or in person has always been far more motivating than 30 seconds of anthemic brand worshipping. It's not that TV and radio programmes are irrelevant. It's the lack of ability to develop a relationship with an ad that makes the medium a less viable marketing tool.

Books on business and marketing are launched weekly. Most are weak adaptations of other people's thoughts. Some authors, like Sergio Zyman, Seth Godin, Scott Bedbury and Marc Gobe, have made bold and meaningful interpretations of contemporary opportunities and helped me to clarify a new advanced perspective on how to be a more successful marketer. Tomi and Alan have done that and, with Communities Dominate Brands will end up shaping our thinking and approach for some time.

Stephen C Jones

"In life you throw a ball. You hope it will reach a wall and bounce back so you can throw it again. You hope your friends will provide that wall."

Pablo Picasso

Acknowledgements

This book is a collective volume combining numerous concurrent trends and themes. Therefore, we have been influenced by a remarkably wide range of experts from diverse fields and areas.

First and foremost we must thank Axel Chaldecott, the chairman of SMLXL, who helped us right from the start when we were planning this book and Axel's influence is in every chapter. We have gained enormously from Jouko Ahvenainen of Xtract in understanding social networking, and from Adriana Cronin-Lucas and Perry DeHavilland of the Big Blog Company about blogging and the power of the blogosphere.

Many experts helped us understand the various technologies. In this area we want to mention Minna Rotko, Matti Tossavainen of Elisa, Tarja Sutton, Ukko Lappalainen, Jochen Metzner of Nokia, Rick Pryor, Stefan Ciesielski and Eva Remerie of Siemens, Anders Dalenstram of Ericsson, Mike Beeston and Olof Schybergson of Fjord, Paul May of Verista and Tom Hume of Future Platforms.

Then we needed to understand marketing, branding, broadcast and advertising. In this field we want to mention Brian Jacobs of Millward Brown, Tim Birt of Osborne Clarke, Mandy Merron of Willott Kingston Smith, John Ranelagh, Adam Singer, Simon Waugh, Mike Smallwood, John Nolan of North One Television, Steve Yeomans, Ross Sleight, Keith Pardy, Myra Landsburg, David O'Hanlon, Ant Liow and Jason Coward, Alan Mitchell, Maddie Hamill, Timi Petersen of hasan & partners, Kate Whalley and Adrian Bailey of People Fan Club, Moira Clark at the Cranfield School of Management, Andrew Swinnard and Rishad Tobaccowala of StarCom Media, Robin Price, Ebba Dåhli, Paavo Aro, Teija Hyttinen, Minna Sainio, Tuula Putkinen, Arja Suominen, Lauri Kivinen of Nokia, Mike Short of O2, Adam Foster of Frost & Sullivan, Joe Grunenwald of Clarion University, and our friend Sara Melkko.

Finally, the most difficult area for us was understanding communities, and in this dramatically developing area we want to thank Teppo Turkki of Elisa, Timo Kasper of Observer, Ilkka Pukkila, Helena Hekku Kahanpää, Russell Anderson, Janne Laiho, Nicole Cham, Paolo Puppoli, Marjatta Forsberg of Nokia, Taina Kalliokoski of TeliaSonera, Voytek Siewierski of NTT DoCoMo, Steve Chan of M1, Steve Jones of the3GPortal, Peter Holland of Oxford University, Matti Makkonen of Finnet, Mark Curtis of Fjord, Kimmo Kiviluoto of Xtract and Greg Chaplan of Clear.

There were numerous authors who influenced us through their writing. We were particularly guided by the thinking of *Howard Rheingold* in his book Smart Mobs, *John Grant* After Image, *Clayton Christiansen* The Innovator's Dilemma, *Timo Kopomaa* The City In Your Pocket, *John Beck & Mitchell Wade* Got Game, *Chan Kim and Renée Mauborgone* of INSEAD, *Alan Mitchell* Right Side Up and The New Bottom Line. *Tom Peters* Re-imagine, *Gary Hamel* Leading the Revolution. And, in a style of his own, we've enjoyed the humour of *Scott Adams's* the Dilbert Future.

We want to thank Ajit Jaokar of futuretext for his assistance and patience in the planning and production of this book.

Finally we want to thank our families for their continuing support in this demanding project. Alan would like to thank his long-suffering partner Tricia, for years of understanding, hard work and the patience of a saint, his children Richard, Emma and Josef, and Axel Chaledecott and Ami Hasan, for being the first to give the opportunity to try out his theories in a commercial environment. Tomi for his part to thank Ulla Brans; Tiina, Jon, Ere (19), Katariina, Maria, Heikki; Ruud; Luca, Leo, Timotei, Hanna, Jukka (Hifki!); Timo, Olli, Salla, Outi; Robert, Mary and Salvatore Abiuso, Jari, Inkeri, Iiris, Aamos; Terttu-täti and Kari; Pirjo, Roni, Kris, Petteri; Kimi Finell. And in memoriam Jan W Brans.

We welcome feedback for this book. Please send it to communities@futuretext.com

Tomi T Ahonen & Alan Moore

"When written in Chinese the word crisis is composed of two characters.
One represents danger and the other represents opportunity"

John F Kennedy

I

Introduction
On the Road to Engagement

If the last 10 years have caused disruption in your business, the next 10 years will cause much more so. Not driven by a controlled introduction of new technologies, but by an uncontrolled adoption of new, radical, unpredictable and even "unfair" methods by an emerging new element in consumption – the *digitally empowered community*. Digitalisation and the falling costline of technology have ripped through our business and social fabrics over the last five years, across all industries, across all countries, altering our economic and social landscapes forever. Yet what we have witnessed so far is only the beginning of a more profound, *seismic shift* in the very foundations of how business is conducted. We can imagine and do things which were just not possible a few years ago. Life-threatening or life-enhancing? This is what this book is about; the Red pill or the Blue pill? Which one are you going to take? One thing is for sure: the structured order of our familiar industrial age has come to an end and it's dying as days do, gasping for every last ray of light.

All the rules are changing

Now, the Age of Connectedness and its newly active communities are altering the way all businesses will market, promote and sell their goods and services. The very first cases are emerging simultaneously around the world, and they clearly give an answer to what the marketing industry has expressed for several years already. Traditional methods of marketing, advertising and branding are increasingly in effective. Something new is happening, only we could not put our fingers on it. Not yet. Not until this book.

Phillip Evans and Thomas S. Wurster state in their book *Blown to Bits* that digitalisation is "deconstructing" traditional industries such as home electronics, business, broadcast, retailing and banking, while at the same time creating new commercial opportunities such as Google and eBay, the low-cost airline industry, online banking, or Closed Audience Networks. These are trends echoed time and again by experts analysing the individual phenomena such as digital convergence and disruptive technologies.

Today, central to young people's discussions are music players, mobile phones, enhanced bluetooth technology, digital cameras, robots, plasma screens and laptops. From Tokyo to New York this is the digital generation, brought up on generating their own content or consuming the content they want, digitally. So profound is their impact that the *Financial Times* writes that companies like Time Warner, Sony and Walt Disney are being forced to rethink their business models. Yes, we know the young are digital, but that is only half the story. There was a digital generation a decade ago, with Playstations, personal computers, digital calculators, portable CD players and Nintendo. *Digital* is *not* what is different this time; digital is not the key. The change is something deeper and more profound.

The new digital economics has removed the need to decide between whether one has richness or reach. Today, you can get both. This changes essentially everything. It changes the way customers can access information and changes the way they use it. It changes the way business can communicate with their customers and it also changes how a business might go to market. It changes the linking between channels, that link businesses, customers, suppliers and employees. It offers opportunity and it offers your once helpless competitors the chance to radically rethink their business strategies and attack vital parts of your business model. New and hungry players are taking every opportunity to enter the value chain, hoping to disintermediate you and your brand promise.

Worldwide population of PCs and PDAs is over 800 Million

We are still observing the very beginning of this, business guru Gary Hamel says: "The least appreciated effects of digitisation is the fragmentation of customer attention. Customers become harder to find and more difficult to keep."

Tomi T Ahonen & Alan Moore

From a Networked Age to the Connected Age

Much has been written about the digital age being the networked age; that we plug into and out of the network and get considerable benefits from being connected to the network. The network age was a good term for the 1990s, as it did describe how we as humans approached "the network" – ie, the internet. We logged on, we accessed our email and we surfed seeking information. Much of what most readers will consider the digital world and digital convergence will consist of that networked model.

The first decade of the 21st century starts mankind's next evolution in delving deeper into the information age. We move beyond the networked age into the "connected age". Typical of the connected age is that we no longer have to physically log on and log off. We are not tied to any single physical place to find our connection. It is not the office or the home where we have our connection, and we do not have to connect at a hotspot. We are always connected and we can instantly access the network. We can be reached at any time, and typical of the connected age, we start to manage our connectedness when we deliberately disconnect ourselves for personal reasons.

The single most visible change from entering the Connected Age, is that we suddenly have permanent access to our peers, our friends, our colleagues and family members. We can start to live with a "lifeline" to those we trust. Our communities, which previously only existed at given points in time, now become ever-present. We are no longer alone. In the Connected Age modern people are able to draw on the community for assistance, information and support. We learn to search, share and interact in a new way.

In the Connected Age people will have public and private – and semi-private – personas, which coexist in the network and are connected independently. We may want to keep our public persona connected only during office hours. We may want our private connection always on, but always with the ringing sound turned off with all personal contacts knowing to use SMS text messaging to reach us. And we might connect and disconnect with our semi-private persona; for example, relating to our hobby or passion, be it football, car racing or opera.

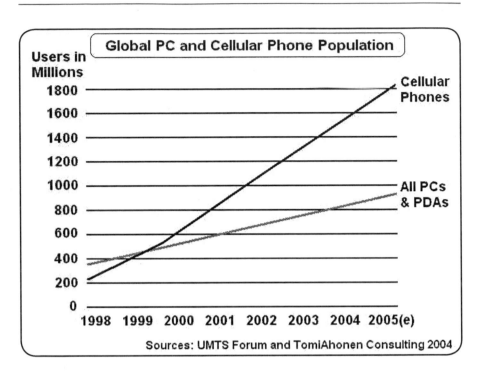

Global PC and Cellular Phone Population

Users in Millions

1800 — Cellular Phones
1600
1400
1200
1000 — All PCs & PDAs
800
600
400
200
0

1998 1999 2000 2001 2002 2003 2004 2005(e)

Sources: UMTS Forum and TomiAhonen Consulting 2004

In the Connected Age the intelligence and ability to customise our gadgets becomes ever more powerful. We will find that most of the novelty of surfing the net has worn off, and we rarely surf just for the sheer joy of discovering new websites. Our devices learn to adapt to our whims and preferences and quickly help us navigate to the sources of the information, entertainment and utility that we seek from the web. That kind of content and related applications will be increasingly consumed on mobile or cellular devices. When we use our cellular devices we will usually be in hurried states and need access fast. For that speed we are willing to pay something, and that payment in turn helps keep the content at our favoured sites current and valuable.

But, with the greatest of threats comes also the greatest of opportunities. So, how do you navigate this newly converged world and what are the strategies that will enable you to do this successfully?

Brands in paralysis

We will show in the book how traditional advertising, marketing and branding are in crisis and how traditional marketing communications are becoming bottlenecks for growth. Brilliant marketing minds of a generation have been harnessed to deliver

Tomi T Ahonen & Alan Moore

marketing from its despair, yet none have shown a sustainable method or tool for the marketing industry to deliver. All experts agree there is a problem, none of the solutions have been found to work. Foster and Kaplan state in a recent book entitled *Creative Destruction*:

> *Corporations are built on the assumption of continuity; their focus is on operations. Capital markets are built on the assumption of discontinuity; their focus is on creation and destruction. The data present a clear warning; unless companies open up their decision-making processes, relax conventional notions of control, and change at the scale and pace of the market, their performances will be drawn into an entropic slide into mediocrity.*
>
> Foster & Kaplan, *Creative Destruction, Currency 2001*

Technology changes the way we interact, the way we shop and consume. It creates new opportunities and destroys businesses that are unable to adapt to a sudden discontinuity with our past. We are moving from a production-driven to a consumption-led economy, where the nature of exchange is different, and this difference is exacerbated by the forces of digitalisation: the internet, e-commerce and the mobile phone.

Our recent history has been deeply affected by the increased speed of technological development plus the convergence and proliferation of the audio-visual, mobile, IT, and personal computing industries, increased internet and bandwidth penetration, and media choice. These developments have impacted on the businesses and the marketing community. As a result of these developments, business itself is faced with a tougher job when innovation and flexibility are the markers for competition, rather than efficiency being the fundamental driver of value.

We see creative destruction from disruptive effects to digitalisation to disintermediation by network effects in industry after industry. The music business, the movie business, television broadcasting, banking, the airline industry and travel, publishing, retail, utilities, government etc. The effects are seen everywhere. Michael Nutley, the editor of the *New Media Age,* says: "Industries which try to dictate how their customers should transact with them are taking a huge risk in the digital age." As a consequence of the uptake of new technology and the way customers' habits are changing there is a lot of "creative destruction" happening across industries.

Enter the community

A key development that has been monitored and noted in numerous instances is the emergence of digitally connected communities. Mostly these have been seen in isolation, as a new "market space" opportunity to harness and harvest, to exploit if you will; to make money from. Communities like eBay's online auctions and shopping, or communities like online dating, music and movie file sharing, friend-finders and job recruitment, etc. These are significant developments by themselves. But they are the earliest visible symptoms of a massive development in human behaviour and change in society. Many more powerful and personal communities are also forming, and these are not limited by the shortcomings of the fixed internet.

Communities that use mobile phones to share, influence, connect and participate are spontaneously emerging in all countries in all areas of interest, from car shopping to birdwatching to anti-government revolt. Rather than the armchair networkers of fixed internet communities, those who connect on mobile phone communities are young, mobile and active. They can suddenly swarm and appear by literally the thousands on a moment's notice. These "smart mobs" as Howard Rheingold wrote in his book of the same title in 2003, can become activists either for or against any authority, politician, company, product or service.

With the first actual evidence of community activities on behalf of some product, services and companies, and of evidence of communities also against companies, we can formulate our thesis: that communities are the counterbalance to brand dominance in the 21st century. By examining what word of mouth, when enhanced by the powerful digital echoes of mobile phone communities and other networked communications such as IM Instant Messaging, email, and increasingly blogging, can do, we see that communities have been an undefined or underestimated barrier to recent marketing success. Furthermore, we establish that by harnessing community power and working with them, a modern marketer can succeed in delivering remarkably positive marketing effects to the intended target audience.

Community activism is biggest change in business in 100 years

In our book we proceed logically by looking at the disruptive trends of technology, chance, digitalisation, disruption, convergence, and societal changes, then how businesses are changing. We examine how branding, marketing and advertising is in crisis. We establish the basis for understanding communities, both in the Networked Age of the past decade and the new Connected Age. We analyse the emerging new type of consumer. Still mostly under the age of 25, this Generation-C is the *Community* generation and we show how dramatically different it is from older generations, and how intuitively it already uses community power to its own gain. We then show how communities and brands interact, and why communities dominate brands. And finally, we show how businesses can thrive in this new marketing environment: they need to evolve from interruptive advertising to engagement marketing.

Tomi T Ahonen & Alan Moore

Bloggers, gamers or Gen-C?

We devote three chapters throughout the book to discuss in more detail the community behaviour of three groups of digitally-aware societies. In the virtual chapter we discuss videogamers. In the blogging chapter we discuss fixed internet bloggers of today, and the likely emerging mobile bloggers of the near tomorrow. And in the Gen-C chapter we discuss the young cellular-phone connected smart mobs. These are not the only digitally connected societies. There are countless more using the digital communication tools of choice most suitable for each community. We discuss gamers, bloggers and Gen-C because these three groups seem to have evolved furthest into discovering community power now, in 2005, and from a business point of view. We must emphasise that digital communities are inherently self-improving; they will evolve dramatically over the next few years. It is safe to assume that all of the power of the exceptionally successful community action that we describe in this book today will be totally commonplace with all communities a year or two down the line. Make no mistake about it: no matter what your business, your customers will behave like these communities.

Why us

We reveal a change to how all businesses need to interact, from the branding and advertising to all core marketing activities. The change is enormous, the biggest single change in business for the past 100 years. Why suddenly is it that the two of us would discover such a profound change?

We have been lucky to be involved in several strategic marketing projects in the earliest markets where this phenomenon has started to happen – the countries where mobile phone penetrations reached young teenagers first; Scandinavia in general and Finland in particular. We have also been lucky to work with those leading companies in those markets whose very core competence and deepest research happens to hit this area where our new Generation-C, with C for Community, has just emerged. We have supported companies that have specifically worked to understand Scandinavian youth and how it interacts with mobile phones. Our customers have included Nokia, Ericsson, TeliaSonera, Elisa, and numerous media companies, as well as support organisations with the deepest customer insights; such as specialist Xtract the user profiling company, or Fjord Networks, the User Interface company.

Even with exposure to the very earliest user patterns, it took us collaborative thinking and analysis and our own research to finally develop the theory that combines the counterbalancing forces of brands and communities. However, with every emerging new finding our conclusions become more firm. The facts solidly support our hypothesis and we can now already claim it to be true, the balance is in favour of the communities: communities dominate brands.

An American angle

Some of the issues in this book, particularly the early parts of digital convergence and disruptive technologies, are very familiar to American readers. The ideas of blogging and virtual environments are also not alien. And, as we all know, Americans tend to be world leaders in innovation in marketing, advertising and branding.

American readers should pay particularly close attention to the issues of the cellular phone, the Connected Age and Generation-C. Because of the early successes of various digital, internet and wireless data solutions, American businesses may be blinded to the "big picture" – the much more dramatic shift happening to communities activated by the cellular phone. It is not a "rival" technology to co-exist with email, e-commerce, IM Instant Messaging etc. No, cellular phone based communication is a *total cannibalisation* of the digital space.

It is very easy to become impressed with the dramatic growth rates of the various digital delivery technologies from broadband internet to digital radio. Yet these all pale in comparison with the pervasiveness and power of the cellular phone. Do not become distracted, the analogy is not railroads vs airplanes – both of which still co-exist in the 21st century. The appropriate analogy is steam-powered cars vs gasoline-powered cars. In 1890 over 90% of all motor driven vehicles were steam-powered. By 1920 less than 1% were so. Understand the shift from the Networked Age to the Connected Age. The future of every business depends on capturing the soul of Generation-C, sooner or later.

It's all about dealing with change

In the final analysis this book is about change. The early parts of the book echo, repeat, summarise and explain the related relevance of several known current trends in changes that affect business. These changes, while significant and disruptive and even frightening for some players, are known. Most organisations should have processes and plans in place to prepare for those changes, to capitalise on any opportunities and make precautions for threats.

The big, monumental idea in this book is that marketing will have to totally change. When we say companies must move from interruptive advertising to engagement marketing, we do not mean that it is one campaign. It is the whole business, a change to the very fundamental way a company's marketing is planned and executed. Engagement marketing, when fully embraced, is a radical thought and bringing about that kind of change will invoke resistance from all parts of the organisation, from the inside – established marketing managers, advertising and product management personnel and branding executives – to the outside partners and suppliers such as the advertising agencies and PR agencies etc.

Tomi T Ahonen & Alan Moore

The benefit to the bold is the rewards of being first to the future. The trends we have identified are proven to be inevitable. All significant authorities in each of the related fields is as near unanimous to the major trends as can be expected. But nobody had shown a way out of that quagmire until now. We show the way: it is engagement marketing, and we give a few early examples of real holistic changes to marketing activities that have been designed to embrace engagement marketing. For the reader of this book, if you find the individual trends to be self-evident, then the final conclusion will also have to be so.

We urge all professionals in marketing to stop projects involved in mindless propaganda of interruption advertising and branding. We urge them to learn how to introduce engagement marketing and harness the power of communities. If it is not you, it will be one of your competitors. That is the final certainty proven in the digital age. Any new good idea will not remain secret for long. When a book like this pushes engagement marketing, if you are not the company introducing it to your industry, your most dangerous competitor is the one to do it.

The future of marketing will not be built around hits, cut through, or attempting to bring as many people to a media channel at a single fixed point in time. It is like applying military strategy from the medieval ages to the battlefields of asymmetrical warfare of today. It is rather by creating compelling reasons for people to engage with your brand and to aggregate audiences over time, when they can come to you when they are ready. This is based upon insights into the fundamentals of human nature, combined with the push and pull capabilities of technology and integrated media channels. It is also potentially a lot cheaper.

Dominate!

You know your marketing, branding and advertising is not working. You know your industry is facing threats if not from actual digital rivals, then your processes face digital disruption. This book reveals the enormous power of the community, if it is not already countering your marketing, it very soon will be. We provide a thoroughly researched manual on how to succeed in the future, illustrated with 13 real business case studies from around the world. If you adopt engagement marketing methods you can succeed in the Connected Age. You can work with communities. In fact you can dominate. But to achieve that you must be bold and change. Not a small change, a huge change. It takes courage. With that we are reminded that it is not the biggest or the brightest that survive change. As Charles Darwin wrote in *Origin of the Species*: "It is not the strongest that will survive, nor is it the most intelligent; but the one most adaptive to change."

"Its easy to get stuck in the past when you try to make a good thing last."
Neil Young

II
Society Changing
Discontinuity, does it hurt?

Culture has collapsed into the marketplace and vice versa. Our concepts of institutions and industry sectors once living in splendid isolation, ring-fenced from
each other today seem antiquated. Pachter and Landry in their book *Culture at the
Crossroads* believe that the spirit of our age is one in which the sciences and economics question and challenge the notion of fixed categories, perceived oppositions,
and impermeable boundaries. This means our culture is closer today to notions of
*flexibility, fluidity, portability, permeability, transparency, interactivity, and engage-
ment.* We will start the analysis of the trends affecting our lives with the general
ones, and then proceed to the more specific. Therefore this chapter will examine how
society as a whole is changing, with institutions and our lives overall facing change.

A VALUES CHANGING

For most of humankind's history the basic values have been consistent, rather than
constant, changing only gradually over time. Furthermore, the geographical distance between societies had kept developments distinctly out of synch. Famously
Bhutan had not had television until the 1990s, and most Bhutanese held totally
different values from most of the rest of the world. But with the introduction of TV,
they suddenly adopted very Western, brand-oriented, spending-oriented status sym-
bol- laden values. While telegraphs and telephones did technically connect "everybody to everybody" all through the last century, there was little practical need to call

---

up a random person in Bolivia, or Burma or Belgium just to talk to them. It was not until the internet in the 1990s that suddenly it became quite common to exchange thoughts with total strangers who could be in any random foreign country.

Starting with radio and more strongly via TV the world started to harmonise its values. It wasn't until the internet that communication in a "world community" became truly viable. This society of the new information age holds surprisingly different values from older generations, and also remarkably consistent values between themselves, globally.

Death of intimacy

Our privacy is being eroded from several different directions. We reveal more and more of our preferences to faceless institutions that collect data on our behaviour. In London you are on closed circuit TV for the police in practically every public place including streets, shopping areas etc. Border controls are becoming significantly intrusive; now the USA already takes fingerprints and digital photographs of everybody who enters the country.

There is an ever-increasing concern over the erosion of privacy. We see individual intrusions everywhere on a daily basis, starting with spam via the internet. The writer Martin Jacques identified three important trends that change society in an article entitled "The death of intimacy" in *The Guardian*. The three trends are 1) the rise of the individual, 2) the spread of the market into all aspects of society and 3) the rise of communication technologies, notably the mobile phone and the internet.

Jacques has made observations which are significant and thought-provoking, and there are important lessons that apply to businesses and brands. If your business wants to offer added-value then you have an increasing responsibility not to be invasive or intrusive. Recent research, such as the British Chartered Institute of Marketing report *You talkin' to me?*, (January 2004) and the Yankelovich *Survey Report* (April 2004) both confirm that people feel that brands are more intrusive today than before. These are but two examples of an avalanche of similar reports.

Self-actualised people

Maslow's *Hierarchy of Needs* suggested that as people grow content with more primitive needs such as food and shelter, they can move up towards the top of the pyramid, to ultimately seek self-actualisation. In 2001 SMLXL conducted research among teenagers in Germany, Spain, Italy and France. The findings reveal that young people today are remarkably self-actualised. In fact a direct statement from an interview sums up the findings: "The other side of fear is freedom." This genera-

Tomi T Ahonen & Alan Moore

tion is the first to grow up without a significant fear of disease and hunger (1910s, 1920s), of poverty (1930s), of war (1940s), or of nuclear war (1950s – 1980s). The findings were remarkably similar in the four different countries.

The current young generation is concerned with behaving authentically. Taking material goods for granted they seek meaning, and create meaning for themselves, through symbolic interpretation of their actions and environment. They take a contemporary existential view. The youth believe in freedom of choice, indeed in the necessity to make their own choices. They live by their own rules, and the rules themselves are prone to constant revision based on experience. Furthermore, the current young generation is content with a portfolio of self-expressions, and forgiving of their own mistakes.

mobile phone ringing tones are 14% of global music revenues

The respondents indicated they are inner-directed, concerned with behaving authentically Not being overly-introspective or introvert, they are determined to engage with the world meaningfully and individualistically. The young generation is not cynical, disappointed, angry, revolutionary, or rebellious, but confidently and optimistically making choices for themselves. Finally, the young people of today respect and identify with people who live by their own beliefs and they have very finely tuned antennae to discern between those people and organisations that do this and those that do not. In 2003 Michael Willmott and William Nelson described the development of individual self-awareness, which they labelled the new individualism in their book *Complicated Lives, Sophisticated Consumers*. They wrote:

> *It is not about the individual as opposed to society, but about how people's sense of identity is increasingly complex, nuanced, and self-aware. The "self" is now something we seek to understand and express, not something we simply accept. This raises difficult issues for individuals as well as our companies and public services who are still struggling to escape the historical legacy of mass provision.*

Willmott & Nelson,
Complicated Lives, Sophisticated Consumers, 2003

We as consumers, employees and citizens want experiences for our lives. As a society we no longer worry only about finding a job and getting a home. Now many are seeking to have meaningful experiences, and shift much of their disposable income from gaining goods to building memories through experience. Jeremy

Rifkin, the American economist, described the change in his book *Age of Access* when he wrote:

> *We are making a long-term shift from industrial production to cultural*
> *production. The meteoric rise of the entertainment economy bears witness*
> *to a generation in transition from accumulating things to accumulating*
> *experiences.*
>
> Jeremy Rifkin, *Age of Access, 2000*

Businesses and other organisations that supply services and goods to the modern consumer need to recognise these changing needs. Now it is not enough to provide simply a product or service; increasingly the customer needs to be fulfilled with feelings of experience. Car manufacturers, for example, are now developing different experiences. We have seen owners' clubs already build events and meets, such as the Ferrari owners, Porsche owners, Jaguar owners, etc. There are similar clubs for Range Rovers, Jeeps, etc. Now manufacturers are becoming increasingly interested in supporting these kinds of activities. Even tyre manufacturer Bridgestone maintains a Winter Driving School.

Fundamental shift for businesses

For businesses the opportunities are clear to become integrated into facilitating those experiences. Think about it like this. Brand image advertising and marketing was based on the premise of "Be like me" as an aspirational desire. But in the 21st century this will not work. Brands have to think about how they can deliver experiences that customers value. Becoming like someone else is no longer enough. Delivering customer value requires a very different mindset.

The industrial age could not cope with a vast amount of complexity. It required simplicity and rigid standardisation to create economies of scale. But in the age of personalised cultural consumption, where value is based and judged upon the quality of the experience, companies can and must become interactive, navigational, enabling, life-simplifying. Martin Raymond in his book *The Tomorrow People* says:

> *It is a world of experience marketing – of content culture and content*
> *brands of knowledge... a world where knowledge is profit and*
> *interconnectivity is power – where enabling and personal empowerment is*
> *key to all business-to-consumer transactions.*
>
> Martin Raymond, *The Tomorrow People, 2003*

Tomi T Ahonen & Alan Moore

This move towards self-actualisation is supported by new communication technologies, so the change is more profound. As Steve Heyer, ex Coca-Cola CEO said, "I am describing a magnitude and urgency of change that isn't evolutionary – it's transformational." This means an age where personalisation and customisation are not only needed; they are expected.

B HEALTHY CYNICISM

With increasing education, enlightenment and experiences, modern consumers have acquired a strong dose of cynicism. The customer of today is faced with more choice than ever before, and has more tools to evaluate the options before making a choice. This produces a steep learning curve of how expectations can be met, by whom, and if expectations were not met what to do to avoid disappointments next time. The consumer of today is vastly more capable of discerning facts from promotional information clutter than ever before.

Geography no longer a limiting factor

The continuous growth of the travel industry and in particular the appearance of budget airlines have shrunk the world in terms of inexpensive travel. Earlier generations thought of international travel mostly within their continent. The latest generations think nothing of going to *another continent* for part of their studies or for tourist travel upon graduation. Previously there was strong mistrust of anything from other countries – still in the 1960s and 1970s, anything coming from Japan was considered of inferior quality, for example, a thought totally the opposite today. Today's consumer is not particularly mistrusting if the manufacturing has been done in Mexico, India, Brazil, Poland, Korea or China. We do live in a global economy.

In the new digital world, location is increasingly becoming meaningless. We are facing a death of distance – our British video game may have been coded in Korea, sold in the USA, on a gaming platform made in Japan, and when you call up the help desk with questions, you talk to a representative in India. With outsourcing and the internet, it is very common for parts of projects to be done in other countries and even continents.

Choice

Choice was a topic that strongly emerged from the findings of the SMLXL research. Young people in Europe had new views on choice and what choice meant to them. They said that we have moved from a time of relatively little choice, through a time of a large *quantity* of options, to today, when *quality* of choice matters. The choices that have to be made now are about what kind of person you are going to be. The concept of choice is encompassing internal life values as well as exterior material life.

What's more, the respondents explained that choice is now a necessity. The old rules and the old patterns of life are no longer relevant. This generation understands the necessity of choosing their own rules. Occasionally the groups felt that the necessity to choose was stressful. Still respondents aspire and indeed often achieve states where they like the fact that they are making their own way; guided by an inner compass.

Map your positioning

John Grant in his book *After Image* talks about how we have shifted from an age of image, to an age of true content. We are a generation exposed to so much, both in messages and in repeated revelations of broken brand promises, that we have evolved to have highly advanced "bullshit filters":

> *A great phase in human society appears to be drawing to a close – the Age of Image...Some called it the society of the spectacle: a time saturated by images from the new media of cinema, magazines and television. These fused with the growth of leisure, lifestyle and mass-produced goods to create a Consumer Society. It's now being challenged by everyone from anti-globalisation protestors to non-conformist geeks. Brand image advertising is the new junk mail.*
>
> John Grant, *After Image, 2002*

We have seen an age of ever-greater spectacle. Already 10 years ago MTV would give away whole islands or even towns – granted it was a ghost town – as giveaways. Five years ago *Who Wants to be a Millionaire?* established the new yardstick for game show awards. If you wanted to get the attention of spectacular advertising you literally had to advertise on a space rocket – which also has been done. Suddenly no level of spectacular was enough. One of the opportunities for advertising and branding is achieving diminishing returns.

Nothing stays neutral for long

It becomes very difficult to be and stay neutral about anything. In this world of shifting attitudes and values, people will pick and mix ideologies that fit their current view on the world. Is the fox hunting ban in the UK a fight about rural versus urban, or about class or about property ownership or about basic democratic rights?

2M Blackberries, 15M MP3 players, 1,600M mobile phones

The point is that we live in an age where issues polarise. People nowadays tend to care a lot, or tend not to care at all. In communication terms you are either faced with apathy or extreme reaction. Very rarely is it somewhere in the middle. Very significantly for readers of this book, recognise that with the available media outlets, people will seek media sources that support their own view.

Communication: guilty until proven innocent

The presumption in the public mind is that communication is inherently tainted. Why is this the case? Because in the public consciousness all communication is now viewed as having ulterior motives. Because no one is sure who to trust any more. Either directly or indirectly, people today are far more sceptical about the precise intent of any form of communication. They look for intention, even if it does not exist. They look for the angle. Recent scandals concerning the credibility of the news media and political spin on both sides of the Atlantic have compounded this distrust of all communication. It has become a society whereby organisations are guilty until proven otherwise.

Always before in the history of mankind, authority had inherent credibility. We trusted our Presidents, Prime Ministers and Kings. Today, especially with the younger generations, there is widespread mistrust of those in authority. Repeated political and economic scandals in all democracies have aggregated this mistrust.

Today, nothing is taken for granted any more. From religious institutions even to our own doctor, we have learned not to trust or defer to these social structures as once we did. Are we so surprised to hear that the world's biggest accounting firm Arthur Andersen went bust due to widespread fraudulent practices of their auditors? Or when we hear a few people in the British National Lottery have turned out to be dishonest? Not really. It is these kinds of experiences that mean today nothing and nobody is beyond public scrutiny. And in marketing terms, people have equally tuned themselves to see through the transparent. To the point where face-value no longer carries any value.

The implications for marketing and communications should be obvious, but it seems that business in general and the advertising industry in particular has been slow to recognise that today you need to stand for something. And if you do, you need to follow through on it. People will not give you a second chance.

Curiosity

Yet another significant change is how society now has an enlightened population that is expert at research. Seeking facts that are real time, digital, global. For earlier generations there was no such empowerment, to find the truth with a few clicks. The way we change with the ability to use the power of online search was described by British branding and advertising guru Axel Chaldecott in his poem "Polemic on Search":

Polemic on Search.
by Axel Chaldecott

I need to re-mortgage
I want a cheap holiday
I want to help my daughter with her homework
I wonder what vaccinations I need to go to India
I want to go dating with a shoe fetishist

Search is pull
Search is 'relevance'
Search is 'context'
Search is life's 'remote control'
Search is in the 'I want to know more about' marketplace.
More about my interests, my passions, my needs.

Search is 'I'm actively pre-disposed'
Search is the start of the 'long tail'
Search is the start of a 'learning curve'
Search is power
Search is instant
Search is potentially at the start of a 'sale'

Search is THE piece of the jigsaw when it comes to 'marketing interruptus'.
Search is the final act of 'completing the circle'.
Search is the mixing part of the marketing mix
Search is 'find'.

Before the internet it was not possible for the average person to seek immediate facts on a random new encounter with any given issue of interest. Today any curiosity tends to start its fulfilment with a Google search.

Tomi T Ahonen & Alan Moore

C DIGITALLY EMPOWERED ACTIVISM

As society on the whole and communities within it become aware and cynical, they also learn they have considerable power. That power had often arisen in the past decade on issues of truly significant societal matters such as on voting rights, against dictator rule, against war, etc. But today, with digitally empowered activism, communities are rebelling against particular individual rules and actions, even against individual companies. These are still "baby steps" like an infant starting to learn about walking. Make no mistake that this power is immense once it is fully realised. Communities are learning the extent of their power against individual businesses, their goods, services and brands.

Brands are punished

Protests were nothing new to major economic summits, but the movement gained global public attention for the first time in Seattle in November 1999, where, among the tear gas and the chaos of the baton charges, 50,000 highly-motivated demonstrators overwhelmed a city and stopped a major World Trade Organisation meeting from happening. The underground networks of activism reared their heads and spoke with one voice. They said: we are in fear of corporations, we are increasingly critical of corporate rule and its consequences, we feel we are being colonised by companies that are essentially a law unto themselves, that exploit everybody and everything around them. As the comedian Bill Hicks once said: "Stop putting a dollar sign on every god damn thing on this planet."

Seattle begat similar mass protests over the past five years in Washington, Davos, Quebec, Gothenburg, London, Genoa, New York, Barcelona, Calgary and so forth. The world seemed to be caught up in a grass roots civil war against big business. You could almost smell the tear gas from your TV set.

> **84% of Japanese subscribe to news on the mobile phone**

Yes, every generation of the past century has had its revolutionaries and mass protests for whatever causes. What makes this latest crop interesting is that large numbers of people were *self-organising* and turning up to events numbering tens of thousands, all around the world. Even though their agendas were often complex they became united. These events made headlines on the TV news, in the newspapers and against the backdrop of corporate scandals such as Enron, Worldcom, AOL Time Warner, etc.

Cannot hide

Businesses today are under greater scrutiny then ever before. Greenpeace has evolved from an organisation that was at the fringes of society to one which has become highly organised and efficient; it takes its protests to shareholder meetings, with a legitimate voice and through the courts. Films such as *Super Size Me, Farenheit 9/11* and *The Corporation* are taking up the mantle in our cinemas. In their book, *Culture at the Crossroads*, Marc Pachter and Charles Landry so accurately describe the converging forces which have changed our motivations, needs and desires:

> *The ascendence of the marketplace as an arbiter of value and taste and the rise of the entertainment industry; the rise of the knowledge-based econo-my; the demand by many publics to participate in defining the values and purposes of society; challenges to the unified canon of knowledge in many fields and a blurring of intellectual boundaries; the growth of multicultural national communities; the reordering of relationships between the sexes; changing conceptions of space, time and tempo particularly driven by tech-nological advances. In its latest stage the market economy has recognised other aspirations in its public beyond consumption alone – a desire for en-gagement, involvement and participation.*
>
> Pachter & Landry, *Culture at the Crossroads, 2001*

We have many examples from the recent past of individuals rapidly forming into powerful communities of protest and influence. For example, Nike – the maker of running shoes – received a very public warning. Nike was punished in the 1990s for its sweatshops, for acting arrogantly as a corporation. Activism, the picketing of Nike stores, forced Nike to rapidly reassess and react to these protests. Nike's reputation was badly dented and its revenues adversely affected when the truth was brought to the world of its economic exploitation of its customers and the abuse of those who made the running shoes. There is no reason whatsoever for businesses not to know of consumer activism, and no reason anymore to underestimate its power.

Good night, Kryptonite

The latest development that is dramatically expanding the power of consumer ac-tivists, is new digital connectedness. New online communities can utterly destroy businesses and individuals almost overnight when the corporate version of the story proves to be false or built upon consistent inaccuracies. The example of **Kryptonite** is a recent and illustrative example. The story broke on the bicycle forum with the head-line: "Your brand new bicycle U-lock is not safe." The original post went like this:

Today I was hanging out with a friend and we got to talking - he said his friend showed him just recently how to open a U-Lock with a ball point pen. Of course I didn't believe it. **That is until just thirty seconds ago when I opened my own Kryptonite Evolution 2000 with a bic ball point pen!** *This has to be the most absurd thing I've ever seen. Try it. Take the end off the pen, jam it in the lock, wiggle around and twist.*

Discussion thread on the Bicycle Forum
www.bikeforums.net/showthread.php?t=67493

The story was picked up within the blogosphere which resulted in major mentions in the *New York Times* "The Pen Is Mightier Than the Lock; A Ballpoint Trick Infuriates Bicyclists" and the *Boston Globe* "Cyclists: Bike locks easy prey for thieves. Kryptonite promises more secure product". The Boston Globe article explained:

Kryptonite, the large bicycle lock maker, said yesterday it will speed the delivery of new versions of its burly locks following complaints that current versions can be picked open with flimsy ballpoint pens. This week cycling enthusiasts have deluged the Canton business with concerns over the security of the locks. The apparent vulnerability is related to broader concerns that have arisen lately against makers of locks used to secure everything from laptop computers to coin-operated laundry machines

Boston Globe, 16 September 2004

Before Kryptonite activism grew slowly and by necessity required activism on the streets, boycotting stores, etc. Kryponite demonstrates how rapidly bad news can spread today, that activism can happen solely in cyberspace, and that people will punish brands if they don't tell the truth.

Naturally, as community power – the new force – is emerging, companies and their brands are instinctively responding. Some companies, almost by accident, are discovering remarkably successful strategies to tap into this new power. Others seize upon the opportunity to use the prevailing sentiment and community power to position themselves against an established icon, such as Blackspot has done.

Nike vs Blackspot

The Blackspot example illustrates at a grassroots level reaction against Nike. People have decided to protest by offering an alternative product or service that challenges the orthodoxy of how businesses normally operate. We could call them "anti-brands". The **Blackspot** is a sneaker or running shoe that from its materials, its logo, and its distribution on is fully organic and grass roots. Blackspot gives ownership in many ways back to the consumer. It is an extreme example but it is out there and it is truly international. This is the Blackspot philosophy from the website:

> *The philosophy behind the shoe: Enter the world's first global anti-brand: the Blackspot sneaker. Made from organic hemp in a Portugese union shop, the Blackspot is an exciting alternative to the commercial, pseudo "culture" of the mega corporations. After years of "brand damage" from anti-sweat-shop activists, we're betting that Phil Knight is now flying the flag of a fading empire. Our business plan is to cut into his market share, unswoosh his swoosh and give birth to a new kind of cool in the sneaker industry. Join us! Become a Blackspot shareholder. Together let's create an authentic, non-corporate cool and change the way the world does business.*
>   http://adbusters.org/metas/corpo/blackspotsneaker/home.html

Blackspot sneakers is just one of many early examples of how brands are defining themselves and how communities are forming around these companies that share the same world view. We will explore many more examples in this book.

D DIGITAL CONVERGENCE

We see convergence happening everywhere, from the dozens of microprocessors built into our cars to the intelligent fridge and the robot pet dog. For the reader of this book, there are three main battlefields where we see digital convergence happening, and those will govern much of your focus in thinking where your current services, goods and brands fit in.

The battle for office

At the office we have seen the battle for the dominant device, and the personal computer has clearly won over typewriters, fax machines, copiers, "binging machines", news feed displays, etc. Today the PC has only the telephone (fixed wireline, wireless "WiFi" or mobile/cellular) as its only significant partner, and increasingly these two are merging in the business world. All of the necessary functions we used to have for the myriad of electronic devices – from accessing information sources, to performing the analysis, to creating presentations and reports, to communicating – can be done on a personal computer. Today the PC is increasingly a laptop computer. The PC and telephone themselves are converging with pocketable devices such as PDAs and smartphones combining functions from both sides. Still, the time of the office computer is not over. While we can do some of our data access and communication with a small handheld device, we prefer to have our large keyboards, separate mouse pointing devices, and large screens. The PC, especially in a laptop configuration, is going to be with us for a long time to come.

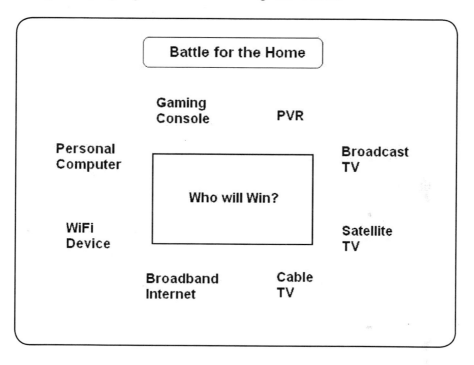

A battle royal for the home

While the battle for the office has been settled, the battle for the home is far from decided. After years of talk, finally the converged vision has arrayed the various contenders – such as the TV, PC, DVD player, video game console, cable TV box, PVR and other portable devices such as personal digital assistants (PDAs), smart mobile phones and gadgets such as the new iPod – all ready to commence battle for the home. The only question seems to be which companies are going to do the linking, and taking the revenue and profits?

For example, Sony's newest PlayStation games console incorporates a TV tuner, a PVR (personal video recorder), a DVD and a broadband link. Convergence does not amount to much more than faster emails and clearer telephone calls unless you factor in content.

Microsoft is eager to make a strong play for this battle. Its XP Media Center turns a PC into a TV set adding DVD, music player and photo album functionality. Microsoft's foray into this world shows just how much our world is shape-shifting. This newly converged world will be a major market contest and what is evident is that business models are under threat, and therefore companies need to rethink how they market themselves and how they differentiate and how do they survive? *The Financial Times* reported that Microsoft has spent $20 billion trying to get into the living room. That's how big a deal it is.

Battle for the pocket, handbag

In the battle for the pocket – or handbag – the victor has already emerged. For a while it was a close call with the PDAs (Personal Digital Assistants), digital cameras, portable gaming devices, music players and the mobile phones, but the mobile phone soon crushed its rivals and established its overbearing dominance in this space. The reason is simple. For all other uses, such as taking pictures, listening to music, making notes to our calendar or playing games, we – as the mainstream public – are not willing to carry the device everywhere always. But for being connected and having the ability to communicate – hence the mobile phone – we are. In fact the mobile phone is the first digital device most people look at in the morning, and the last device before going to sleep at night. It is the only digital device many take to the bathroom, and the only one we carry with us all day.

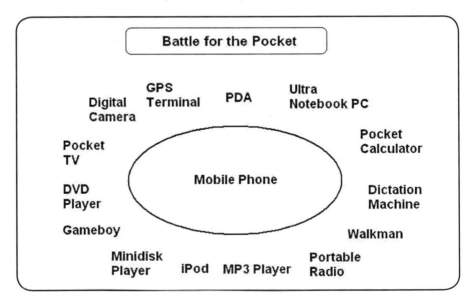

Because the mobile phone is the dominating device carried upon our person, its global penetration numbers are mind-boggling. By the end of 2004 there were over 1.6 billion mobile phones worldwide. In contrast at the same time there were about 60 million PDAs, 100 million digital cameras, 50 million portable gaming devices, and 15 million iPod and equivalent "MP3" music players (only about 10 million of those are actual Apple iPods).

E MOBILE CULTURES

We have talked about the digitally converged society. We will now take this opportunity to start on one of our main themes for this book. While all other digitally converging technologies are significant, one is above all others. That is the mobile phone.

Our main tool for contact

Within the context of changes in society, the mobile phone is becoming an important social medium. Our recent history has been deeply affected by the increased speed of technological development plus the convergence and proliferation of the audio-visual, mobile, IT and personal computing industries, increased internet and bandwidth penetration, and media choice. These developments have impacted upon us all, changing the way people interpret and consume communication. As a result of these developments, business itself is faced with a tougher job when innovation and flexibility are the markers for competition, rather than efficiency being the fundamental driver of value.

In Japan, on the BS-i channel, there is a TV detective programme called *Keitai Deka* the cellphone detective. Each week she solves crimes with the help of her high-powered DoCoMo smartphone. Smartmobs commented on this TV show on 28 July 2004: "Westerners might find the premise implausible, in Japan, where multitasking teens can thumbtext faster than you can type, it's practically a documentary."

The idea of sending text messages to strangers in their cars – fancy the blonde in the BMW? – requires car owners to register their licence plate with a mobile phone to participate and then pay premium text message rates to communicate in this way. The idea seems doomed as a business. Yet in the UK alone this idea generates one million text messages per month and some £3m ($5m) in annual revenues. Similarly, nightclubs, pubs and discos in the UK have installed public texting boards, that patrons can send messages for all to read. Yes, premium SMS of course. These deliver over 100,000 messages per month.

In Finland if you turn to any of the commercial TV stations at night you will not find the test pattern or an info-mercial selling some fantastic slendering gadgets. Finnish commercial TV runs all night SMS-to-TV chat boards, on all commercial channels. The premium rate is over *nine times more expensive* than regular SMS text message prices in Finland, yet the channels are full of chatting messages all night. And if you think you are the latest wordsmith genius rapper and want your lyrics broadcast, the latest Finnish variant of the SMS-to-TV show is the "text the rapper" show where viewers send their lyrics to the virtual rapper who raps them outloud. These get charged at over 20 times the regular rate of SMS text messages. Two human hosts comment on raps received and rate them.

Who is digital gatekeeper

Finally, our changes in society will see an emergence of a new player controlling the information flow related to our society, its members, and increasingly, the communities. That entity is the mobile phone operator (wireless carrier, cellular telco) which almost by accident has become the dominant player controlling the access to services on the most preferred personal device – our mobile phone. Furthermore, in complete contrast to all the players involved in the internet, mobile operators *control* a digital environment with a rigid and powerful payment system and because of the design and technology of cellular networks, they continuously collect data into their billing systems. This makes the mobile operator the aggregator of the most complete, in-depth and intimate knowledge of all economically viable persons on the planet, amounting to the most in-depth user data on the viable part of the global population.

The mobile operator/carrier will yield enormous power in deciding who gains what information and at what cost. Even more significantly for understanding the behaviour and power of digitally connected communities, the mobile operators can track and analyse social network communications. For those who are interested more in the economic functioning of the mobile telecoms business, including the business case for the mobile operators and the various content and application partnerships that form modern mobile business, we refer to the business book of the telecoms industry; Tomi T Ahonen's *m-Profits*. Suffice to say here, that the mobile operator/carrier will grow greatly in importance to the market understanding of end-users and their communities.

Summing up Society

In this chapter we have examined the "big picture" changes in society. We showed how end-users are becoming enlightened, self-actualised, more cynical and literate with digital search tools. We offered a few cases of community power both against companies and on behalf of them. We discussed digital convergence in the office, the home and in our pocket. We gave a few examples of how the mobile phone is becoming the predominant communication tool, and we concluded with a brief discussion of the new gatekeeper for information, the mobile network operator/carrier. While our book is about advertising, marketing and branding, it is important to understand that all of society is changing, not only the marketing side of business. When you read further in this book remember what motivates you and what you learned about motivating others in the past. Money is no longer as obvious as it had been, as Mary Kay Ash says: "The two things that people want more than sex or money are recognition and praise."

Case Study 1

The Transistor Project

The biggest cost of the popular music industry today is the amount of effort devoted to discovering talent that can succeed in the charts. All major record labels employ large armies of talent scouts, who try to evaluate future band prospects from various demo tapes and listening to bands live, etc. For all prospects that the record labels sign up, they then spend a lot of marketing effort to try to build an image and sound and market buzz for the band, to help its chances of succeeding in the chart. The music business is very much a hit business. For every Jennifer Lopez or Robbie Williams, there are literally hundreds of artists who did not make it. Each was given marketing support by a label – some more, some less, but regardless, each such prospect was given resources – in other words money from a marketing budget, to try to make it.

　　The problem from an analytical point of view, is that each prospective artist is dependent on the luck with which a talent scout happens to hear them. Famously, the Beatles were, for example dismissed by one of the major record labels. The Darkness, though perhaps not in the same league as the Beatles, decided to use the route of becoming self-published because they could not find anyone to back them. This kind of myopic view is diminishing the chances for any truly talented pop artist to make it. Equally the talent scouts can be strongly influenced by their own preferences, tastes and desires, giving opportunities for bands which really do not have a chance at making it.

Engaging a community brings a totally untapped, new and immense power to the process of finding music talent that can make it. Rather than depending on the skills of a single talent scout, if a whole community is activated to consider future music, a much better overall success rate can be achieved.

In a recent article the *Financial Times,* "A virtual lift-off to fame", Paul Sexton describes a recent venture driven by Dave Rowntree, drummer with Blur, and Jim Beach, manager of Queen, which shows a dramatic departure from the traditional talent search, and the utilisation of new technologies to tackle the problems of talent discovery. Rowntree and Beach have created a digital platform designed to break new acts onto the music scene and help others who have been discarded by the majors. They call it the "Transistor Project".

> *The project's goal is to develop "cost-effective, long-term and creative" digital marketing campaigns to generate the biggest possible online fan bases for artists. Services include helping previously well-known acts to reconnect with lapsed audiences, and introducing successful overseas acts to the UK market. But it is their development of unproven names that may appeal to rock wannabes. The Transistor Project works with fledgling artists as a facilitator rather than a traditional record company. All its initial marketing energies are driven online to seek, find and recruit the act's crucial first 1,000 fans and build a buzz that will have big and independent labels calling.*
>
> *Financial Times* September 15 2004

The idea behind the two rock veterans in the Transistor Project is to radically alter the status quo of the business. Now this project aims to work with upcoming music hopefuls and work with the artists with the Transistor Project acting as the middleman, to recruit the initial core fan base of about 1,000 fans to support the growth of the prospective band.

When this fan base is activated and supports its band, there is a much greater chance for the music to become a hit. 1,000 fans can create a considerable "buzz" around a new band, and help them with early concert attendance etc. Equally if that 1,000 first fans are not there to be found, a prospective band is clearly not going to become a hit over longer periods of time, even with more marketing push by a major record label.

Tomi T Ahonen & Alan Moore

"The future always arrives too fast... and in the wrong order."
Alvin Toffler

III
Business Entities Transforming
From Dinosaur to Puma

There is a theory that in extreme cases people can feel and taste fear; it apparently feels cold and tastes metallic. Across all industry sectors legacy businesses are in crisis. IBM, Kodak, Sears, Marks and Spencers, WH Smiths, Virgin record stores, Nokia even. Once the dominant force in their respective sectors, they now face one of the biggest issues that can bring any business to its knees – the crisis of context and meaning with their customers. The weaker the notion of context and meaning someone has with a brand, the greater the probability that they will abandon them for somebody new. There are a number of forces at work which have brought about this crisis for legacy brands – we start with digitilisation.

A DIGITALISATION

The digital revolution has hit businesses, hard. From acting as a disruptive technology, altering decades-old stable industries such as the film-based photography business, or music recording industry etc, and expanding competition to a global base, the digital revolution has also altered internal processes. Some companies are boldly entering new fields, such as Apple going for the music business with the iPod and iTunes, while others leave potentially significant digital industries for others, such as IBM shifting from computer manufacturing to consulting and service businesses.

Technology changes the way we interact, the way we shop and consume. It cre-

---

ates new opportunities and destroys businesses that are unable to adapt to a sudden discontinuity with our past. Napster took billions from the music industry. Digital cameras crippled Kodak. The first news of digitalisation seemed to be of cannibalisation and disruption. After a few years of disappointment and mistrust of hi-tech, suddenly in 2004 new media technologies and related new business models were in favour again. Legal music downloads are generating significant revenues, TV on the computer screen and mobile phone, the expansion of video gaming etc are generating positive news for the industry.

Not by TV but broadband

We have many technologies that are part of the digital revolution, but only those technologies that have a natural feedback element can truly be the full conduits to the digital age. Our traditional means of consuming content tend to be outdated. Stephen Carter from UK regulator Ofcom writes:

> *Television cannot deliver a digital society. Only broadband can do that. The move to digital broadcasting and to broadband means that media literacy depends on a willingness to embrace new technology. That can be a challenge for many people. Changes often bring great benefits, but they can also bring added complexity. Ultimately, the real value of technology is what it can add to our daily lives.*
>
> *The Sunday Times* July 11 2004

The way to business advantage is discovering clear customer benefits such as ease of use, time saving, lower cost etc. In short, an enhanced customer experience.

Punctuated equilibrium

While over longer periods of time change is a constant, change itself does not occur at a constant rate. In fact Stephen J Gould has explained in his theory of punctuated equilibrium that in evolution there are periods of stability punctuated by a change in environment that forces relatively rapid adaptation. In other words there are lengthy periods of minimal change with sudden bursts of several dramatic changes. We see this all around us in the airline industry, which had been stable for some 70 years and was suddenly in chaos with discount airlines from the 1990s. Similar effects are seen on TV through HBO's effect and in the newsprint industry in the UK from digital economics.

70% of owners of Personal Video Recorders (PVRs) skip ads

Digitalisation brings about opportunities for disruption, cannibalisation and the creation of new marketspaces. These introduce the opportunity for a period of rapid changes. The punctuated equilibrium causes fundamental changes and disruption all throughout the society, from the culture and the political world, to businesses and industries.

B MUSIC MOVES ONLINE

The global music industry used to be worth well in excess of $30bn in worldwide revenues. Music revenues have been shrinking for three straight years now nearing the $25bn level, mostly due to piracy and file-sharing. The industry is in turmoil, seeking a unified position on the trends of file-sharing and piracy, while seeking to profit from the surprising success of music on the mobile phone.

Music on digital front line

Music is the soundtrack to young people's lives and these young people are targeted by practically all brands. It is easy to see why brands have jumped on music as a means to open up a direct channel of communication with their customers.

The current trend at end of 2004/early 2005 is direct downloads of music, either to a PC or the mobile phone. Just between January and August 2004 legal, paid internet-based music downloads increased fivefold worldwide to about half a million per month. Apple was the pioneer with iTunes in America, but Coca-Cola is one of the big players in the UK, and Sony has partnered with McDonald's. And while the quality of the "music" is appalling, mobile phone ringing tones are a much greater business, already delivering over 14% of the total music industry revenues.

For the music industry, disruptive technologies such as peer-to-peer networks, music ringing tones, direct downloads, etc, introduce opportunities for new value propositions. Generally, disruptive technologies underperform established products – such as the music CD for the music business – in mainstream markets. But they have other features that a few fringe (and generally new) customers value. Products or services based on disruptive technologies are typically cheaper, simpler, smaller, and, frequently, more convenient to use.

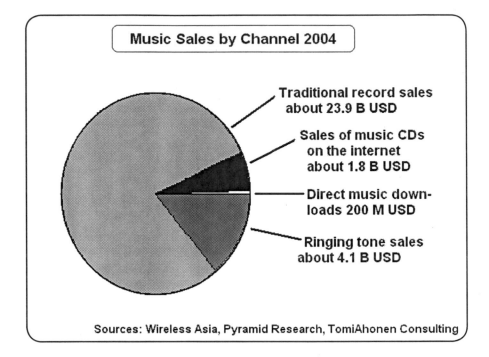

Music Sales by Channel 2004

Traditional record sales
about 23.9 B USD

Sales of music CDs
on the internet
about 1.8 B USD

Direct music down-
loads 200 M USD

Ringing tone sales
about 4.1 B USD

Sources: Wireless Asia, Pyramid Research, TomiAhonen Consulting

Revenues will come from intelligent packaging and delivering other value based offerings: limited editions, merchandise, discounts, e-coupons, "first to know" type of information, the ability to become a virtual and physical community etc. These will aggregate revenues over time. The intelligent use of digital platforms offers up so many opportunities to build a very different relationship with your customer base. It is all about richness and reach.

A look back

200 years ago music was consumed only in live formats. The wealthy might invite a chamber orchestra to perform some music by a composer or a musically trained family member might play some of the latest songs on a piano etc. With the ability to record music onto vinyl records and broadcast music via the radio 100 years ago, music became more broadly available and multiple formats were created for the same music.

The emergence of the tape recording and then the popularity of the C-cassette allowed users to record favourite music and store it to replay it. But the formats were all analogue and incompatible. To transfer music from one format to another

---

Tomi T Ahonen & Alan Moore

required recording (or re-recording) of the music through a conversion - such as connecting a tape recorder to a record player and these kinds of conversions invariably degraded the quality of the music.

Digitalisation opened Pandora's box

In the 1980s music CDs replaced vinyl recordings and digitally stored music entered the mainstream. With the internet and file-sharing technologies such as Napster, at the end of the last decade users were suddenly able to share digital quality music via the internet. While Napster was closed down through legal action, numerous other similar services such as Grokster and KaZaa carried on the sharing traditions.

The digital convergence in other industries opened new avenues for music. Hollywood movies and TV broadcasting had already discovered the use of music recordings from the analogue days and movie soundtracks were often released with movies. Now with digital processing of motion pictures, the soundtracks are naturally also digital, on music CDs. Newer opportunities appeared with video games, where in the late 1990s most video games still had sound effects and music backgrounds that sounded like a cheap Casio keyboard. Today most games have digital recordings of popular music that appeals to the gamers. For example *Tony Hawke* skateboarding videogames have hip hop culture music on the backgrounds, typically rap and heavy metal music. This is emerging as a new marketing medium for pop stars who want to have their music on cool and popular games.

Music is also increasingly consumed as video, on music video TV channels such as MTV and VH1, and by consumers buying music DVDs, with video clips of their favourite artists. Music videos are also becoming hit successes on advanced 3G mobile networks in Korea and Japan.

Ringing tones best success in music

Another channel is the mobile phone through ringing tones. Ringing tones – the service invented in Finland in 1998 – have exploded to over $4bn in business worldwide in 2004, and deliver over 14% of the total revenues to the music business. The rap artist 50 Cent broke the American sales record with 500,000 copies of the ringing tone version of his *In Da Club* hit. In the UK the sales of ringing tones earn more revenues for chart-topping pop artists than the sales of their traditional singles.

While the IT industry has been raving about iPod and iTunes, in South Korea a more profound revolution is taking place. Music songs and music videos are sold directly to 3G mobile phones. Ricky Martin was the first major artist to test this channel, by pre-releasing several tracks from his newest album as MP3 files direct to the mobile phone in the summer of 2003, six days before the album was released for sale in stores. Ricky Martin sold over 100,000 songs this way. As the advanced mobile phone penetrations in Europe climb to reach Korean levels, such music distribution opportunities will also emerge in all countries.

The mobile phone is increasingly becoming the pop musician's channel of choice. Robbie Williams made his latest album available on a memory chip via the Vodafone mobile network in 2004. Some artists, like Celine Dion, have built the launch of a new music CD album not on traditional advertising and promotion, but solely around mobile advertising and promotion.

Music kiosks

A specialist company, Inspired Broadcast Networks, has introduced music vending machines that will allow people to buy and download songs at railway stations, in stores and shopping malls or in the pub. The kiosks transfer tracks to a mobile phone or personal music player for about £1 ($1.75). This innovation brings music downloading to the majority of people for the first time, dramatically increasing the potential reach of paid downloads past the young and technically clever iPod users. The company launching the vending machines initially hopes to offer two million songs. It expects to add another 300 tracks to the catalogue each day.

Disintermediation

The traditional music business is caught in a dilemma. They can see a new future but their whole business model – employed, real people – are all dependent on the old way of developing talent. The profits are being squeezed out of an industry with cut-throat competition as the overall global music sales market is shrinking. This leads to shorter commitments into ever more manufactured hits that seem to be most shallow and incapable artistically of sustaining themselves over time.

> ## In just 4 years smartphones cannibalized 80% of PDA market

Where are the creative powerhouses going to come from? Bands like U2, David Bowie, The Clash, Bob Marley and the Wailers etc are all carved out of the equation to allow more short-term populist acts to provide short-term immediate revenues for the music industry. TV reality shows like Pop Idol and American Idol and today's manufactured groups sell reheated versions of hits from previous decades. The traditional music industry is increasingly locked into a vicious cycle of short-termism, where ever faster sure hits are built, that burn out fast and need to be replaced. The major labels still have the muscle, but for how much longer?

C CREATE MARKETSPACE

The future for brands should really be about the creation of branded content, assets or services that are unique to that brand, that deliver enhanced customer value, either as experience or as something that we can describe as broadly enabling. Digitalisation allows existing competitors to rapidly encroach upon each others' markets and customers. The easiest solution is to stay and fight. Unfortunately this mostly leads to market wars and ever lower levels of price. The more challenging road is to create new opportunities where there is no offering, and no competition. Brands need to create "marketspace", rather than competing on the same terms as the competitors. A new marketspace means building a new game where your brand gets to set the rules. A new marketspace allows generating new revenue streams, providing a greater return on investment. Creating value for customers via information, entertainment, experience, speed of delivery, flexibility of distribution etc.

Requires vision and courage

A new marketspace is not the same as a new market. A new market arrives when a totally new product is introduced, such as the introduction of the automobile or mobile phone or the personal computer. A new market can also be created when sales are made available in a new place, such as museums adding museum stores, or the emergence of the internet. A new market*space*, however, is finding a new opportunity within the existing product and sales opportunties.

A good example is the **discount airline** business model. Discount airlines entered what many thought was a saturated market and one which many analysts thought was already cost-optimised. Airlines of the 1980s had perfected passenger routing with a "hub-and-spokes" structure. Airlines optimised their traffic routes by having passengers change planes in hub cities like Chicago or Atlanta rather than flying directly between every possible city. Passengers had more flights from their home airports, – but mostly to hub cities, and airlines could optimise the traffic and run high-capacity widebody jets for the major routes between hub cities. For the airlines this seemed like the logical end-state of decades of cost-cutting and capacity-optimisation. There could not be an opportunity for rivals, in particular as the landing slots at the major hub cities were in extremely short supply. Passengers were inconvenienced by having to change planes and airlines turned to profit-maximising by focusing on specific routes and regions.

| **World's bestselling digital camera brand is Nokia** |

Discount airlines came and broke all the rules of the existing airline business, and created a dramatically big business opportunity. They opened up the skies for many passengers who otherwise could not afford to fly. Discount airlines started to fly direct between cities, rather than via hubs, avoiding the congested hubs and their precious landing slots. They operated smaller jets so they could efficiently fly on lesser routes. They standardised on only a few aircraft types to optimise maintenance and crew training and typically focused on a given geographical region. With drastically pruned standard services and charges for everything from snacks and drinks on, the low-fare airlines were able to sell airfares at levels dramatically below those of the mainstream airlines. The discount airlines also emerged at a time to capitalise on cost savings of internet-based ticket sales. By thinking creatively, discount airlines were able to create a new marketspace within what most called a mature industry. Today discount airlines account for nearly all the growth in the airline industry and a lion's share of the profits. To further validate the concept of a new marketspace, many of the major airlines have responded by launching their own discount airline brands.

When a business builds a new marketspace it creates new and initially uncontested markets for itself. Today, for these to succeed, a brand will need to offer a value-add that was not available before. It is increasingly likely that the traditional marketing emphasis on creating effective brand communication strategies will need to be extended and dimensionalised to create effective *brand experience* strategies which allow the customer to meaningfully connect, experience and interact with a brand. The rapid acceleration of these will be crucial to success in any market.

Need creativity

Finally, we believe we are, as Richard Florida writes in his book *The Rise of the Creative Class*, living in a creative economy that is drawing the spheres of innovation (technological creativity), business (economic creativity) and culture (artistic and cultural creativity) into one another, in more intimate and powerful combinations.

Creating a new marketspace is not that new as an idea. It does, however, require a different approach, some courage and some lateral thinking. The **Tour de France**, for example, was originally invented in 1903 as a circulation-boosting promotional device for French daily sporting newspaper *L'Equipe*. Today, it is a global sporting event annually attracting 1,200 journalists from 350 publications and news agen-

---

Tomi T Ahonen & Alan Moore

cies. The audience has active participation of 15 million people who line its route and the Tour de France is broadcast over 75 channels in 170 countries and results in 2400 hours of programming.

Marketspace is not about benchmarking your competition. It is about looking outside your industry sector, and rethinking what your core capabilities are and how these can be leveraged. Who is it that is coming into your industry that could disintermediate it the same way as DVDs and PVRs (Personal Video Recorders like TiVo and Sky+) have done to terrestrial television? So if you are the Discovery Channel, are you a broadcaster or are you in the content distribution business? What are the cultural and business touch points that would be relevant to you and your viewers? How can you grow your brand and business beyond the box? How can you capture your community?

D NEWSPAPERS INTO THE ABYSS?

Newspapers, humbled by the new digital economics, are potentially in a decline which is irreversible. The introduction of free dailies funded solely by advertising eat away at the ability to charge per issue; while the rapid growth of internet advertising eats at the newspaper revenues from advertising. The best that owners can do is to manage the decline as profitably as possible until traditional newspapers simply expire.

At wrong end of digital divide

The newspapers are among the oldest media and show their age in contrast to the latest digital inventions. The industry seems to be overloaded with bad news. The readership is in decline; competition is appearing from new media which readers see increasingly as more immediate, convenient, cheap and compelling; traditional advertising revenue, from recruitment, housing sales, personal ads etc, is under threat. Newspapers are not even considered as multi-channel content delivery vehicles. Furthermore, new mobile media and commercial partnering do not fit naturally into the editorial process. There is also the critical issue that readers of newsprint are ageing, and young people are learning to increasingly access content via digital platforms.

The mobile phone is the exact opposite. On the fixed internet few newspapers have managed profitable web editions, but on the mobile phone the money is much easier to make. In Japan, the country that was first to introduce digital news services to mobile phones in 1999, today 84% of mobile phone users subscribe to some kind of news service for their mobile phones. It is not an isolated pattern and cannot be ruled out as the Japanese being somehow different from the rest of us. Similar patterns are starting to emerge in all other countries that were early to introduce news services to mobile phones, from Korea and Singapore to Scandinavia, Italy and Israel.

Change, driven through convergence and the falling costs of technology, coupled with changing customer behaviour, can be seen as either terminally life-threatening, or life enhancing. Most newspaper groups are struggling to integrate digital communication channels into their editorial content or advertising packages. Yet these multiple channels can be used much more optimally to engage "readers" beyond the printed page and at the same time build the core business of circulation and advertising revenue. Much like shipping, which had to learn different seafaring skills when moving from wind power to steam power, so too must newspapers now master skills with new media and interactivity with readerships.

Customer touch points

Between 1985 and 2000, US advertising spend grew from $95 billion to over $240 billion. The biggest piece of the pie went to TV advertising. In the UK in 1987 there were 500 TV commercials aired every day, by 1997 that had increased to 11,000. When most people think of marketing or advertising, they tend to think of TV advertising. The explosion of interruptive marketing communications and our subsequent rejection of it is why it is important to understand that there are many ways in which a brand can reach its customer.

In a paper for Admap, "Changing consumers: Rethinking your strategy" in May 2003, Chris MacDonald discusses what he describes as the "connections wheel", which charts the touch points that a customer can have with a brand. TV spot advertising is but one of those connections that MacDonald lists.

These customer touch points can be reconfigured as combinations. They can be deployed in both paid-for and non-paid-for media. And touch points can be utilised to offer a "value-plus" to customers. Understanding the touch points and deploying the appropriate messages through each is the way to generate greater efficiency in the marketing communications.

Tomi T Ahonen & Alan Moore

Modern Touchpoints for Most Brands

Television	Public affairs	Mobile phone
Radio	Investor relations	Direct response TV
Newspaper	Entertainment	Loyalty programmes
Music	Publicity	Mail ambient
Magazine	Corporate comms	Directory
Internet	Consumers	Speakerships
Computer games	Business	Outdoor billboards
Cinema	B2B	Retail
Books	Cause related	Taxis
Training	Contests	Public transport
⚹ Store	Coupons	Sonic branding
⚹ Product design	Cultural	e-Mail
Point of purchase	Festival	Word of mouth
Packaging	Sampling	Editorial
ID Design	Sport	Service staff
Experiential	Sweepstakes	Virtual
Brand extensions	Call centre	Special events
Off-trade	Custom publishing	Telemarketing
Sponsorships	Direct response	

Adapted from Chris MacDonald's 60 Touchpoints

As we live in an increasingly information-rich world, there is an economic need for brands to deliver "value-added" content or services to their customers. These value-added services must deliver on each individual's personal needs and desires.

Power of personalisation

Not everyone in the newspaper industry has thrown in the towel. There are exceptions, surprisingly successful examples of newspapers responding to the changing business climate. A vital key is engaging the community, bringing in participation. Roy Greenslade in an article in *The Guardian* described several local British weekly newspapers as bucking the trend as he wrote:

> *Four of the weeklies that have substantially grown their sales recently – the Doncaster Free Press, Derbyshire Times, Wakefield Express and Mansfield Chad – are owned by Johnston Press, the fourth largest chain. The Barnsley Chronicle's editor, Robert Cockcroft, famously pioneered the use of non-journalists as reporters and has gone from strength to strength ever since, as yet another set of excellent sales figures prove. Now lots of papers*

are doing the same, including the Derbyshire Times, which has 30 village
correspondents filing reports.

Guardian, September 1 2003

This is what we call engagement and we will have a whole chapter on it later in
this book. Get your readers involved in generating your product or service, such as
these local newspapers have done.

There is no doubt that the newspaper industry has to evolve to survive. Regional
and local newspapers, vital parts of their communities for decades, need to embrace
change or die. This must include using digital channels to create audience contact and new revenue streams. For example, the price of TV distribution is falling.
Taking a position on the Astra satellite just to serve a few hundred thousand people
is now viable. The emergence of new satellite broadcasting options like *Free Sat*
will make it even more so. Do not forget broadband internet. In this digital world
the guiding principles are content, richness and reach. So, we know that newspapers
have online sites and services – but are they "me too?" and have they truly taken the
technology to the limit of what it could truly deliver?

What business are you in

The classic cliché is that the railway industry failed because it saw itself as being in
the railway business, not in the transport business. While railroads worldwide grew
all through the last two centuries in coverage area, train car numbers, total transport-
ed people and cargo, they were seen as losing out to other forms of transportation,
to airplanes on long distance, and cars and trucking on shorter distances. Clearly,
from a technical point of view, a high-speed bullet train can be a superior transport
solution for travellers on distances of short-haul flights, and still a viable competitor
on some medium-haul routes. But the railroad industry never caught on to the wider
competition in transportation, and only considered other rail as its competition. In
a very similar way IBM in the early 1980s did not see the potential of the personal
computer opening new and over time much larger markets than its traditional mainframe business had been up to the 1970s. Today local press has the same problem in
that they see themselves as in the print business, not the information business.

Community generating material

Local newspapers are particularly suited to benefit from the emerging community
dimension. Local print can use a wide range of community services to build their
new value proposition. They can set up contributors that can comment on events,
a "territorial army of journalists" around the county. The newspaper could set up a

Tomi T Ahonen & Alan Moore

blogsite for the local community to share and swap information. Gardening questions could be supported by the local garden centre, and then add the local gardening club with online and offline community. A chat room could be introduced for debate on the the local topic such as expanding the local school or revising parking rules etc.

600 Million mobile phones sold every year

People like to have the opportunity to "have their say"; local news could facilitate this using interactive digital platforms via email, MMS picture messaging and, of course, SMS text messaging. The strategy would be to drive very hard the two-way debate so local news becomes a dialogue. They could also harness the democratic power of the blog. Hot topics could drive debate; the sacking of the local football club manager, is the local council corrupt, etc. If such topics were to be aired in an audio-visual format via cable, broadband, the mobile phone etc, it would make local news more immediate, more vital, attracting local advertising.

This is merely scraping the surface of the potential of broadband and mobile services for the news media industry. There are vast opportunities but they can only be captured by those willing to make the effort. Certainly continuing with newspapers as they have always been is a certain road to ruin.

E SELECTED OTHER TRENDS

There are numerous other issues involving business that are causing disruption or change, such as ERP (Enterprise Resource Planning) and CRM (Customer Relationship Management) and the globalisation of competition, etc. It can also be argued that the *increase* in speed of change is itself a disruptive force. As these tend to be areas rather well covered in earlier business texts and published research, we will assume the reader is well aware of those. We will want to address a few other examples of further disruptive business forces here briefly.

Providers become commodities

Telecommunications is about to become a commodity industry like water or petrol. The telecoms operators/carriers are facing the prospect of becoming commodity providers. The competitive stakes are rapidly being raised as advanced mobile service propositions are increasingly attracting competitors from outside telecoms.

In the meantime Music Television (MTV) launched its own mobile service in Sweden as an "MVNO" (Mobile Virtual Network Operator) – in other words a mobile telecoms service provider. They sell MTV branded mobile phones and subscriptions, and make money on the regular voice minutes and text messages of their customers. Why? Because voice and digital data are globally worth a trillion dollars and the MTV brand is perhaps the strongest brand for the youth segment hooked on the mobile phone and music. Many youth brands are rushing to enter into the mobile phone sweepstakes, including hamburger restaurant chains (Hesburger in Finland), youth magazines like Cosmo Girl, pop bands like Twins, and video games like Super Stable, in Hong Kong.

The competition does not stop there. It is Vodafone vs AOL; electric power utility vs telephone operator/carrier; the music industry vs online retailers; retailers vs multiplex cinemas; TV vs the retailers. We even see the consumer taking on industries such as with peer-to-peer sharing and digital piracy. Draw your own map of what is going on in your industry. Your marketplace is changing at the speed of light. In the middle of it all is an empowered and enlightened consumer asking "and what's in it for me?"

Differentiate or die

Most branded mass-market products and services are near-indistinguishable without their branding. Yes, a passionate Pepsi drinker can tell the difference between Pepsi and Coke, but most do not care enough. Is there a significant difference between Pepsodent and Crest? Between Mobil and Shell? Between Citibank and HSBC? Or Marriott and Sheraton? Branding attempts to build value to distinguish between similar offerings. A more profitable opportunity arises if a new marketspace is created.

In the mobile telecoms world the fortunes of Orange and One2One (since renamed T-Mobile) in the UK can be compared financially. At the time it was sold Orange had a remarkably strong brand loyalty, a rapidly growing customer base with industry average revenues per subscriber. One2One had the poorest customer evaluations and a miniscule average revenue level, as it has been trying to buy customers offering them near-free calls to counter the bad image. Certainly Orange could be claimed the best customer-focused network of that time in the UK. Being customer focused and generating significant customer advocacy will drive business success for companies. The valuations the two rivals achieved when they were sold tells a compelling story, as reported by Barwise and Meehan in their article "Making Differentiation Make a Difference" in *Strategy & Business*:

> *Orange and One2One, another start-up, received their licences at the same time. Both were well capitalised, and they were equally regulated.*

*Neither had a technological advantage over the other. But while One2One
stuck with the practices that gave the mobile phone service category a
bad reputation among consumers – many calling plans, confusing billing
approaches, and quirky networks – Orange sought to change them. In
1999, both companies were sold: Orange to Mannesmann and One2One to
Deutsche Telekom. Orange fetched £20 billion, a premium of £13.1 billion
over One2One's price.*

Strategy & Business 30 September 2004

There are many ways for many different types of companies to significantly
differentiate themselves in today's crowded marketplace. But that involves a lot
of work to identify the market opportunity in the context of existing competition,
and then even more work to shift the business into pursuing the new direction. A
brand's palpable sense of its higher purpose must be communicated to its customers. Service or enhanced value offerings that simplify, enable, or help customers
are keys to success. The opportunities afforded by richness and reach of digital
platforms in conjunction with other forms of media can deliver that differentiation.

Just in time vs just in case

We are also seeing the shift from traditional advertising into new areas. We will
examine advertising in detail in the Advertising chapter later in this book. One specific area of the shifts in how advertising can be used relate specifically to the new
value-propositions of business. That is worth examining here.

All traditional advertising is "interruptive" and therefore premised upon the notion of "just-in-case" you might be interested. TV shows and radio programming
is interrupted for ad breaks. Magazines and newspapers interrupt the flow of their
stories to make room for ads. Yet today consumers are fed up with the interruptions
and are actively voicing their displeasure. In the USA 56 million Americans are
signed up to the "do not call me" register which forbids telemarketing. 70% of all
people who own a PVR (like TiVo or Sky+) skip the TV advertisements.

Consumers do not want interruptive advertising. There is a gaping need for
something new, something better. Brands need to develop strategies where customers will actually request information. Yes, that is not easy, but the easy interruptive
TV ad is not working anymore. Brands must innovate to create services that are
useful to consumers as part of the process of moving towards a sale and creating
differentiation. What businesses need to do is understand that people are today seeking out more information before they buy. There is an opportunity for "just in time"
marketing communications, enabled by converging digital technologies.

An end to business

This chapter looked at how changes are affecting businesses. Starting with digitalisation we looked deeply at the issues facing the music industry. Then with new marketspace we used the example of discount airlines. We listed a long list of touch points that brands have with customers, proving that there is plenty of life beyond TV advertising. The chapter then examined print media and how it might engage its readership using new media. Finally we closed with a few other trends. No doubt businesses are facing tremendous challenges, but with every problem comes an opportunity. Any business today must accept change as a given and be willing to reinvent itself to meet the changes. As Alfred P Sloan, the former chairman of General Motors said: "When you are through changing, you're through."

Case Study 2

Apple iTunes

The Apple iTunes business idea fits well in what we now describe as creating a new marketspace. This is not the first time that Apple has built a new marketspace. They invented the opportunity of the "Windows computer", bringing the personal computer from the desktops of business analysts and word processing secretaries, into mainstream business and the home. While Windows is, of course, a Microsoft product and available only on IBM-compatible computers; it was in fact Microsoft's rush-project to enter Apple's radical new marketspace, created with its Macintosh. Let's go back 20 years.

Apple, one of the creators of the personal computer industry, had been involved for over two decades in a battle for the market in personal computers. For over 10 years its share had lingered well below the 10% level. Apple products tended to be more expensive than the industry average and by the mid 1980s many analysts felt Apple had to abandon its proprietary technical solutions and join the IBM-compatible standards to survive. Apple had other ideas.

At that time in the late 1980s, personal computers were extremely clumsy to use (who remembers the "DOS prompt"?), and there was no graphical interface, no hypertext links, printing never looked on paper what it appeared on screen and, while technically they existed, nobody really used

---

Tomi T Ahonen & Alan Moore

a mouse. The Macintosh changed all that. The Apple Macintosh was the first mainstream personal computer with a graphical user interface, pointing with a mouse, hypertext links, "WYSIWYG" printing (What You See Is What You Get), sound and multimedia graphics support etc. Suddenly the Apple brand computers invaded several industries that had resisted the early IBM-compatible computer. Whole sectors of industry, such as the creative advertising, graphics, and music industries embraced the Macintosh type of computer.

Where previously Apple computers competed head-on with the less expensive IBM-compatible computers, now suddenly Macintosh found a vast market that wouldn't even consider any alternative. It was not until Microsoft launched Windows that it had a foothold into the new marketspace that Apple had created. Microsoft insiders used to call Windows its product of "Macintosh envy", showing how seriously Microsoft took the new opportunities.

Lets consider the new marketspace aspects of Apple iTunes and its device the iPod. When the iPod was launched, the personal computer industry had been involved in over a decade of shrinking profit margins. The strongest competitors were companies like Dell that competed on price. Competing with a high-priced product in an industry of increasing technology harmonisation, Apple needed to find new opportunities.

The amazing thing is that Apple selected the music industry and portable music players. At the launch of iTunes and the iPod, the music industry was an old industry in decline. After years of life as a mature industry, the global music business was among the first to feel digital disruption. It was battling piracy and file-sharing. Most would have suggested that the industry was headed into a bad decade and only a deranged fool would attempt to enter the business at this time.

The portable music player was another business model that seemed to have lived through its best days. The original Sony Walkman – itself a new marketspace bringing to the portable cassette dictation machine market a new music enjoyment dimension, dramatically expanding the sales of portable cassette players – had created the portable music opportunity. But by the year 2000 there were numerous digital solutions, from portable CD players to minidisk players to MP3 players. The Apple iPod was, from a technology point of view, nothing different from already existing MP3 players, themselves considered an inferior technology to the minidisk recorders/players.

The most astounding feat, however, was the iTunes proposition. Rather than selling music by the CD, Apple allowed downloading individual tracks and paying 99 cents for each downloaded song. Bear in mind that iTunes was launched when Napster and free file-sharing were the rage around the world. It took a lot of vision and courage to enter a mature market in decline, with a technology many thought was inferior, with a billable product to a market where free alternatives existed. Yet Apple succeeded. By the end of 2004 Apple had sold 10 million iPods.

A side-effect of the iTunes and iPod success is the interest in and sales of Apple Macintosh personal computers and laptops. The computer range has much higher profit margins than iPods. A buyer of an iPod would be a good target to sell Apple-branded computers. And existing Apple computer owners would easily see the iPod/iTunes offering as convincing reasons to remain with Apple for the next upgrade of the computer, rather than switching to a rival brand.

Six Design Lessons from the Apple Store manifesto contains thought-provoking yet actionable strategic advice on designing and delivering compelling experiences for customers.

The six Apple lessons are:
- Create an experience not an artifact
- Honour context
- Prioritise your messages
- Institute consistency
- Design for change
- Don't forget the human element

The advertising and marketing of the Apple iPod and iTunes merely reinforces the popular groundswell of enthusiasm for this little device, rather than delivering advertising and marketing communication messages which stretch beyond the bounds of credibility what the real customer experience is going to be.

Tomi T Ahonen & Alan Moore

"Nothing is forever except change."
Buddha

IV
Services and Products Fragmenting
A street brawl without any rules

Digitalisation allows services and goods to designed, packaged and delivered in new ways. An ever-increasing proportion of the global economy is based on digital goods and services. Digitalisation harmonises the competitive world, and allows copycats that appear with alarming speed to capture your customers. Even if digitalisation is not affecting your market directly, it is certainly affecting how you go to market and what route you might take. So, how do CEOs of existing companies, trained and familiar with their traditional business value systems, embrace the disruptive new environment of the digital universe? This chapter will look at how digitalisation alters the competitive environment for services and products.

A SPEED OF CHANGE

Kodak has finally succumbed to the meteoric rise of the digital camera and the camera-enabled mobile phone and is getting out of the business of traditional film for consumer cameras. Lufthansa has sold its stakeholding in the airline ticket booking system Amadeus, as it no longer sees the value in a technology that has been disintermediated by the internet and the low-cost airline business model. IBM has shifted focus from making computers to selling computer services. The history of business is an ever-faster substitution of goods and services by ever-better technologies. Transistors gave Sony the chance to eclipse that valve-based giant RCA, wireless meant that Vodaphone became the new British Telecom and, ironically in MP3, Apple's iPod is the new Sony Walkman.

Disruptive technologies

Clayton Christiansen, the Harvard Business School professor, discussed the idea of "disruptive technologies" in his book *The Innovator's Dilemma*. Christiansen studied the pattern of well-managed companies, considered very innovative within their industries, that surprisingly stumbled with technological change. After studying a number of examples, he identified a leading reason why great companies fail. He summarised it as follows:

> *Disruptive technologies bring to a market a very different value proposition than had been available previously. Generally, disruptive technologies underperform established products in mainstream markets. But they have other features that a few fringe (and generally new) customers value. Products based on disruptive technologies are typically cheaper, simpler, smaller, and, frequently, more convenient to use.*
>
> Clayton Christiansen *The Innovator's Dilemma 2003*

We can see this thinking everywhere around us; Skype the internet telephony service, iTunes on iPod, Freeview digital TV service in the UK, etc. One recent innovation is instore TV – where 80% of all purchases are made within 10 feet of the item to be purchased. These all represent the falling cost of broadcast technology. Not to mention the dramatic shift of retailing online. This all can be termed "creative destruction".

Is creative destruction an opportunity or a threat? This depends on how one decides to look at the world. Embrace it or ignore it until it is too late. A significant thought to hold is that if the future will cannibalise your product or industry anyway, then is it not best for it to be *you* who cannibalises your business, rather than your competition?

In addition to digitalisation, we are seeing simultaneous convergence of many technologies, delivery platforms and industries. Converging content and delivery, the internet with gaming and broadcasting, of voice and data in telecoms, etc. Convergence of these technologies means that businesses are beginning to cannibalise each others' industries. Sony Electronics' chief operating officer Hideki Komiyama puts it plainly: "Five or six years ago home electronics was a peaceful market. Now people from the outside are coming in like hunting tribes."

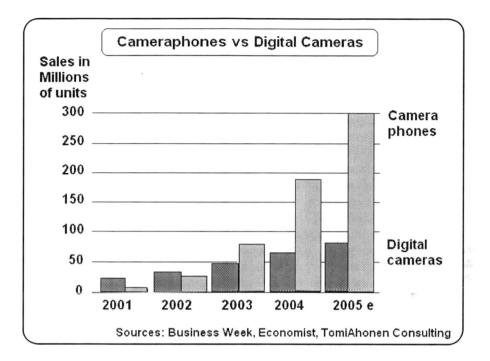

Sudden success of cameraphones

On the surface of it, trying to patch together a voice telephone and an optical camera seems like trying to combine an airplane with a submarine. But as mobile phones converted from analogue to digital systems in the early 1990s, and as cameras entered the digital age about the same time, it became technically possible to create digitally converged devices combining both. Even so, there was little practical areas of synergy during the 1990s as both technologies were relatively bulky and there was no excess capacity in processors, storage units, battery capacity, etc.

Then at the turn of the decade smartphones introduced colour screens for internet surfing, and digital cameras started to abandon the optical viewfinder for the digital colour displays to be used as viewfinder. Now suddenly part of the digital camera was in existence on the advanced mobile phones, and thus it was no longer a prohibitively bulky converged product to add the camera functionality to the mobile phone. Japanese mobile phone operator J-phone (since renamed Vodafone KK) was the first to take the strategic step into cameraphones and had 60% of its 12 million subscribers adopted to cameraphones by 2002.

The growth of the sales of cameraphones has been nothing less than breathtaking. In 2001 the global sales numbered less than two million units. The traditional digital camera market felt very safe as its sales were well over 10 times that amount. Cameraphones were ridiculed as being of very poor picture quality, having limited storage ability, poor graphics of the displays, poor optics, etc. During 2002 the sales of cameraphones climbed to 18 million units worldwide. Suddenly the traditional digital camera market took notice but as traditional digital camera sales kept growing, the industry was not particularly concerned. They were introducing multimegapixel cameras and ever more advanced systems and most in the industry felt assured that their technical dominance over the cameraphones would keep them safe.

In 2003 the sales of traditional digital cameras did again increase, to 48 million units. But cameraphones rocketed past those numbers, selling a whopping 84 million units in 2003. Already by 2003 the world's bestselling brand name on digital camera devices was not a leading camera brand like Minolta or Canon or Nikon, it was phone maker Nokia. In just three years mobile phones had invaded the digital camera market and totally crushed the established competition within it. In 2004 the mobile telecoms industry shipped so many cameraphones that they now, four years from launch, amount to more than all digital cameras ever shipped.

Wedding photos on cameraphone?

It is important to note that for specialist and professional use there will always be a "real camera" market. A professional wedding photographer will not show up at the wedding with a cameraphone. A sports photographer will use a real Canon or Nikon with the massive 300mm telephoto lens. Professionals such as fashion photograhers, news photographers, nature photographers etc will buy professional photography tools. These may be digital, or they may even be film-based, by photographer preference. These kinds of specialist markets will remain and high-end specialist cameras will be made for these markets.

Our point is that the mainstream digital market, the mass market, will inevitably converge to the predominant digital device. At the moment the clear champion is the mobile phone. Thus in the contest for any function that can be added to the mobile phone, the phone will hold a near-insurmountable lead in its attractiveness. We saw it already before the cameraphones with the brief battle between the stand-alone PDAs (Personal Digital Assistants) and the smartphones, which the smartphone won easily. Next for 2005 we are preparing for the next battle; between the stand-alone music player like the iPod and the music-phone. We expect this battle to be as easily won by the mobile phone as it did with the PDA and the digital camera.

Music and new media

The music industry is one of those on the leading edge of the disruptive effects of digitalisation. With the ever-increasing capacity of mobile phone memory storage and battery life, it seems music companies are indeed looking to embrace the digital age. Will it be enough? Will enough people want all their content on their phone?

A special case is the new type of "3G" phone, that has been on sale in Japan and Korea for three years and is now appearing in most Western markets. Most 3G phones have storage ability for at least a modest library of music files, and the ability to "stream" music; ie, play music from live feeds much like a radio. Significantly 3G phones are better than the current crop of iPods in that all 3G phones can play music *videos*. Again the mobile phone trumps the existing contenders and pretenders. The pop culture clearly proved how much more appealing a music video is to young generations rather than simply listening to the same music on radio, fulfilling the theme of the Buggles hit Video Killed the Radio Star – the song that famously launched MTV in 1981. To put the numbers in context, both technologies are about three years old, but while iPods number about 10 million globally at the end of 2004, there are already 32 million 3G phones worldwide.

Will these new superphones be an iPod killer? The answer is yes and no. For the die-hard music fans – especially those with sophisticated digital music systems on Apple computers or IBM compatibles, who efficiently "burn" music CDs to various digital formats – the iPod, and its close rivals, will be the supreme portable music device. But yes, for the mass market we are convinced the dominance of the mobile phone, with 600 million sold every year and phones replaced every two years, means the moment the phone industry decides to take over the music player market, it can do so. The mass market is doomed to be dominated by the mobile phone.

B FRAGMENTATION

As goods and services become digitalised, they are easily replicated or modified for multiple channels. Variations of the same content can be tailored for given customer segments. This results in fragmentation.

Repackaging

One of the considerable benefits of having content in digital form is that the content can be easily altered, by digital processes. A movie that was originally in black and white can be colourised, like the vast collection of classic movies owned by Turner Broadcasting. Creating still images from video clips, generating TV format versions, small-screen versions, and internet versions are easy to do. If you want to build a video game and own video rights to a movie or sports, it is easy to use video clips as part of the gaming experience. *Forrest Gump* was famously the first major movie where the modern character was digitally inserted into a real historical news-clip so that Forrest Gump could be seen to meet the president.

Apple iPods are being used to store X-rays in hospitals in the US. This is one ex-ample of how digital technology is changing our behaviour. But digital technologies have invaded many other common devices around us too. Our kitchen gadgets tend to operate on microprocessors. Our car typically has dozens of separate digital process-ing units. The PVR and the digitisation of broadcast, broadband penetration and mo-bile PCs all expand broadcasting and TV, video, radio and movie opportunities.

32 Million 3G phones in the world at end of 2004

The more relevant point to the reader of this book is how much digitalisation allows one player from one industry to expand the offering into other industries by using different distribution channels and outlets. Some of the early obvious pio-neers were, for example, Disney, which even before the digital age were bringing the cartoon characters from movies and comic books to television, branded toys, the Disney store, even prints on t-shirts and men's ties. Disney soon capitalised on digital games, screen savers for PCs and mobile phones, etc.

TV news

Nowhere is the fragmentation of audiences seen as strongly as in the mass media. In a world of over 200 TV channels we can literally spend a whole half hour surfing from one channel to another, spend 20 seconds on every channel to decide if we want to watch that show, and by the time we are done surfing through all channels, the programming has hit the next half hour show times.

20 years ago TV everywhere was dominated by the main broadcast stations. Today viewers seek channels that support their personal views. For some, perfect accuracy in news is not as important as the news focus fitting with our personal values, opinions and beliefs. "No, I don't watch the nightly news, I only watch MTV news" is what a teenager might say. "My regular news broadcast is the financial news twice a day" might be a businessman. "Only Entertainment Today" could be a reply, as would "I never watch the news, I get my news from the monologues of David Letterman and Conan O'Brian".

Today fragmented audiences, the growth of political and niche interest blogs, plus alternate news sources such as the fixed internet and the mobile phone news alerts, have all combined to disintermediate the traditional broadcast networks. In a blink of an eye the once all-important news anchormen seem as though they were from another age. It has been argued that news has become more a mere profit centre than a key element of democratic process.

Certainly soon we will see plenty of evidence that the democratic process has shifted with the same shifts we outline in this book, from a regimented hierarchical system with few in control – in this case the news media – to the pluralistic user-generated community content systems, such as blogging and reader-generated content for newspapers etc. These broaden the web of people participating.

Television broadcast is in transition from a system of centralised provision to a market economy of demand. We have changed from passive viewers to active consumers of programming. The question for brands in a media-fragmented world is: "Where is my audience and how do I talk to them?"

Can the can

Closed Audience Networks (CANs) are TV systems designed for a captive audience ranging from the student union to retailers. The ex-CEO of UK broadcaster Flextech Telewest and founder of the consultancy Cordelia, Adam Singer, says: "The cost of transmission has fallen so dramatically that anybody can start a TV station. There are no barriers to entry." One example is the UK's biggest retailer, Tesco.

Tesco TV is getting a lot of publicity for its innovations. The big European advertising company JC Decaux, best known as being the biggest operator of billboards in Europe, claims that advertising on Tesco TV generates 10% better performance, on average, across the 62 brands involved in trials: "The extensive trials of Tesco TV have demonstrated that customers value its content as an aid to their shopping experience. And, advertisers see it as the first media format to work in the last 10 feet – which is media where it matters – encouraging customers to choose their brand at the point of purchase," it adds.

Tesco TV is so successful that Tesco announced it will no longer use traditional cardboard displays at the aisles after successful trials of its in-store TV service. This is a significant early blow against the prevalence of traditional point-of-purchase material, and on 10 June 2004, *Marketing Week* went as far as proclaiming it the beginning of the end for the retail marketing staple.

Non-traditional competitors

The competitors to existing services can come from any direction. In Japan and Korea the mobile phone operators give subscribers access to most TV channels that are available on broadcast, cable and satellite TV. Similar solutions have also been introduced in Europe with TIM of Italy one of the pioneers. The operators between Thailand and Singapore announced a roaming system that allowed mobile phone users to access home TV stations when visiting the other country, in real time, on the mobile phone – and at very expensive international data roaming costs. There are also several technologies to install TV tuners to mobile phones with the first coming online in Korea in 2005.

Another example comes from a surprising candidate. Mainstream airlines had been providing an outlet for movie distribution, and for a while were in the telecoms business with phones in planes – although the pricing model mostly destroyed that business. Now discount airlines like Ryanair have entered the video rentals business by renting video players to passengers to consume video content on planes. Rather than bundling the price of the movie into the airline ticket, discount airlines can make much more money by renting the individual viewers to passengers. Is the airline becoming a broadcaster?

60% of USA car buyers use internet for research

How long can the traditional broadcasting industry hide behind its infrastructure and broadcasting licence protection. Already today many use broadband internet to access radio and TV programming from other markets. Some of the TV content bypasses the broadcast route, and goes directly to end-users via DVD. This happened, for example, when some markets did not show programmes like *South Park*, or when viewers suddenly wanted to see "next year's" episodes of a series that had not yet broadcast, such as *Sex in the City*, *Sopranos* and *West Wing*, etc.

Sky, in releasing its PVR, the Sky+ (like TiVo in the USA) certainly would not be offering a technology for viewers to skip TV ads if it did not have research which demonstrated that people don't like to watch TV advertising. Its aggressive activity into this area to clearly differentiate itself from commercial terrestrial broadcasters is based only on growth and creating and defining an ever-larger marketspace.

This one statement should put the fear of god into advertising agencies and terrestrial broadcasters. In fact, when one pauses to consider the turning off from analogue for commercial broadcasters, this will mark another era-defining moment and the death of a number of business models. Remember digital is different.

Digital, different: TiVo. Now it's TiVoToGo. We know that "to TiVo" is about customer choice and a desire to edit out TV spot commercials. TiVoToGo is an extension of enabling technology that allows people to start to move recorded content from the TV hard drive to a variety of other devices and ultimately out of the home.

Tomi T Ahonen & Alan Moore

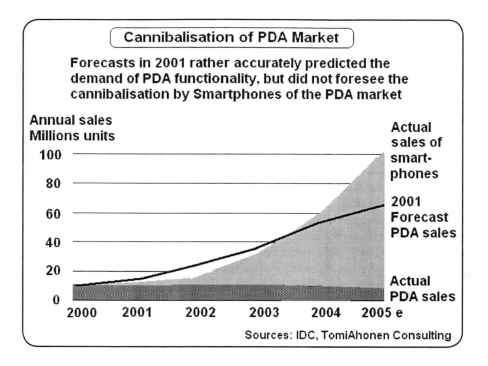

Cannibalisation of PDA Market

Forecasts in 2001 rather accurately predicted the demand of PDA functionality, but did not foresee the cannibalisation by Smartphones of the PDA market

Annual sales Millions units

Actual sales of smart-phones

2001 Forecast PDA sales

Actual PDA sales

100 80 60 40 20 0

2000 2001 2002 2003 2004 2005 e

Sources: IDC, TomiAhonen Consulting

If you want to watch the last episode of *Six Feet Under* while taking the train to work, you can. If you want to watch that interesting documentary as you fly to Washington, you can. What and how we consume information is going seriously mobile. And this is what technology has done. Today it is not about why, it is about why not? Whereas before we just accepted that was the way it was.

C MARKET EFFECTS

More competitors, stronger offerings, faster rivals. The effects of digitalisation, fragmentation and disruption overall is that the market becomes an ever-more hostile environment. Stable industries suddenly become unstable. Dominant brands suddenly falter. Previously unknown players suddenly emerge and succeed. These are not isolated incidences, and they will never go away; it is how the rules of the game have changed. For everyone.

Ever faster speed to market

Digitalisation allows the delivery of content and services on an ever faster cycle in time to market. Digital tools allow rapid "processing" – eg, we do not have to wait for a film to be developed. More importantly, once the content is in digital form it can be converted to other media efficiently and with speed.

Any digital manipulation tools that find a market will tend to get ever cheaper. A good example is the "morphing" technology, by which for example late night TV show host Conan O'Brian shows his "If they mated" comic routines of what children of celebrities might look like. The idea of combining two images, and morph a third, as a mixture of the initial two, was a very exclusive, expensive movie production special effects technology in the 1980s, and done manually in the film laboratories. The first digital technologies to allow morphing were introduced in the 1980s and were literally run on the supercomputers of the time. During the 1990s the first of the most advanced photo manipulation software for the PC introduced morphing ability. Today morphing is a basic feature available in numerous freeware or shareware image manipulation software.

Another key benefit of digitalisation is that the content can be created anywhere in the world, and transmitted instantly without any loss of quality. A developer might work in India, another in Korea, a third in the UK, and all three collaborate on the finished product without ever meeting. This allows all content industries to benefit from the global talent pool rather than the nationally, often very limited, specialist pools of before. Also, obviously this brings down the costs of deploying digital innovations.

In the case of advertising, movie editing, music producing etc, now an expert in one country can use a specialist in another country and quite cost-effectively gain access to top talent and skills. As digital development methods tend to be controlled with similar tools – typically the personal computer – skills in one industry become more easily transferred to other industries. An expert editor of music can be rapidly retrained to edit movies or video games or printed pages, as the tools and processes are now similar.

A special case is the "free" duplication of digital content. Peer-to-peer networks, pioneered by Napster and now living further with KaZaa, Grokster and others, are emerging as a new and potent distribution channel, as well as a serious threat for content piracy.

Increasing variety

The net effect of the ability to spread the same content digitally is that familiar content brands spread into ever more markets and media. *Dilbert* the daily (and thus "free") cartoon strip on many major newspapers around the world has been published in book form in about 20 books already. Beyond that, the author of the strip, Scott Adams, has released several written humourous books on business and management, illustrated with occasional Dilbert cartoon strips. Meanwhile Dilbert has been released as a TV series. Apart from competing in the newspaper free comic strips "category" of content, the Dilbert brand has expanded into books and TV.

Movie actors and musicians have often wanted to expand into each others' domains, starting with Elvis decades ago, so it is not surprising that Jennifer Lopez is succeeding both as a singer and actor. What is more interesting is that she has expanded her brand into non-digital spaces by releasing clothes under her brand and now offering a perfume etc.

500,000 videogamers play simultaneously in EverQuest

These examples show how existing brands can enter new fields and become competitive there. The digitalisation has dramatically increased the markets of where services, products and brands can compete. This means that all markets and industries will see more competition, by more players, more strong brands, and supported by ever more professional and competitive marketing.

Airline inventory efficiency

Norway based discount airline **Norwegian** has adopted the rapid innovation of mobile check-in, allowing users to use SMS to purchase tickets, do check-in, and use as a boarding pass on its flights. Norwegian is not only doing this for revenue purposes, but to prolong the maximum amount of time it can sell seats on the next departing flight, and to open a direct marketing channel to its travellers. Such innovation will radically change the marketing of the travel business.

Beauty on the web

A Body Shop survey of 1,509 working women aged from 18-54 in the US found that 54% of the women relaxed by shopping on the internet *every day* as a way to escape their day-to-day pressures of their jobs. New web stores and services are appearing to feed this need. One example is **HQhair.com**, which offers a fly and deliver service for all of its beauty products. The beauty of the web lies not just in bringing some of the world's most sought-after products to your door, but also alerting you to their existence – and whether or not they are really worth buying – in the first place.

All other industries beware

We have seen some examples of truly rapid cannibalisation by new digital devices. The same can happen in any industry where the main service or product is digital, as we are seeing in music, videogaming and movies today. But the same effect can happen to any *process* that is digital as well. The need for growth, coupled with convergence, both forces and enables business to think beyond its own market sector in search of increased revenues and profitability. This scenario is played out against a culture in flux, with different needs and aspirations to those of a generation ago.

The role of digital information processing has altered most industries where digital can have a significant effect, such as entertainment, information, banking, etc, and has dramatically altered aspects of other businesses. For example, the travel industry has almost no digital element to transporting humans from one city to another by jet plane, yet the sales of airline tickets are now increasingly done via the internet and, in an emerging form, by mobile phone.

There is no question about how broadly digitalisation has altered traditional businesses, such as the music industry, newspaper publishing, movies, television, banking, etc. It is important to note that still today these industries have not fully utilised the benefits of digitalisation within their own fields.

D CUSTOMERS CHANGING

The change in customer behaviour is one of the most powerful trends today. Customer behaviour can make or break a company. Companies need to develop customer advocacy by understanding the rationale for their behaviour but do not know how. Increasing disquiet regarding the effectiveness of "interruptive" communications has led to a focus on media cost-efficiencies.

In the US 60% of car buyers use the web for research. We are not at the end of this shift in behaviour, not even in the USA, definitely nowhere near as far in the rest of the world. If this is how consumers learn to behave in expensive purchases, soon they will do this for all significant purchases.

Compare with bricks & mortar goods

Much like the original innovation of mail order shopping – pioneered by Sears in America over 100 years ago, by which the Sears mail order catalogues were most popular in the rural areas far removed from major shopping areas – so too today internet shopping is becoming most popular in rural areas removed from shops. According to the Hitwise Holiday Shopping Series 2004, online Americans in rural districts were 16% more likely than all other social segments to visit a shopping site. Bill Tancer, Vice President of Research, Hitwise, said: "With the holiday shopping season well under way, internet users in remote, rural segments are taking advantage of the convenience and comprehensiveness of online retailing."

Embracing emerging media

The digital opportunities are enormous. One channel option receiving very little attention is digital radio. That is likely to change with perhaps the best-known radio personality, shock jock Howard Stern, ending his association with terrestrial broadcast radio and moving his show to the digital airwaves on the Sirius standard. Digital radio is one of the many alternate options emerging. Everyone does not have to try to squeeze onto the tiny screen of the mobile phone.

Virtual gaming property sales on eBay worth 880 Million dollars

---

Video on demand (VOD) is another new opportunity reaching critical mass, and advertisers have taken notice. Michael J. Wolf, global head of the media and entertainment practice at McKinsey and quoted in *The New York Times,* believes that video on demand will become a significant way for consumers to find and watch programmes. But of course this means that people are not watching the ads, they want to be in control of what they watch when they watch. Ian Bezoza, a cable analyst at the New York office of Friedman, Billings, Ramsey, says:

> *People using TiVo and other digital video recorders expect to be able to fast-forward through commercials, and people who select free on-demand programmes on cable expect to see no commercials at all, unfortunately, they're used to it by now.*
> *The New York Times*, November 22, 2004

Advertisers worried about the impact of this behavourial change are now actively investigating how to embed commercial messages into the broadcast media.

Customers surf between media

As brand experiences increasingly have digital elements, and as digital services are delivered on an ever wider range of digital delivery platforms, customers are learning to optimise their experiences. Customers use interactive tools to pull con-

---

tent from digital channels, to consume content in parts, and increasingly filter out advertising. In this customer-focused environment an experience/community-based economy has emerged.

For a large part of the past century the balance of power between companies and their customers had been solidly on the side of the companies. Today we are witnessing the shift of balance more towards customers, from filtering message hype to relying on other consumers for opinions on what to purchase. The consumers are also communicating with each other after purchase to discuss satisfaction with a good or service. A new digitally connected generation is emerging. We describe Generation-C in its own chapter later. Marketing to these people by interrupting them with image advertising will not work. The only way to convince this generation is to join them, share in their interests, activate them and engage them.

The examples we cite in this book of community behaviour are still the very early ones, happening much by trial and error. But the trend is inevitable. A connected community learns its power remarkably fast. The true empowering technology is mobile telecoms and, as such communities get involved with consumer action connected by mobile phone, soon all communities learn of the potential that communities wield. The mobile phone, however, is not the only communication method, and communities will use increasingly multiple channels to share.

Sum up the fragments

We have looked at how services and products are splintering into ever smaller fragments. We discussed several different industries from cameras to music, from movies to newsmedia, from airlines to cosmetics. The modern services and goods market is one with ever more choice. With global players trying to outsmart each other, encroaching upon each others' markets, and all attempting to deliver a compelling value proposition to the end-user. Modern competition is like a street brawl. You cannot rely on the rules to protect you. You have to be willing to adjust to the changes. If you don't embrace change you will become obsolete, as General Eric Shinseki said: "If you don't like change you will like irrelevance even less."

Case Study 3

Guinness Visitor Centre

Guinness is probably Ireland's best known beer brand. They wanted to show community involvement and expand the experiences related to the beer brand by opening the The Guinness Visitor Centre in 2001. It is firmly established as Ireland's number one tourist attraction, now known as Guinness Storehouse (The Guinness Visitor Centre).

Many different elements come together in this extraordinary building – a unique visitor experience, retail store, gallery and exhibition spaces, with first-class events venue, restaurant and bar areas, the Guinness archive and state-of-the-art training and conference facilities. Guinness Storehouse, in Dublin, reimagines how a brand can perform for customers, employees, and the community. Its primary purpose is to be a tourist attraction but it manages to be much more than that.

The project transformed a vacant, outdated fermentation plant into a seven-storey visitor and conference centre. Today the Guinness Storehouse is a working building, offering the Irish and international business communities a range of rooms, spaces and facilities to hold seminars, private dining occasions, parties, product launches, fashion shows, lectures, conferences, etc. "Around 42% of all holidaymakers to Ireland come to the Guinness Storehouse," proclaims Paul Carty, the attraction's general manager. "This compares to our estimate of 38% of London tourists who visited Madame Tussaud's."

Visitors are greeted by the thumping drums of a celtic river dance. A roaring man-made waterfall surges over slabs of Lucite suspended overhead. A bank of monitors flash images at the speed of REM sleep that are quintessential Ireland – emerald hills, a raucous rugby stadium, a sheep herder. Escalators and moving walkways whisk visitors up a seven-story hive of glass and green I-beams to various exhibits and, eventually, to the 130ft-high Gravity Bar.

Every visitor receives a plastic lozenge that encases a dark drop of Guinness. It can be traded at the end of the tour for a free pint of stout or soda. From an island workstation in the middle of a large, circular room, bartenders serve 2,000 pints on a weekend day – twice that many on St. Patrick's Day.

An exhibition tells the story of brewery founder Arthur Guinness and shows visitors what goes into making and distributing Guinness using multimedia, film and large-scale graphics applied directly to the interior walls of the building. A six-storey glass atrium shaped like a giant pint has been carved into the middle of the building – at the head of which sits the Gravity Bar, offering drinkers a 360 degree view of Dublin.

According to Brand Strategy, The Storehouse attracts around 700,000 visitors a year, 60% from the UK and 20% from the US. It also lures an additional 100,000 corporate clients and operates as the site for Diageo's internal training centre. It is more than a tourist attraction. Guinness Storehouse is an example of how Guinness has combined live events, architecture, design, advertising and other skills to create an overall brand experience.

With increased tourist numbers as only one vital statistic a piece of brand engineering has benefited the wider social and economic community. More income for taxis, bars, restaurants, hotels etc and a facility that can be also used by the local community. The Guinnness Visitor Centre demonstrates the economic and social power of engagement marketing.

Has it returned on its investment? According to brand strategy, Guinness Storehouse broke even in its first year and has been in profit since its second year of business. How does Guinness view the "success"? Aside from visitor numbers, the success of Guinness Storehouse is measured in terms of affinity – an internal measure created by Diageo. According to that definition, affinity leads to increased awareness and admiration of the drink. Aine Friel, the Storehouse's marketing manager, was quoted saying: "Everything we do must be aligned to the global brand and increasing awareness and driving sales of Guinness." She adds: "We can prove that we recruit 45,000 new Guinness drinkers per year, who've never drunk Guinness before and have their first pint in the Storehouse."

Paul Carty, believes that Guinness's link to sociability and entertainment make the brand a natural fit to extend into experiences. "This isn't Guinness's core business but we're adding to the success of Guinness's brand," he insists. Carty explains his ambitions: "We're going back to the drawing board. We want to attract one million annual visitors, we want to be the world's must-see-now attraction, not a once-in-a-lifetime attraction, and we want to be the world's favourite brand experience."

More improvements and investment in the attraction are in the pipeline. Guinness Storehouse has just rewarded Imagination with the project of updating the visitor centre. It will be creating new exhibitions to represent Guinness on a more global level and turn the centre into a more enriching experience for the visitor.

"It does not do to leave a live dragon out of your calculations, if you live near him."

J.R.R. Tolkien

V

The Emerging Virtual Economy
Magic kingdoms for us and our children

"I have commanded armies, built civilisations and destroyed them, seen the seven moons of Orion, and cried inconsolably when I died in mortal combat." Welcome to the interactive, addictive, never-ending world of the virtual economy. And we thought the universe was big. The emergence of the virtual economy is a very recent phenomenon that evolved with the personal computer. Many early creations appeared such as virtual goldfish that could be viewed on the PC screen. The tamagotchi phenomenon brought about the first virtual pet and taught a generation to care for and play with a virtual toy and one which had a life – and death. The true power of the virtual economy started to assert itself through networked gaming. Early networked games were built for a small number of users but with the advent of MMOGs - Massively Multiplayer Online Games – the virtual gaming world started to mutate into a true economy. Hang on, we're going in.

A SIMULATORS

The virtual world can trace its roots to the world of simulators. In the 1960s, as jet fighter airplanes were becoming ever more expensive to build and less forgiving to fly, jet manufacturers started to build simulators where a pilot could sit in a perfect cockpit replica, with all the correct levers, buttons, meters and gauges, and operate the simulator just like flying a real jet fighter. The simulators soon added displays to allow displaying, for example, a runway of an airport etc.

Jet pilots

The benefits from jet fighter simulators soon expanded to other areas of aeronautics. Commercial jet airplanes soon developed simulators for the pilots of the main jet airliners and today all commercial jet pilots are trained via simulators before they take their first flights in the control of an actual big jet plane. Astronauts had special simulators built to train on rocket controls. There are even special simulators that allow air crash firefighters to train in how to fight the fires and save lives of an air crash.

Simulators soon spread to many other areas where the actual operation – and crashing – of the real world equipment would be remarkably expensive. Today submarine crews train on simulators, as do battle tank crews. Race drivers use simulators to familiarise themselves on the exact braking points of a new race circuit etc.

Business simulations

Simulators are also now expanding into many other fields. With the advent of Lotus 1-2-3 and then Microsoft Excel, spreadsheets allowed the analysts in the financial markets to develop ever more complex "What if?" models for the financial markets. These are simple simulations. Today many investors expect to see scenarios developed using real market data for any new ventures, to suggest likely market development for a new business idea. Senior management in business is often trained in the industry using complex computer models that simulate the market. The management teams are competing against their peers, taking the roles of the main players in their industry, to see which company can win in market share wars etc.

While simulators are increasingly a part of the lives of highly trained professionals, they are still a case of where a real world situation exists that is closely modelled into a computerised world. We try to paint an accurate picture of the real world and replicate it precisely in the virtual world. This limits greatly the scope of what can be done in the virtual world. Because in the real world we have real laws of nature to deal with. There is gravity, time, money and size restrictions. If we were to capture the full opportunity of the virtual world we should not be limited by these earthbound real world restrictions. In the virtual world we can go way beyond the rules and limitations of our world today.

Modern young generations are increasingly comfortable with virtuality in harmony with the real world. The reason is that the young generation of today was the first to get to play with virtual toys. The older readers may recall with considerable trepidation the phenomenon of the tamagotchi.

Tomi T Ahonen & Alan Moore

B VIRTUAL PETS

The first case of a truly virtual product or service hitting the mainstream mass market was the tamagotchi. The tamagotchi initially was a cheap toy pet. The tamagotchi was launched in 1996 by Bandai in Japan and by the time the global craze had passed, a massive 40 million of the toys had been sold.

Tamagotchi

The idea behind the tamagotchi was to create interaction between the gamer – a child – and the virtual pet so that the gamer has repeated play by feeding, nurturing and playing with the tamagotchi regularly to keep it healthy and growing. Each tamagotchi would develop minor variations, such as becoming overweight or unhappy, depending on how often and how the interaction was had with the toy. Many a family faced the trauma of the child returning from a weekend away to find that the dear tamagotchi had died because older family members had not grasped the importance of the toy and the need to nurture it.

> **GDP of virtual world of EverQuest would make it 77th richest country**

While it may have seemed odd to adults watching their kids, those children with their tamagotchis grew very fond relationships with a virtual pet. They formed emotional ties with what was, in effect, computer programming algorythms. Children named their pets, took them to school and showed them to friends, and played with the tamagotchis of their friends etc. All of the behaviour relating to the tamagotchi was similar to that with a real pet, without the "moral" trauma of the child forgetting to feed the dog and having the real family pet die.

Tamagotchi Mutations

As the first generation of the tamagotchi phenomenon was passing away, the same principles behind the game were being introduced in various games for the mobile phone. The first successful variation of the tamagotchi theme was the **Sumo Wrestler** game introduced in Japan on NTT DoCoMo's i-Mode service in 2000. Exactly like the earlier youth tamagotchis, now older (mostly boy) gamers would need to feed and train (ie, play with) their virtual sumo wrestlers so that these would become strong and capable fighters. The Sumo Wrestler game then added a new powerful activating and motivating element to the toy: network play. Now, these virtual sumo wrestlers would be scheduled to fight other virtual wrestlers on the network. The tamagotchi was back, in Japan.

Being close to Japan, the Hong Kong market got interested in the idea, but did not want to deploy a sumo game, as sumo wrestling is not that popular in Hong Kong. In Hong Kong the game was adopted and adapted, being reincarnated as a kick-boxing karate fighting network game. Again the kick-boxers were fed and trained so that they could fight successfully against other such karate combatants on the network, exactly like younger children fed and played with their tamagotchis a few years earlier.

As word spread of the strange mobile network fighting games in Japan, the game idea spread to Europe. The mobile operator/carrier Orange adapted the idea but targetted the game for younger users who were interested in dinosaurs, by releasing the **Dino Island** game in 2002. Again the players would grow, feed, nurture and play with their dinosaurs. There was a fighting element for those who wanted to fight dinosaurs. Orange reports that still in 2004 the game is a favourite revenue-generator among its target age group.

Virtual friends

Meanwhile in Hong Kong and Japan the tamagotchi idea was developed even further as the virtual girlfriend/boyfriend. Rather than feeding food to the "pet", now the virtual girlfriend of boyfriend needed caring SMS text messages on a daily basis. These could be love poems and other shows of affection so that the relationship would grow and flourish. The virtual partner would react in predictable ways, so if the gamer has annoyed the virtual friend or ignored the partner too long, then the virtual girlfriend/boyfriend would become annoyed. To fix matters, the gamer would then need to send virtual flowers, chocolates etc to make the partner happy again. The concept is still the tamagotchi, only the setting is a bit different, and the target age group obviously teenagers. For those who think this idea is so silly it can only work in the Far East, it may come as a surprise that the British version of this game generates tens of thousands of premium SMS text messages per month in the UK alone.

Here we see the first real interplay with the virtual world and the real world. When interviewed on why they spend money on a virtual girlfriend or boyfriend, users, typically young teenagers, respond that this is practice. They do not have a real boyfriend or girlfriend – yet. Young people at that point in time are very insecure about their personal appeal, appearance and skills in being able to perform "correctly" in the first relationship soon to appear. So they practise being a good boyfriend or girlfriend, with a virtual partner.

The idea is not far-fetched. In some of mankind's most intense areas of capability, such as fighter pilots, submarine crews, tank crews etc, trainers use simulators to train.

Tomi T Ahonen & Alan Moore

Young people today are very astute, will naturally gravitate to anything that could give them the "edge" or to help them overcome what to them is the most traumatic near-future scenario, the first real romance. But returning to our theme, this interesting relationship tutor is actually just a variation on the tamagotchi. A virtual pet.

Bees and horses

The tamagotchi was also being introduced to adults. In Austria in 2002 the tamagotchi reappeared as the network game **Killer Bees**. In this game the "tamagotchi" was not a live pet as such, it was the beehive (castle) that gamers would build with worker bees, and then gamers would grow an army of killer bees to attack the beehives of other networked gamers. The game soon became popular with teams such as colleagues at work. The idea was that colleagues would know when one of them was stuck in a meeting or otherwise unable to defend the beehive, that was the ideal time to attack. With a national leader board displaying who are the national masters, these were the continuous targets of rivals, which meant that there was also a lot of variation with the top rankings as the best players got to be attacked more than the rest.

While the Killer Bees was mostly an entertainment game, in Hong Kong the local more money-oriented culture developed the tamagotchi idea into a money-making and gambling opportunity. The game **Super Stable** was introduced in 2002 and now the tamagotchi returned as the virtual racehorse that you nurtured, fed, grew, groomed and trained. The aim was to get the horse ready to enter races against other virtual horses. The virtual races are broadcast in Hong Kong just like real live horse races with, of course, all the related aspects such as race track conditions, the weather, breeding and trading of horses, and very importantly for the region – betting.

Superduper stable

Super Stable has hit the Hong Kong passionate horse racing community and has become so popular that its users spend more on their mobile phone than heavy business users spend on regular voice and messaging. The gamers are not teenagers interested in video games. These gamers are adults, who are passionate about horses, but cannot afford a real horse. Through Super Stable these owners get many of the benefits of owning a real horse at a tiny fraction of the cost. Meanwhile the game developers and network operators collect all kinds of service fees from special horse feeds, grooming and training etc, services they offer to the gamers, always, of course, at a fee.

Super Stable demonstrates that people today want *interactivity and engagement* that today life is built around more intense and profound personal experience. The game has already spread to neighbouring Taiwan, allowing gamers of both countries to enter horses to international meets of virtual horses with the races broadcast live. But keep in mind this also is only the tamagotchi, reborn. As Timi Petersen of Hasan & Partners said: "If you're into something, why not get more of it?"

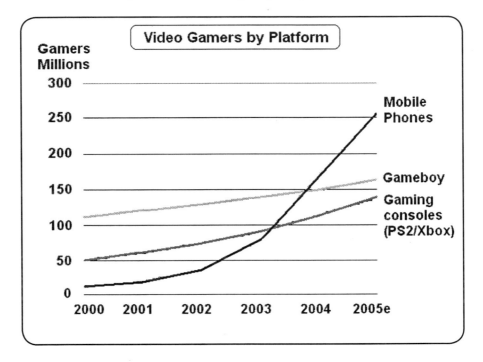

Real money out of games

Gaming is about to undergo a dramatic change. The previous generations of gaming platforms were designed for single and dual play. Now new game innovations are all about increasing the interactivity and enhanced experience. And is there money in gaming? Already today the videogaming industry is bigger than the music industry, and bigger than Hollywood movies.

C VIRTUAL WORLDS

The tamagotchi-type virtual pet world changed dramatically with the advent of the MMOG (Massively Multiplayer Online Game). The first MMOG appeared in 1997 with *Ultima Online*, which had 250,000 subscribers. Today games such as

                    Tomi T Ahonen & Alan Moore

EverQuest have half a million active players each paying $13 per month just for subscription fees. *EverQuest* earns $78m per year, which places it in the class of a successful Hollywood blockbuster.

MMOG environments are unlimited by the "realities" of the real world. Players typically set up characters and can have characteristics that are different from themselves – such as a male user taking on the role of a female – and depending on how the gaming environment is set up, players can have magical and superhuman powers. In fact much of the MMOG world capitalises on the virtual world's escape from reality; magic spells and supernatural powers are typical of these environments.

Users often create avatars, virtual depictions often but not necessarily in the shape of a human or animal. The avatars are the playing pieces in the games and depictions of the players themselves to interact and communicate with other players. These discussions can often spread into the real world, where discussions are taken off-line to talk via the phone or email with the other player.

Most MMOGs have been developed for the fixed internet, and tend to work best on broadband connections. But following the trends of ever more powerful mobile phones, MMOGs are also appearing in the mobile phone space. *Pocket Kingdom: Own the World* is an MMOG developed for the Nokia n-Gage gaming phone. The game has most of the typical MMOG elements, but one of Nokia's gimmicks is a 24-hour news channel on the Nokia n-Gage gaming phone dedicated to what is happening and relevant to Pocket Kingdom.

Economics of Virtuality

A game world can set the boundaries of what can be done; ie, what it costs in a given game's money currency to buy a given good or service, such as buying weapons, a home, some furniture, or to book passage from one part of the MMOG world to another, etc. The virtual world collides with the real world when there are enough players to try to "cheat" and in MMOGs there invariably are so many players that real rules of the economy come into play. Currently on major MMOGs many players may want to purchase some goods or services using real money rather than accumulating gaming money. This is like if playing the traditional board game *Monopoly*, you suddenly go to a friend's home and buy his game to get more Monopoly money – paying real cash for the play money – so that you can return to your game and be rich again.

This may sound like behaviour of the seriously deranged if you are enjoying a few hours of family entertainment with a board game. On MMOGs the players spend weeks and months developing their gaming experiences. This makes the time invested quite significant and motivates players to shift real world resources into the game. Bizarre? Perhaps to us of an older generation, but for the gaming youth familiar with virtual worlds, this is rational behaviour. How serious is it? Just on eBay in late 2003 there were 28,000 trades every week on virtual properties on just one MMOG, *EverQuest.*

eBay transactions for MMOG goods and services involve the exchange of typical virtual properties such as weapons, ammunition, real estate properties such as castles, as well as more obscure gaming "valuables" such as spells. Most relevantly, the gaming currency can be bought and sold on eBay. The sales transactions just on eBay amount to over $500,000 per week with global sales on all real world trading markets worth about $1.5m per week. The trade in virtual goods for MMOGs was reported to be worth $78m per year in 2003, according to *The Financial Times,* and by 2004 the real world market for virtual properties of MMOGs had exploded to $880m according to *Wired* Magazine. We are on the verge of a billion dollar industry where all of the value is virtual, and the value was completely created by the gaming community in their spare time. Imagine if you had that kind of productivity from your staff? *Wired* reported on the development:

> *For years, companies like Sony Online Entertainment have prohibited the buying or selling of goods from games such as EverQuest. Despite such rules, which are commonly spelled out in MMO's terms of service, the secondary market for virtual goods is estimated at $880 million annually.*
> *Wired* December 20 2004

Better yet, with the sales of virtual money on eBay, an exchange rate has emerged for what the gaming currency is worth in real money. The exchange rate for the "Norrathian Platinum", the gaming currency in *EverQuest,* was 1.538 to a dollar at the end of December 2003. Now properties in the game can be valued in dollar terms and real values established for virtual goods. These are determined by laws of supply and demand and reflect economic realities in the gaming environments. *The Financial Times* reported that the virtual GDP of *EverQuest* could be calculated per (virtual) capita and at $2,266 per capita, the virtual gaming world has created wealth that makes it the 77th wealthiest country on Earth.

26% of American adults post ratings on internet

We want to stress this point. In just one MMOG virtual world nearly two years ago, its gamers had **created** an economy so wealthy, it produces the annual equivalent to the **total domestic product** of a vibrant country the size of Croatia, Cuba, Ecuador, Liberia, Slovakia, Sri Lanka, Syria, Tunisia, Uruguay and Vietnam. The virtual world opportunity is immense, and growing at unprecedented speeds. Many real world start-up companies exist already to provide goods and services within that virtual world and the opportunities are there for mainstream business to get involved and active. The virtual environment is the new "gold rush" of this decade. Anyone can join in.

Real fans for virtual stars

The MMOG virtual gaming worlds have introduced yet another strange twist on reality meeting virtual world. There are now young but experienced players, who become stars that attract fans. Fans sponsor their star players, support them, and then encourage their stars to play against other famous players. The fans may go and "scout" the intended rival by fighting them to find out how they do battle (and typically suffer death in the process of such encounters), and then report to their stars on how it went. The key here is to bet on the success of your star. Stars then get paid a part of the loot won on the battle. Very much like the Wild West, there are new gunslingers coming to town; some like the chances of the local sheriff, others bet on the stranger. Again this would be a quaint sideline of a gaming environment for a few who are way too addicted to gaming, until we bring in the conversion ability of changing virtual properties to real world cash, dollars, via eBay. Remember it's already a billion dollar business today, and growing faster than any industry in the history of mankind.

D CHEATING WINS

The big impact for the digitally aware generations is that gamers have learned about the digital aspects of gaming. That there are certain game rules - which often can be circumvented. Some games have "god states" that can be achieved if the gamer discovers hidden keys etc, and most games have "cheat codes" that allow bypassing some of the normal rules of play. Games can be saved and then games can be cheated by not saving at a critical point.

Rules made for breaking

For example, in the videogame *Gran Turismo* gamers race against the computer and collect gaming money based on how they finish in the races. The money is then used either to tune-up the current car or cars owned by the player, or to buy ever better cars, which can then be customised with even more gaming money. Any car purchase or tune-up will, of course, then deplete the gaming bank account and the gamer has to start collecting money again by racing more. If the gamer saves the game after the money is won, but before the next cool car is bought, the gamer can in effect buy many cars. Buy one car, play the game with that car for a few hours, then *not save*, but shut the game. This cheats the system. The next time the gamer opens the game, the game will give him all of his money again, and he can select another car to buy or customise, etc.

This kind of thinking may seem like "cheating" to us, and since it would never work in the real world, older generations would not instinctively look for these kinds of loopholes in a virtual world. Gamers, on the other hand, learn to live in a digital world where software rules and virtual world rules dominate, rather than the rules of the old, physical world. This gives them a considerable advantage in any kind of activities with the ever more digital world, from web design to running a virtual team.

Copying illegally and legally

Napster brought to the mass-market the idea of copying among communities. I have this in digital form, I can share it with you, and I still have it. Older generations also had copying ability, such as taping music from records to music cassettes, but these produced inferior copies. The broadcasting and publishing industries were not alarmed by these as there was a serious degradation of the content if a copy of a copy of a copy was made. And the copying equipment tended to be expensive, such as using two VCRs to make copies from one to another. Now, with digital content, it has become possible to make perfect copies time and again, generation after generation. And copying software has become so intelligent to remove some of the initial blemishes that may have been introduced in the transition from the mechanical original, such as film, and in some cases it is possible to generate better digital copies than the original mechanical master, such as an underdeveloped still picture.

Napster and its many subsequent followers like Grokster, KaZaa, Morpheus etc, introduced to the masses the idea that, rather than just sharing from music and movies of your immediate friends, you could join an electronic community of millions of people and gain access to all of their stored digital content. While this idea of sharing naturally appealed to young people who had a much larger appetite to consume music and videos than they had funds to pay for them, and also appealed to the "purists" of the fixed internet, in that all content on the fixed internet should be free, there is the obvious issue of content ownership, copyrights, royalties. Even though it was technically possible to share content, and nobody had bothered to fight against it with music cassettes and video tapes, now with digital copying a very serious threat had emerged to paying the owners of the music or video content.

Tomi T Ahonen & Alan Moore

E VIRTUAL MARKETPLACES

So far we have looked at virtual equivalents of real world concepts, such as pets, people and whole worlds. The virtual environment is also a fruitful ground for the spread of ideas. Ideas themselves are intangible. They used to be expressed in speech and writing. Now increasingly new ideas emerge and are spread by the internet and the other digital delivery means. One of the most powerful new means is blogging, which is so significant we will discuss it in its own chapter later in this book.

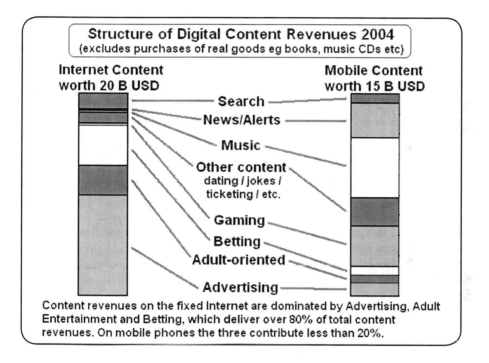

Structure of Digital Content Revenues 2004
(excludes purchases of real goods eg books, music CDs etc)

Internet Content worth 20 B USD

Mobile Content worth 15 B USD

Search
News/Alerts
Music
Other content
dating / jokes / ticketing / etc.
Gaming
Betting
Adult-oriented
Advertising

Content revenues on the fixed Internet are dominated by Advertising, Adult Entertainment and Betting, which deliver over 80% of total content revenues. On mobile phones the three contribute less than 20%.

Search

When researchers started a new project a mere twelve years ago, they headed for the library. Today, any research starts with Google, Yahoo or the preferred search engine of choice. And it will become even more powerful as whole libraries are starting to be digitalised and placed online. People are now using the internet as "the first port of call" for accessing information. The internet is now a "mass medium" and in the knowledge economy the internet is the research tool. Search is a vital part of the new marketing communications landscape. It is the single most significant contributory reason businesses have to move from "push" to "pull" marketing communications and more subtle engaging ways of communicating.

Rating systems

eBay and Amazon have also used trust and community based two-way feedback on their sites. To put this into perspective, the Center for Media Research in the US released the statistic in December 2004 that already one-in-four adult Americans have used some internet-based rating system:

> *Twenty-six percent of adult internet (about 33 million people) users in the U.S. have rated a product, service, or person using an online rating system. These systems, also referred to as "reputation systems", are interactive word of mouth networks that assist people in making decisions about which users to trust, or to compare their opinions with the opinions expressed by others. Many websites utilise some form of this application, including eBay, Amazon, Moviefone and Amihot.*
>
> *Center for Media Research* December 2004

The user numbers are most impressive. There is a need inside of us to rate products and services, to give our opinion, to effectively "have our say", Without a doubt the rating system that eBay devised and used from its earliest days, demonstrates how powerful the rating system is. Premised on trust, the individuals' interest in the welfare of the wider community should not be underestimated in the digital world. Regardless, the trends to rating indicate a willingness of consumers to become actively involved in bettering the market environment. They want to warn random customers of bad experiences, and also to reward good companies and publicise good experiences. These findings suggest a continued trend of the growth of the internet as a two-way communication network where users create and share content online, rather than acting as mere content consumers.

It is important to remember that this user-generated information has value. People seek the information, the opinion. Kevin Kelly wrote about Amazon's community in the book *Ultimate Telecoms Futures*, edited by Stephen McLelland:

> *Amazon.com has several under-appreciated aspects; one is the fact that Amazon.com ultimately sells information about books. That information comes from reviews, and the reviews are done by the customers, who are actually creating value at Amazon.com. These customers are co-creating a lot of value. The idea of the customer creating his own car had been unthinkable before this technology came along, as was the idea of*

Tomi T Ahonen & Alan Moore

customers writing an operating system. Now, we see one coming along
written by nobody, but actually by everybody.

Stephen McLelland (editor) *Ultimate Telecoms Futures 2002*

A good example of an internet site using customer feedback for its products
outside the usual suspects is **MakeupAlley**, a cult website in the USA on which
users review their most and least liked products. Here you will find the sort of
information that you do not get in women's glossy magazines. Each item is rated
by the number of users who would buy it again – information from which one can
draw one's own conclusions. For example, 96% of subscribers would buy MAC's
266 Small Angle Brush for eyes a second time, but only 50% would come back for
more Bioré Ultra Deep Cleansing Strips.

In most cases on the fixed internet the ratings and evaluations are free but new
systems are starting to emerge, in particular on the mobile phone, by which users
will actually pay for viewing such ratings and user-generated content pages. In the
UK one of the first such systems to go live is **Kwickee Guides** offering reviews
on a wide range of goods and services. Being on the mobile phone, each Kwickee
Guide page has a cost, but the innovation is that a good fraction of the actual payment of the page fee goes to the author of the page. Now reviewers and authors and
commentators are actively motivated to create the best possible content, on to pages
that can only be accessed by mobile phone, because for every time a random reader
hits the page, the actual author is paid again another about 30 pence (50 cents) into
his/her account.

m-Learning

Another obvious "tenant" of the virtual space is "education". Knowledge is an intangible service. We acquire knowledge, data, information, analysis and insight.
Yes, we can attend a course at Oxford or Harvard to gain such knowledge or buy
a reference book, but the modern digital networks are very potent at delivering
information.

RTV China has launched a new service allowing people in China to learn English
in an innovative way. The company is launching a "Cool English" service that will
include a radio programme, interactive TV, and the "Slang of the Day" via SMS, as
well as video and audio MMS. The RTV China Press release reveals:

Learning English is trendy and even receives increasing governmental
support: over the next 8 years, 62% of Shanghai's citizens shall speak
English – that's the goal. With RTV China there now is a Chinese/German
media company supporting this effort with a new campaign. What's special

about it is the approach, NOT to teach boring school English but cool slang and trend talk about topics ranging from dating to sports and travel in a radio program called "Talk da Talk". The radio program is only part of a true cross-media campaign, which is unique not only in China. The campaign also includes the "Slang of the Day" via SMS, as well as video and audio MMS. It is further enhanced by cooperation between radio stations, magazines, book publishers and SMS providers of China telecom all over China.

Source: RTV China Press Release

Young people are learning to use the virtual world in experimental ways that also seem very foreign for older generations. We explained the attraction of the virtual girlfriend/boyfriend earlier in this chapter. Similarly young gaming people are most comfortable in thinking about and trusting the results of simulations, using gaming theories to test real world responses etc. The point is that for most adults these theories need to be explained, their track records and success rates exposed. For young generations the benefits are *instinctive*; of course gaming helps improve performance.

Buy and sell

"I hate to shop but I love eBay" is a sentiment shared by many. eBay is an excellent example of benefits of communities to business. Here is not a faceless digital virtual impersonal world. No, at eBay there are clearly real people with real products (or at times virtual services) to sell, and the connection enabled by eBay is very real. Enabling communities to form, connect, share information, trade. The whole notion of eBay's staggering success is based upon trading on trust, customer feedback, communities (virtual and physical), connecting the many people to the many people; on being uncynical, idealistic, libertarian.

And just in case any reader thinks that all this wishy-washy idealism doesn't wash commercially, it does. Second quarter 2004 revenues at eBay were up 52% to $773m. eBay handles more daily trading volume than the NASDAQ. 430,000 people make their living from eBay.

180 Million cameraphones sold in 2004

Companies need to recognise that the value of their product or service is increasingly in the role it plays in consumers' lives. It is in the everyday that real value is

Tomi T Ahonen & Alan Moore

found. Companies that are information-rich have an asset which they can offer to their customers in more meaningful ways. Be that retailers, financial services, travel companies, media etc. It is more of a question of sitting down and thinking through what this value is that can surround a product or a service.

Real goods sold through virtual worlds

Real goods can be sold through virtual environments as well. The gaming world has rapidly found itself as a new marketing channel for young, mostly male, gamers. With digital games on Playstation 2 and Xbox etc, games have rapidly gone from the casio keyboard-type of simplistic music soundtracks to real recorded music used with permission. Music artists have noticed that songs preloaded as the background music for games like *Tony Hawke's* skateboarding games sell well in the same age groups in the real world. Games like *Need for Speed* now feature support from the car manufacturers to get the cars looking and feeling right, as these users will in a few years be old enough to buy their first cars. Through game product placement the brands can strongly influence young minds as they play their favourite games.

The mobile phone and intangible services

We should mention, that because all economically viable people on the planet carry mobile phones on their person at all times, and it is the only digital communication device with this level of adoption, the mobile phone is particularly suited for any virtual goods and services. In fact any intangible service is exceptionally suited to be delivered via the mobile phone. This includes lotteries – the lottery ticket is only proof of participation, but the selection of numbers is an intangible service – no numbers are actually given to the buyer. Lotteries are migrating in all countries to the mobile phone, following the early examples from China and Scandinavia.

Licences are yet another class, such as a fishing or hunting licence. In Finland Oulu was the first region where fishing licences were offered via the mobile phone. Taxes and fees for the government are still another one. In Abu Dhabi the police will accept payment of car speeding fines, paid by mobile phone. In the UK a local council send late warnings of rents due via SMS. Any intangible services can be sold on the mobile phone, and the buyer can have the proof of purchase delivered to the mobile phone.

Real end to virtuality

Where will it all end? The digital networks, overlapping, global in reach, and increasing in capacity offer a backbone for rapid expansion of virtual goods, services and, yes, virtual worlds. This chapter has outlined a few of the very first phenomena but virtuality is so new, that likely the biggest virtual opportunities still lie dormant, waiting to be discovered. Be that as it may, this chapter has clearly proven that whole new opportunities are emerging in the virtual world to make dramatic new business opportunities. Virtual worlds also provide room for expansion for established brands, goods and services. What is needed is bold vision by companies willing to capitalise on these clearly emerging, clearly lucrative opportunities. We are encouraged by the vision of a man 175 years ago, who was riding on the longest and fastest railroad of the time; the Manchester Railway. The ride at 20 miles per hour was so jerky and uncomfortable that it was not possible to drink coffee without the beverage spilling. "The time is not far off when we shall be able to take our coffee and write while going, noiseless and smoothly, at 45 miles per hour," said Isambard Kingdom Brunel, considered the greatest engineer of all time, who then went on to achieve that incredible accomplishment with his Great Western Railway only a few years later.

Case Study 4
The Habbo Hotel

The fixed internet is notoriously poor at generating payment for content. As the fixed internet has no built-in payment mechanism, any payment will need cumbersome other arrangements from subscription models to payment by credit cards, to establishment of virtual wallets and e-cash. Part of the problem is that young people – those most likely to try out new opportunities on the internet – are also those with least financial instruments to pay for anything.

In Finland an innovative mixture of fixed internet game and mobile payment has been introduced as the Habbo Hotel. The Habbo Hotel is a virtual hotel or visiting place where any internet users can establish a persona and then visit with each other. Users can hire a room in the hotel and then personalise the room.

Any visitors to the Habbo Hotel can do so for free, this is typical of the internet culture. But the hosts – the friend whose room you visit – will need to pay for the room and any decorations and entertainment etc in the room, in concept similar to hiring a room in a real hotel. So if you want background music, posters, furniture, etc, these all will then need to be paid for.

The payment gimmick with Habbo Hotel is premium SMS text messaging. All young users in Finland who might have internet access at home,

---

in school or at a library, will also already have personal mobile phones. In Finland over 90% of 10-year-olds have mobile phones. Thus while the kids are years away from their first credit card, they have a viable payment tool for the Habbo Hotel. The hotel environment is becoming very popular in the 12-17 year old segment. Very much like personalising their mobile phones with interchangeable covers, ringing tones and screen savers, now the young people can personalise their Habbo Hotel room.

While all decorations and items do cost, the costs of the virtual goods tend to be a small fraction of what the real items would cost. Thus rather than inviting friends to visit your real home, you can bring them over to the Habbo Hotel and visit with your virtual room, one which can be significantly more "cool" than your real room.

The phenomenon is rather interesting. Children could meet in reality, face-to-face, with their friends, go to the home of any of them, and share in playing with real toys. But rather they all go online, visit the rooms of the Habbo Hotel, and share playing and interacting with purely virtual toys and goods. Children in Finland are most comfortable with this type of interplay between the real world and the virtual world.

There are certain things that may be easier to accomplish in the virtual world, and those are best experienced with friends in a familiar environment that the children can control – their own room(s) in the Habbo Hotel. Other matters – like celebrating a birthday at McDonald's – are obviously more enjoyed live, in person with the very same friends.

In Finland there was even a case of the theft of some virtual property from the Habbo Hotel towards the end of 2003, when the real police were brought in. It is believed to be the first case of a real policeman attempting to solve a crime performed purely in the virtual space.

"The best mind-altering drug is the truth."
Lily Tomlin

VI
Delivery Channels Splintering
Battle of the channels

Another revolution happening with digitalisation and networked connectivity is the splintering of distribution channels. Services and goods are packaged and delivered in new ways. This creates opportunities to deliver existing digital services but also creates threats to existing ways of doing business. Monopolies that once held the keys to access to specific distribution channels are under threat as their competitors see new ways to circumvent them. It is disruptive and it is bloody. The explosion of cable and satellite TV has fragmented audiences and each new digital outlet forces choice upon us – eroding our familiar analogue world. This chapter will look at delivery channels both physical and digital. We start with examining how we have both splintering and converging channels.

A SPLINTER AND CONVERGE

We have seen how digitalisation will produce a vastly fragmented market with countless copycat services. At the same time the traditional mass media channels have multiplied and are increasingly encroaching upon each others' focus areas.

Multiple channels

Once content has been made digital, it becomes very easy to duplicate across multiple formats. For example James Bond, content was initially only offered in the

1950s and 1960s via printed books and motion pictures. With the success of the movies, the soundtrack was released also as music records. By the 1970s Bond had arrived on TV. As the secret agent remained popular even after the original author Ian Fleming died, new books were commissioned by further authors. This was all in the times of analogue technologies. But now, with the advent of digitalisation, Bond, James Bond can be distributed across a wide range of channels. 007 has invaded the internet, video games, and a vast multitude of custom content in specialised magazines, DVD specials, and a wide range of new books – not with new adventures of the hero, but books about the existing movies and books about the secret agent.

Converging

Distribution channels are also converging. Only 10 years ago a bookseller was very distinct from a computer store that was distinct from a gaming store, which was different from a music store, again, different from a video store. These were all self-contained ecosystems. Today, increasingly, stores expand their offering where major booksellers can sell also music CDs, video games, movies and TV shows on DVD, as well as computer software. The same is true of record stores, computer stores, gaming stores and video stores.

Another example is Amazon. Starting out as a bookseller, Amazon has expanded its offering to a wide array of goods and services that it now sells from the obvious such as the same music, games and movies as in more conventional booksellers, but also perfumes, toys and a wide range of other goods.

Disintermediation

The simultaneous splintering and converging of distribution channels are creating opportunities for disintermediation in the distribution chain. Or, in layman's terms, part of the value chain is eliminated. If we shift a major part of our music and book purchases to the internet, the traditional music and book stores will get less of our money, and some of them will go out of business. If music is consumed directly as digital file downloads, there is diminishing demand for traditional music CDs. They may go the way of the vinyl records and C-cassettes. Disintermediation is happening in almost all industries to a greater or lesser degree. Traditional ways of delivering goods and services are adapting and reorganising into less rigid and formal ways, resembling value webs more than value chains.

Tomi T Ahonen & Alan Moore

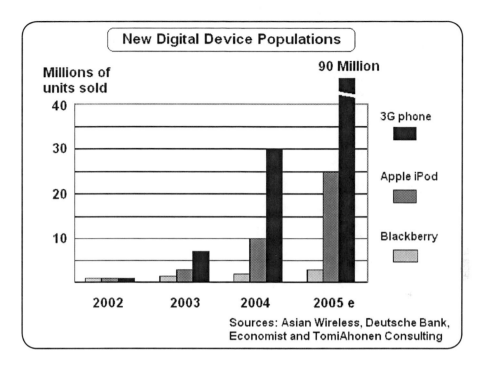

New Digital Device Populations

Millions of units sold

90 Million

3G phone

Apple iPod

Blackberry

2002   2003   2004   2005 e

Sources: Asian Wireless, Deutsche Bank, Economist and TomiAhonen Consulting

B RETRAINING RETAIL

When we were young we remember experiencing the strange but curiously won derful smell of the tobacconist, or the lure of the sweetshop, with its dark wooden counter and rows and rows of exotic jars of sweets. Or, the practical fascination of the hardware store, or the cavernous furniture store. Each, had their own sense of adventure, each had their own myth. Even as the "high street" (British) or "main street" (American) gave way to the shopping malls, still those specialist stores carried their own brand promises; record stores, blue jeans, the electronics store chain, etc. That old retail shopping experience is now facing change.

Where is the old store I used to know?

The physical effects of digitalisation have seen many traditional storefronts literally disappearing. From the first steps by banking cash machines (ATMs, Automated Teller Machines) to the internet and now mobile phone banking, we've seen a continuous erosion of physically manned bank branch offices. In Finland already less than 10% of all banking transactions are done in the bank offices – and traditional cheques were phased out three decades ago.

With digitalisation rival methods have appeared; there now are independent third party cash machines – usually charging a premium for withdrawals – and some supermarket chains have started to allow cash advances etc. At the same time mobile phones and credit cards have started to merge, such as in Korea where the market leading SK Telecom offers Visa branded credit via its mobile phones. Many stores and vending machines now connect wirelessly with mobile phones, for example with infra-red, to allow credit card purchases.

The same trend of vanishing high street stores seen with travel agencies suffering because of internet bookings. Similar effects are seen with booksellers and music stores. Soon we expect similar effects to be seen across most traditional establishments on main shopping streets around the world.

Encroachment everywhere

For example, British newsagents and stationers WH Smith has seen its customers escape to more convenient retailers. These might be the generalist stores like megastores and supermarkets, or specialists like bookseller Waterstones or HMV the music store. Increasingly, the growth is with retailers operating on digital platforms whose business models are beginning to realise the opportunities of technology, networks and the more refined needs of the consumer. We may listen to a new album at HMV or Virgin superstore, then go on the internet and buy the album at a discount. We might buy the song as a ringing tone for our mobile phone, or we might go to iTunes or Rhapsody and pay to download our favourite tracks.

> ## From 2004 the most used gaming device is the cellphone

Let's consider WH Smith's value proposition a bit more deeply. Beyond the rows and "spines" of magazines, newspapers, candy, books, DVDs, CD's that WH Smith sells, lies the latent potential and excitement of populist culture. WH Smith is a business all about "knowledge distribution". It is, in fact, its biggest strength. And that "knowledge" or "content" has to be aggregated totally differently and presented in the most exciting way possible to capture future profits and cash flows.

WH Smith is seen and thinks of itself as a retail store. It is, in fact, a knowledge and entertainment distributor. It could be: a creative facilitator, a community facilitator, an education facilitator, a hobby or interest facilitator, a lifestyle facilitator. In this way a store like WH Smith could start to create the cultural context, and package its content in a way that customers would find entertaining, useful and hopefully

Tomi T Ahonen & Alan Moore

a reason to spend more time and money in their store. That bundles and leverages their assets in more entertaining and meaningful ways.

Virtual hair cuts?

Some retailers seemingly struggle to understand the profound implications the digital future has for them, other than to know they are under siege. Others experiment and discover community dimensions almost by accident. Today, for example, most major bookstores have their own coffee shops so patrons can come, browse books and spend time in the store. A more modern, digital example comes from the British hairdresser chain Toni & Guy. They have developed a mobile phone service where you can try different hair styles digitally, sending them to your friends to get their approval or howls of laughter. But it is a service which frees the hairdresser from a physical space, and offers up an "added value" service that expands a customer's experience. It is a niche example, but it points to possibilities, and opportunities to reach out with "pull" media as opposed to interruptive communications.

Pay to buy?

We are starting to see a premium of making purchases in the retail store. The airline industry was the first to do this, where the price of the airfare is set based on the internet fare and an e-ticket. If you want a paper ticket you will be charged extra. Traditional travel agencies are feeling the squeeze as their customers are transferring the purchasing to the internet. We may well see a parallel pricing standard for many goods, where bricks and mortar store prices are above the web shopping prices.

Certainly we as consumers still sense a value to going to a store. We like to see and touch the items we buy, especially those which are not purely digital content. So if we want to compare two plasma-screen TV sets, we want to see them side-by-side to compare the picture quality for ourselves. Yet for such expensive purchases, our preference is to take the often significant savings from the purchase made online.

Atypical digital pioneers

Museums are knowledge distributors and have adapted to survive, as Darwin would say. They are doing so by engaging better with their public. The Science Museum in London or the Exploratorium in San Francisco are both good examples. Even the Natural History Museum, London, has opened a space where children can touch, feel, learn and explore. Interactivity is not a digital concept; it is the way children play and learn, it is a fundamental aspect of our social makeup.

Libraries are another such entity in search of a role in the digital age. A good way to see that future is to visit a typical library in one of the pioneering digital countries, Finland. In Finland all libraries include internet access personal computers that can be booked for 30 minutes or one hour at a time, for free, on a pre-order basis. You can make one booking with your library card, and only after your session is done will the digital system allow you to make your next booking. This guarantees nobody can hoard the computers for hours on end, and the libraries have a good measure and clear data of how they are being used and by whom. Understandably paid-for internet cafes are hardly viable in Finland.

The libraries have also innovated in many ways to help their customers benefit both with traditional books and more digital media. You can make book reservations online, but you can also order music CDs and movie videotapes and DVDs, and have them shipped from the library of record to your local branch, all by a click of the mouse. If an item is currently on loan by someone else, you can have your branch send you an SMS text message to inform you when the book, CD or movie has arrived. And also, if your loaned item is becoming due to be returned, you will get a notification by SMS text message. Better than that, if the item is not ordered by someone else, you do not need to return the book, CD or movie to the branch; you can extend your loan simply by reply SMS text message.

Video rental going virtual

Blockbuster Video was once a great business model, putting its video stores on most street corners in most towns. When access to movies on video was limited, the idea of a rental "library" system for video was a great business model. But last year that business model hit a brick wall when cable behemoth Comcast and children's programme creators PBS and Sesame Workshop did a deal with London based HIT Entertainment to make a 24-hour digital cable TV channel for preschool children. The killer punch is that a parallel video-on-demand (VOD) service aimed at preschoolers was part of the deal.

Why is this bad news for Blockbuster? Because it is these children that take their mums and dads, uncles and aunties to the video store. Children with access to video-on-demand are not going to want go to the local Blockbuster for what is ultimately a limited choice of films. The VOD service is to be launched in early 2005 and available to any cable operator in the US. One can imagine that this is but one example of VOD. Sky in the last quarter of 2004 launched a massive campaign in the UK offering its subscribers films on demand.

We are not predicting that video rental is dead, yet. We do suggest that it is no longer a growth opportunity. Would you consider setting up a traditional travel agency or music store at your town centre or megamall? The internet has already

Tomi T Ahonen & Alan Moore

turned these traditional store concepts into a shrinking opportunity. Video rental is one of the next to go.

C RETHINKING CONTEXT

Entertainment is as much a part of today's high street as it is in the multiplex cinema. Entertainment, edu-tainment, info-tainment, these are all things we willingly consume. The key is that consumers not only want goods and services. They increasingly want to be entertained as well. Today there is no distinct "leisure". Brands are what people "do", and customers are bored with products and "same-old, same-old" brands. They are demanding experiences. They are content hungry; you do not come out of a computer game and put up with the sliced white bread that is all too often the current high street experience. Retailers today have no choice but to engage.

Shoppa-tainment?

We are already familiar with info-tainment, the mixing of information and entertainment, or edu-tainment, making learning and education more entertaining. Might the retail store be next? Are we on the verge of "shoppa-tainment"? So companies like British newsagent chain WH Smith facing the need to rethink why they exist on the high street, must realise; more advertising, more design, more conventional and incremental changes will not solve their problems. They need a transformational strategy. Vittorio Radice, the visionary behind the reinvention of the UK department store, Selfridges, says: "We are not in the retail business, we are in the entertainment business. We compete with all the other places our customers go to." Retail will need to find a new role, new meaning, new value proposition to its customers, if it wants to achieve its objectives.

D REBEL NETWORK

It has become common that the young generation rebels and takes part in activities that their elders disapprove of. From the beginning of the last century, young people have had their jitterbug, jazz, rock and roll, punk, rap etc. A particularly rebellious generation was that of the 1960s, the first to form a global force, for "flower-power"; the hippie movement. Hippies believed in sharing, communities, and hippies wanted everything to be free. As we know, the movement died out as one commune after another closed down. The hippie parents who grew up in the 1960s had their children grow up in the 1980s who now are now starting to have their own children, making the hippie generation already grandparents.

It is important to bear in mind that before the hippies there was no overarching concept of sharing for free, of combining as communities to serve a common good. Arguably communism was supposed to be like that, but socialist governments in Eastern Europe and Asia were centrally governed and in economic terms they were strictly "centrally controlled economies", not community-controlled systems. Thus they were neither true communists, nor communities as we discuss in this book. We certainly are not suggesting our communities to be anything like communism. And also, while the hippie movement as such did not survive, some of their philosophies did, and now find support in surprisingly strong numbers. These range from sharing for free to combining into communities for common efforts. The hippie philosophy found some of its early successes, power and reputation on the internet.

The anarchy-net

Nobody will doubt the overwhelming effect of the internet to society today. In addition to doing many of the older things more efficiently, such as "mail order" type of sales, or email or research, the internet has introduced radical new market opportunities, from file sharing to Skype internet phone calls to eBay etc. As most internet analysts will say today, we are still early in realising the full effects. The internet over time will become a much more significant factor to mankind than what it has done so far. Itt is expected that during 2005 internet-based business-to-consumer e-commerce will exceed traditional mail-order sales.

The internet is but one in a long series of technological innovations, such as steam power, railroads, electricity, the automobile, telegraph, telephone, the airplane and TV. But in stark contrast to all the others, the internet is an inherently disruptive force. Drastically differing from all previous technologies, the internet is *not controlled*. All others are tightly regulated, on centrally controlled systems such as electricity, telephone and TV; or on rigidly defined and expensive routes such as railroads, automobiles and airplanes. Railroads and highways for cars cost millions to build and maintain, and while airplanes do fly rather freely in the air, they are totally dependent on airports, which again are immensely expensive to build and maintain, and airplanes are tightly controlled by air traffic controllers so that two planes don't crash into each other in mid-air.

Dog-net

On the internet there are no rules, and the system is not confined to any space. You can go to the computer store today, buy the components you want, construct the system as you design it, and then build a dozen extensions to the internet yourself. Nobody will require a licence or permit, and you will have grown the internet further. If you then want to use your IP devices to control your pet dogs and cats, it is your right. If you want to put up a server to show video feeds of your wife cooking, or put up a joke site to make fun of the President, or whatever, you can. On the internet it is as if anarchy rules.

Interestingly, as we will see throughout this book, there are certain rules even in anarchy, as communities form, and communities generate their own informal standards, leaders emerge as do forms of behaviour. And, as we will also see in this book, all that seems so revolutionary and significant on the fixed internet today, pales in comparison to the much more magnified effects of the mobile phone-based "internet" of tomorrow. We will see that the fixed internet will have been only a transitionary technology, much like steam carriages were to cars, dirigibles (airships, zeppelins) were to airplanes, or mainframe computers were to the PCs, laptops and PDAs of today. The next evolution in digital connectedness will be based on the mobile phone (cellular phone), not the PC/PDA-based internet. That future exists already in Korea and Japan.

The hippie-net

From a technology point of view, the internet was a development strongly influenced by the hippie culture mentality. The internet roots come from the US military Arpanet project of the 1960s to design a communication network capable of surviving an attack in nuclear war.

80% of fixed internet content is Advertising, Adult & Betting

---

By the 1970s the first connections were being brought online. The most distinguishing differentiating aspect of how the internet differs from our telephone network, is that the internet is designed to work without centralised control. All telephone networks are centrally controlled, thus a (nuclear) attack on a few key control centres would completely disable the national telephone grid. But the internet works on a decentralised, uncontrolled basis. Every node on the network attempts to control the near area. Thus if ten major cities are bombed, the internet would cease to function of course in those cities. But in the rest of the country the internet would continue to function and the internet would automatically reconfigure itself to bypass the faulty areas of the network (the bombed ciities). You would have some areas you could not contact but the whole network would not go down.

The philosophy for what was still not even called the internet in the 1980s, required thus from the start the recruiting of massive amounts of data communication centres in the USA. The US military installations and government sites were obvious first parties to join. Their mainframe computers were connected, and the internet had dozens of contact points and connections. But, interestingly, the second wave was to get the American university campuses connected. This was still the time when personal computers were at their very infancy, and nobody yet even imagined PCs to be part of this massive computer network. Who owned mainframe computers at the time? The governments, big business, and universities. It was a lot easier to convince the universities to open up their computers to this network than business corporations. So universities came next. With the universities connected, suddenly the internet had thousands of contact points.

Network of networks

The basics of the current internet standard, that has hundreds of millions of users, traces its roots to this time, to what was then an obscure data networking standard, called TCP/IP (Transmission Control Protocol/internet Protocol). Here is where the "internet" name comes from, it was part of the name of the standard to interconnect networks to each other, to connect the government, military and university campuses.

By the time in the late 1980s when the majority of connections, users and data traffic on the internet was between universities, the internet was seen as the perfect information storage, organisation, search and sharing system. Universities are in the information industry; this was their big leap into the digital age. Researchers started to share ongoing work with colleagues across the USA and Canada, and very soon also the UK, Scandinavia and gradually much of the rest of the university world as it connected.

Free forever

Because universities carried the bulk of the communciation infrastructure cost – this was still the time of mainframe computers being the dominant members of the internet – and they had limited budgets, they decided to build the data sharing principles to be on a free, shared principle. The idea of instituting some kind of accounting system to track what was stored or borrowed or – heaven forbid, bought and sold – on the internet was immediately dismissed as unnecessary overhead. No need to. The system was designed on the principle of information is free for all. A very hippie-like thought. Let's all share in the information. Let's not bring money into the equation. Money corrupts.

Tomi T Ahonen & Alan Moore

By the time in the 1990s when email systems were coming online in businesses, and the personal computer started to have powerful modems, the interest was to connect not only to your local little network, either at work or on a "BBS" Bulletin Board System, but also soon the interest emerged to want to connect with the big network. The internet. Up to this time all information on the internet was supposed to be archived by a standard for an archiving system called "Gopher". Using Gopher was powerful if you knew how, but it was not at all user-friendly. By 1994 we had seen the first releases of web browsers, Mosaic and Netscape, and now a tool was there for surfing the WWW, the WorldWide Web, or what we now call simply the web. Because there were no monetary limits, and people could access the internet with standard PCs, the development of the internet took off rapidly.

The PC allowed individuals to program applications that could be run on their computer, and on other PCs. They were either IBM-compatible or Apple/Macintosh compatible, but millions of devices could run the programmes. Again here the internet saw the clash of hippie philosophies with the business community. Some companies were obviously in the business of selling software, Microsoft the obvious example. The internet introduced the idea of freeware and shareware, of free software that could be shared. In a perfectly hippie-like philosophy, if we had programmed a simple computer application, we could give it for free to our friends. There are literally thousands of perfectly functional computer applications that exist today that are freeware.

Since it cost nothing to transmit even large amounts of data on the internet, we could easily do so. And with university students still the majority of the early users of the internet, they were, of course, strongly drawn to anything that was free. Microsoft is still targeted. Linux, one of the only computer operating systems today that is a viable alternative to Microsoft's, is the product of collaborated freeware effort started by Finnish programmer Linus Torvalds in the 1990s.

Why internet so disruptive

Why does the internet seems so disruptive to some business and often fatal to new ones? Doc Searls and David Weinberger in *World of Ends* believe this is because the three internet virtues are the antithesis of how governments and businesses view the world:

1. Nobody owns it: Businesses are defined by what they own, as governments are defined by what they control.
2. Everybody can use it: In business, selling goods means transferring exclusive rights of use from the vendor to the buyer; in government, making laws means imposing restrictions on people.

3. Anybody can improve it: Business and government cherish authorized roles. It's the job of only certain people to do certain things, to make the right changes.
Searls & Weinberger *World of Ends,* 2001

Business by its nature is predisposed to misunderstand the internet's nature. The internet comes with its own culture and it is not the one you are used to. Yet people do want to hear what you have to say, provided you give them cause to feel they can trust you. Therein lies the rub: if your company has a pervasive culture of micro-managed "consistent messaging" subjected to endless PR department scrutiny, the result is all too often that people will simply not believe what you tell them even if it is true.

If they continue to buy your products it is in spite of, not because of, what you are saying. It does not have to be so. Unlike e-commerce, the benefits or failings of which are immediately observable (either you are moving product or you are not), the value of conversing with customers in a human voice may not be directly quan-tifiable. However, those benefits are no less tangible – credibility has lasting value.

How can you take your legacy bricks and mortar retail footprint and turn it into something that will offer added value to customers? We have discussed eBay and Amazon and other online retailers, we have shown that their influence continues to grow, we have passed the tipping point of the trust required to make payments on line thanks to eBay and Amazon. What this means internally is that companies have to be fleet of foot; dominance over a market will not be protection for long. A per-fect example is the sudden collapse of Encyclopedia Britannica's business model. That long-standing staple and standard of knowledge crumbled as the information industry went online.

Biggest community rules

The evolution of the internet holds several lessons, such as the effect of the domi-nant community on the medium. When the universities became the dominant play-ers over the military, they formed the use of the internet into a research vehicle. The research tools such as Gopher dominated. But as user numbers shot past the university crowd, web browsing and person-to-person email became the dominant uses with their tools, the web browsers. Similarly when businesses first came to the internet they were the distinct minority. Early attempts to bring any commercial uses to the internet were strongly frowned upon. Today, of course, businesses rule, and much of the traffic on the internet is based on accessing commercial websites like eBay, Amazon, Yahoo, Google, etc.

E   THE FUTURE OF TV

Television is trying to find its place in the world of multiple overlapping channels. There is a view that we are changing from passive viewers to active consumers of TV programming. Our culture is moving from the rigid system to a demand culture. Mark Thompson, Director General of the BBC, was quoted as saying, "We're going to move to a world where people will be able to enjoy BBC content in lots of new ways, delivered through lots of new channels into the home and to them on the move and on demand."

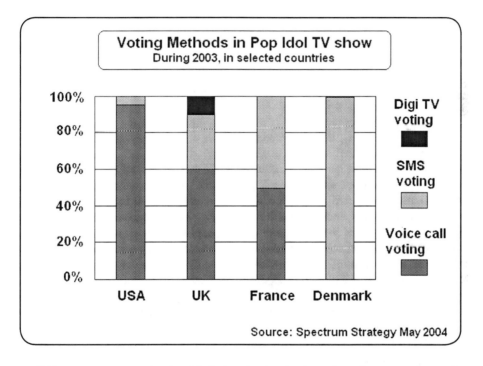

This announcement by the BBC signals clearly that a broadcaster understands its traditional boundaries are evaporating. And that to survive it must embrace the new digital age, with its new digital economics. It also signals the sea change in the role of the consumer or customer. In a media-fragmented world, companies are going to have to work very hard to keep their customers and to keep their customers' advocacy. Creating an "enhanced experience" and adding value to customers is the way this will be achieved.

The end of the TV schedule

Research recently conducted on the PVR (Personal Video Recorder), like TiVo in America and Sky+ in the UK, shows that already today television has become more personal with users taking control of the schedule. The studies clearly indicate that people are using PVRs to skip past the advertisements. This means, of course, that the conventional business model of revenue generated by TV spot advertising is under threat. The chairman of UK regulator Ofcom, Lord Currie, speaking at a Royal Television Society event said:

> *The rapid growth of first multi-channel, then digital, then PVRs and soon higher-speed broadband are simply the pre-tremors of the real volcanic eruption that technology is about to unleash," he said at yet another RTS event. "At the risk of being over-dramatic I would say that most traditional television broadcasters are today standing about the equivalent of one mile from Mount St Helens. When it blows, frankly, that will be too close and it will be too late to run."*
>
> Royal Television Society Fleming Memorial Lecture 2004

It used to be that the broadcast spectrum was a scarce resource. Only a few licences were awarded, and TV broadcasting could not sustain dozens of channels. With only a few channels, there was also only a very limited amount of programming. With cable TV and satellite, the availability of channels expanded, and subsequently the range of available programming exploded. Today private and captive audience TV channels have been launched, such as those on airlines with their multi-channel broadcasting. Campuses have private TV, grocery stores have them, in America channels provide advertising-funded programming for high-rise elevators in skyscrapers. With the advent of digital broadcasting, suddenly the limits of the broadcast spectrum are no longer the bottleneck, and the cost of going on the air has suddenly fallen to a small fraction of what it used to be.

That is all before we include broadband internet and mobile phones as delivery methods for TV and radio broadcasting. Definitely we are seeing the splintering of the broadcasting business into ever smaller niche channels, which each siphon off viewers from the main channels. When the cost of broadcast technology is so cheap, businesses and their brands can become their own broadcasters.

70% of mobile internet content is Music, gaming and News

The relevant business impact of all this to the reader is that the viewer, not the TV broadcaster, is now in control. The most precious commodity for TV viewers is their own time. They are managing that time and are not allowing a TV broadcast schedule to mess with it.

End of the thought monopoly

Why did the world sit at attention 20 years ago to watch *Dallas* and collectively held its breath to find out who shot JR? This was at the height of the golden age of TV. When every household had a TV set, the programming had evolved enough to generate addictive content. But very importantly there was no Playstation, no internet, no cable TV, no DVD players, and even video recorders and video rental stores were the rare exception. What shows were put on, we all watched. *Roots, Hill Street Blues, Coronation Street, Cheers, Happy Days, Fawlty Towers, Are You Being Served?, Dad's Army, Mork from Ork, Star Trek, Doctor Who.* The gospel according to ABC, CBS, NBC and BBC. What they said, we all took in, attending our private domestic church, with the living room arrayed around the TV set. Niall Fitzgerald once said:

> *Digitization, the new technology, the convergence of computing and telecommunications sciences, the plunging unit costs of equipment, rising levels of disposable income and the de-regulation of the airwaves all mean that simple, one-way, mass communication has its best and biggest days behind it... I do not believe that this great change will be mourned by real people – by our consumers (customers). Nor will it be mourned by companies such as mine. Because the opportunities that the new world offers are more exciting – and in some important ways more satisfying – than the very limited nature of the world it replaces.*

Niall Fitzgerald
European Association of Advertising Agencies, Dublin 1997

Up to the Middle Ages the church was able to preach its lessons as the only authority. There was no way for the common man to find any enlightenment by himself. Few could read, and there were no books. Gutenberg changed all of that. Suddenly the congregation was empowered, they were in charge They could go to the bookstore and buy a book, or a magazine or newspaper. The monopoly on thought was broken. With the shift in control and power from the TV producers to the viewers and consumers, we are going to see as dramatic a shift in the role. The TV will no longer be the dominant element in the home. And what is on TV tonight will no longer control our personal schedule.

End of the channel

We have ever more channels for goods and services to reach us. The increase in the number of available channels increases the abilities of business to optimise, to reduce costs, and bring those savings to the consumers. The new channels also introduce opportunities for new competition, often from surprising entrants. In the end it comes down not to a channel of preference, but to our time. As Herbert Simon wrote: "What information consumes is rather obvious. It consumes the attention of its recipients. Hence a wealth of information creates a poverty of attention...The only factor becoming scarce in a world of abundance is human attention."

Case Study 5

SMS to TV Chat

Chat boards are nothing new. The fixed internet has had so-called "IRC" or internet Relay Chat-based chat rooms for over two decades already. The idea with chat is that a virtual room or chat board is set up, and everyone who joins in the chat can post comments. They are displayed in time sequence, with the most recent posting appearing first. Typically chat rooms have a general theme and numerous "threads" of discussions are interweaved between the overall chat discussion. So while the general chat discussion might be about movies, a pair of friends could discuss the rock concert they both attended last night. Chatting is found to be a very addictive service and many internet services have adopted chat boards to build loyalty and repeat visits. What is typical of chat is that on the fixed internet, chatting is essentially free.

On commercial TV there is a general model where the mainstream income comes from "prime time" advertising, typically between 7pm and 10pm. That is when the biggest audiences typically view TV programming. The smaller the likely audiences, the cheaper the advertising minutes, so into the late night the ad rates drop. At some point many commercial TV channels find that it is not worth showing old movies or sitcom reruns, and they show "infomercials", the kind of half-hour shows which are prolonged advertisements for example for dramatically effective exercise equipment or remarkably powerful washing detergents, or hits of old music, etc. Of course, many commercial TV stations simply shut down for the early mornings of the day or broadcast a test pattern.

Tomi T Ahonen & Alan Moore

In Finland in 2001 the biggest local commercial TV station experimented with a new kind of chat board for the late night viewers. It was based on SMS-to-TV chat. Viewers were encouraged to send premium SMS text messages to the special phone number to see their messages displayed on the TV chat board. This innovation combined the addictiveness of chat with the celebrity of TV. Participants loved seeing their name and comments on TV. Early on the premium SMS prices were relatively low, at 3 times or 4 times the cost of regular person-to-person SMS text messaging. A number of active chatters from the internet were invited to join in the early introduction of the service to keep up a familiar "chatter" of discussion on the TV chat board.

What started as an experiment turned a profit in its first weekend. The programming was an immediate success, generating much larger incomes than infomercials. Very soon all three commercial TV channels in Finland had SMS-to-TV chat running all night. One of the channels even stopped running late afternoon soap operas to capture the young viewers when they came home from school, and started running SMS-to-TV chat in the early afternoons, before prime time.

The economic impacts to the TV industry were enormous. In two years SMS revenues earned by TV stations – not only SMS-to-TV chat and SMS games, but adding also the various voting services etc – generated more revenues than the total commercial advertising spend on TV in Finland. One should bear in mind that Finland has one of the longest traditions of commecial TV in Europe, dating from the 1950s, so this was no immature or trivial market.

Meanwhile SMS-to-TV chat kept evolving. The level of the premium paid on SMS-to-TV chat grew to *nine times* that of person-to-person text messaging by end of 2003. Typical person-to-person SMS rates in Finland were about 10 Euro cents in 2003, with SMS-to-TV chat costing 91 cents. With three channels all offering this service, even that did not curb the appetite of Finnish TV viewers, and avatars were introduced to capture even more money. If a viewer sent a message to the avatar, to read the message in its robotic voice, the price premium was *18 times* that of regular person-to-person SMS. The programming was incredibly addictive and profitable.

Today in Finland the concept has evolved into a wide range of SMS-to-TV games as well, from football scoring games to puzzles etc. Meanwhile as word has spread thoughout the world, SMS-to-TV chat is seeing similar successes everywhere from Belgium to Singapore. Many music video programmes have added SMS chat to run concurrent with videos, so viewers can send comments on videos - and have various other unrelated chat discussions – and, of course, pay by premium SMS.

"No army can withstand the strength of an idea whose time has come."
Victor Hugo

VII
Blogging
Everyone a journalist

Depending on whether you are reading this book in Europe, the USA, or elsewhere, will strongly influence how much you appreciate or even understand blogging. The important thing to know is that Bob Lutz blogs. Bob Lutz is the Vice Chairman of General Motors. Jonathan Schwartz, the CEO of Sun Microsystems, blogs. The engineers for the Ford Mustang blog. Armies of bloggers have faced up to US politicians, US news anchormen and humbled them with the truth and unraveled their careers. Bloggers have shamed large companies into global recalls of products. The Iraqi blogger, Salam Pax, gave us insights into what was going on in Baghdad from the individual's vantage point. *The Guardian* newspaper has its own blog. Why all this blogging? Because they have a point of view that they want to share with the world, they feel there is no one else to tell their side of the story and simply because they can. Perry de Havilland of the Big Blog Company puts it succinctly: "People will talk about you whether you like it or not: the good the bad and the ugly."

A BLOGGING FOR BEGINNERS

Blogging is short for "web logging", a form of online personal publishing that allows individuals and companies to articulate and "broadcast" their message into cyberspace. The major advantage of the blog format is the ability to communicate with an audience in a rapid but casual manner. The style of writing used by bloggers combined with the flexible format makes it an ideal tool for companies to communicate the "official" message to their customers in an informal and credible fashion. Blogs tend to attract people based on specific areas of interest. Their readers are, in effect, highly targeted markets and can have a disproportionate effect on a company's public image. Fundamentally, blogging is about interaction, transparency and persistent conversation carried out online.

How blogging works

Blogs are exceptionally interconnected. Blogging activity involves linking to other blogs and conventional websites as linked proof of information. Thus interesting items may be picked up by many other bloggers creating a snowball effect that can lead to big exposure. Links were already available and used in traditional fixed internet websites, so this is nothing really new, but with blogs there is a significantly larger amount of links. What makes blogs so powerful is a shift in how content is presented, so-called "permalinks." Blogging differs from internet publishing also in the frequency of content contribution. As content is frequently added, that invited regular visits and interaction. Embedded links and hyperlinking is far more prevalent in blogs than in traditional web pages. This brings about a permanence, credibility and speed to any new blogs added to the "blogosphere".

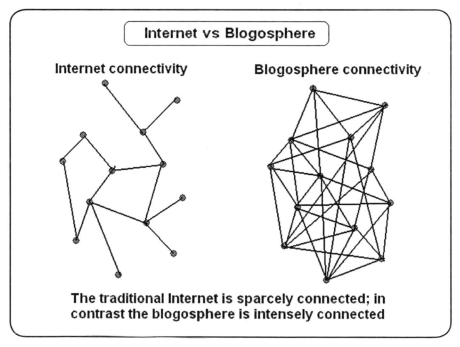

Internet vs Blogosphere

Internet connectivity   Blogosphere connectivity

The traditional Internet is sparcely connected; in contrast the blogosphere is intensely connected

Tomi T Ahonen & Alan Moore

Blogs differ from other online communication and interaction tools in several important ways:

• Chronologically updated entries

A visitor can immediately see at any blog whether it is frequently updated. If it is then blogs are identified as being information-rich and drive frequency of visits or a desire to return.

• Links in the main text and sidebars

Links in the main text mean that readers who want to check sources or want to delve deeper into the point being made can immediately link to that source. This deepens the connectivity and richness of the experience. Links on the sidebars allow the reader to pursue the interests of that specific blogger. They demonstrate what type of community a blogger is involved in and helps define what focus point the blogger takes on the issue.

• Dynamic and flexible content

Conventional websites are the industrial age of the internet. Blogging is real-time publishing, it is immediate, and its immediacy around breaking events makes it a far more powerful medium as it can filter vast amounts of information in near real-time.

• Informal style

Blogging is deeply personal, representing the point of view of an individual or a small group of individuals. The writing style is often compelling and the character and personality of the author emerges over time. This plays an important role in the popularity of blogging among ordinary, non-technical people.

• Permalinks

Permalinks are probably the single most important feature that enabled the blog network to arise. Each entry on a blog has its own unique URL (Uniform Resource Locator, the internet address such as www.futuretext.com). This acts as a "handle" on each discrete "packet" of information on the blog and allows others to "pick" it up and run with it around the network. The result is one of the most powerful emergent distribution systems.

• Credibility

One of the effects of blogs has been to supercede the credibility of traditional journalism. This is because bloggers link to the sources from which they take their information, so that their readers can verify themselves what slant any given blogger is giving to a story. Over time, the readers satisfy themselves as to the blogger's position and trust can be built upon that understanding.

• Syndication feeds
With syndication feeds based on RSS, content is updated in real-time. Syndication aggregates information. It is the advantage that syndication gives to blogs – by removing the need to visit a specific web site regularly, blogs have increased their traffic.

• Comments
Blogs often allow the reader to leave comments, which builds discussion and debate. The commentor will also leave their URL so that interested parties can then go to that blog site to read more about what they think. Information in this way is passed rapidly through the blogosphere. It all adds to the exponential interactivity of blogs and the blogosphere.

• Trackback
Blogs can also see if another blog site has mentioned them and so again interested parties will go to see how their content has been used. Trackbacks reinforce the network effects as they allow the blogger to trace who is linking to his content.

What blogging delivers

Blogging allows users to express their own opinions for the world to see. It may seem trivial and certainly many blogs may be of inconsequential relevance, but consider this blog from a disgruntled Saab owner in the USA:

> **My saab sucks**
> *Good Lord, you want to know why my SAAB sucks? Well, for one, it is a SAAB (damn foreign made cars). I got it about 6 months ago and the first thing that was screwed up is that some stupid "SRS" light keeps blinking on and off and on and off and it won't quit!! It took forever to get it inspected because I ended up having to take the fuse out so it would turn off, but I need that fuse for the turn signals so I have to see that dang light every time I get in the car. Then the power steering belt was screeching cause it was loose and I tightened it and I have to continue to tighten it every single week, at least once a week because it won't stay on right...*
> www.mycarsucks.com/rants/saab/1991_Saab_900_S.htm

The blog goes on and on with several subsequent complaints. The difference to previous complaints and communications is that an individual had little chance of

Tomi T Ahonen & Alan Moore

getting his or her personal grievance heard by the masses. With blogging suddenly the world is potentially reading. The links and rapid distribution and updates on the blogosphere can have the comment explode to massive audiences. An example of a complaint blog from a game developer's wife, whose husband was working for EA Games, drew instantly *tens of thousands* of hits – mostly by spouses and girlfriends of similarly overworked IT engineers. From the world of politics, Senator Trent Lott was forced to resign his position after making racist remarks in a speech that was glossed over initially by the mainstream media. Mazda was forced to take down a pseudo blog, when it was discovered by the blogosphere was breaking the cardinal rule – pretending to be something you are not.

Blogosphere grew from 500,000 to 4 million in 2004

From a corporate perspective, the essence of successful blogging can be understood and recreated for the benefit of companies who want to engage their customers in a new and interactive manner. Blogs offer true interaction without loss of standards and control over the content. They enable companies to find their authentic voice and teach them how to use it to address their audience – customers.

Blogosphere

The features specific to the blog format have given rise to the social phenomenon, the blogosphere. The blogosphere is a community of blogs, interlinked and emergent. Blogs as we have described are powerful aggregators of information and content, they drive phenomenal amounts of interactivity, because they are real-time multi-flows of information, knowledge, views and opinions. They provide for individuals and for companies very different ways to communicate with their audiences.

By late 2004 there were already 4,305,245 weblogs, as reported by Technorati. What is relevant is that the growth is incredibly fast. The blogosphere is eight times as large in 2004 than the same time in June 2003. *Business Week* is already convinced. They write:

> *Now advertisers are realising there is a market emerging in the blogosphere. Already, the growth in regular online advertising, estimated to be about 35% this year, will far outpace the spending increases for any other sector of the media world. Add to all this the fact that about 11% of internet users today are inveterate blog readers, and the blogging scene starts to get mighty compelling for marketers.*
>
> *Business Week,* December 13 2004

The potential of blogging goes beyond the conventional understanding of marketing – for companies it could be the most powerful CRM tool ever invented, the best PR, or at least the most potent. Think about it, compelling content will always drive interest, it is just that in today's world this will be done as mass-micro communications rather than mass communications.

Comment on non-commercial blogs

Blogging is not always commercially valuable – unremarkable content on blogs is not uncommon (see the UK blog scene eg "kitty" blogs or a large portion of the navel-gazing US blogosphere). However, there are some phenomenally successful blogs whose commentary reaches beyond the online world into the political, business and media sphere. These include Instapundit, Command Post, Chief Wiggles Operation Give and Boing Boing.

B TRUTH POLICE

The first time that blogging crossed over from the techno-geek circles to the mainstream media happened in the USA Presidential election of 2004, with Dan Rather of CBS caught using doctored evidence in a news story. The bloggers caught up to the deception in a matter of hours while it took days for the mainstream media to come around to the truth. Dan Rather was forced into an apology. Suzanne Goldenberg writing for *The Guardian* on 21 September 2004 explained how this new "Truth Police" was a credible and potent source for mainstream news media:

> *CBS television issued a humbling apology yesterday for a report on an investigative programme, saying that its story claiming that George Bush had been given special treatment during his stint in the Texas air national guard was deeply flawed and should not have gone on air. CBS was doubly at fault. It failed to appreciate the force of the thousands of voluntary fact-checkers out there on the web (let alone trying to harness their power in advance), while also failing to interview bloggers after the event as part of an ongoing story. In fact, bloggers are often people very expert in their own fields who attract other experts when issues in their domain are newsworthy. Stories in old media can be fact-checked instantaneously and the journalists and their newspapers held to account.*
>
> *The Guardian*, 21 September 2004

There is no doubt that the tectonic plates of journalism are moving. There is awesome potential in the internet as a gatherer, distributor and checker of news - not least through instant delivery channels such as mobile phones. This does not mean old media will die. But it will have to adapt quickly to what has so far been an asymmetrical relationship. Blogging, or probably its more commercially minded sibling nano-publishing, is destined to be an integral part of journalism.

Most newspaper and TV stations have been slow to embrace blogging. We may see that the hype around the CBS story will be the watershed point with the mainstream media taking blogging seriously. Founder of the political blog Samizdata.net and one of the partners of the Big Blog Company, David Carr comments: "This is the first mainstream media admission I have encountered that has been willing to admit that the mainstream media itself is under serious assault."

Reporter or blogger?

Blogs undisclosed the myth of objectivity long held within traditional journalism, which insisted on neutrality and an unbiased position when, in fact, it is impossible to be entirely objective. On a blog entry there will be permalinks and a history of previous blogs. The bias or slant in the "reporting" can be easily determined. Remember we are in an age when new consumers distrust all sources and assume all are biased. When combined with a hunger to seek answers themselves, actively, rather than accept passively what comes from the newsmedia, the young generations are poised to embrace blogging as their newsmedia.

11% of internet users are blog readers

To us it seems obvious that if bloggers can become the ultimate truth police and have already toppled globally respected news personalities, then blogging will play a major role in the newsmedia business. Many journalists are likely to initially view blogging as an opponent, a competitor, a rival. Those will be quick to mention all the frivolous, erroneous, opinionated or simply boring blogs that exist in vast numbers. But journalists are naturally curious and instinctively gravitate to good, credible, knowledgable information sources. Already today many leading journalists are keeping close tabs on what is going on in the blogosphere.

We believe that the professional journalist will naturally become a blogger, and also that many bloggers will find some role in what journalism will become in the future. This is not the catastrophic scenario of what email and the personal computer did to typists. This is more of what happened to secretaries who had to learn to use new tools like Windows, schedulers, messaging, voicemail etc, and are immensely more productive today than 10 years ago. The key lesson is that for a journalist to survive, the vital tool to learn now is blogging.

C MOBLOGGING

When English soccer star David Beckham made a visit to Japan in 2003 a thousand cameraphones snapped his visit for digital prosperity. After all, the star helped launch the mania for cameraphones, with the footballing pin-up appearing in ads promoting the daddy of the cameraphone in Japan, operator J-Phone (now renamed Vodafone KK).

Some of this new swarm of amateur paparazzi then zapped his picture off to their home page, weblog, moblog or whatever you want to call it. Such instant (if amateur) publishing is a possibility only dreamed of by the "official" media crews who were jostling for their best shots of the England midfielder alongside their new, potentially threatening, newsgathering rivals. Shortly after the excitement of the Beckhams' whirlwind Asian tour had settled down, a group of brave new bloggers inaugurated what was to be the world's first conference dedicated to mobile digital publishing.

Over 200 participants representing Tokyo's high quota of wireless-adept locals and foreigners alike squeezed into a hanger-like space in downtown Tokyo to discuss the commercial and social impact of moblogging at the First International Moblogging Conference held on Saturday, 5 July 2003 in Tokyo, Japan. Its aim was to attempt to define moblogging and explore the total experience of mobile web publishing.

What is Moblogging?

Moblogging is a blanket term that covers a variety of related practices, suggests the conference website:

> *At its simplest, moblogging (ie, mobile blogging) is merely the use of a phone or other mobile device to publish content to the web, whether that be text, images, media files or some combination of the above. Location-specific content goes one step further – it relates and connects to the specific physical place where it was created and published. This permits any particular set of real-world Co-ordinates to be "tagged" with relevant information, from instant restaurant reviews to ski-slope hazard warnings to contextual jokes.*
>
> http://marginwalker.org/1imc/

Moblogging is attracting players large and small to offer technical solutions, from Phlog.net to Nokia and its Lifeblog. Many may quibble over what exactly is moblog-

         Tomi T Ahonen & Alan Moore

ging and whose product conforms to what. The significant point is that at the end of 2004 there were 294 million cameraphones already – more than laptop PCs and PDAs *combined*. Every one of those cameraphones is technically able to generate simple text content and simple picture content for a website, either traditional or blog site. As the blogosphere is so strongly embodying the speed of content delivery, it is inevitable that bloggers will soon be doing their content postings via the cameraphone.

Moblogging is very much in its infancy. But as cameraphone numbers increase – by the end of 2005 there will be more than 600 million of them, more than all computers, laptop and desktop – and software for instant publishing becomes more popular, the wireless world is on the verge of a moblogging boom.

Mobilising Brighton Virtual Festival

In 2003 The Brighton Festival undertook an experiment, together with the mobile service specialist Future Platforms. The festival provided a service that allowed selected members of the public to submit reviews, opinions and photos live from festival events using their mobile phones. The contributions were then instantly published onto the official Brighton Festival website, where they could be read and commented upon by visitors.

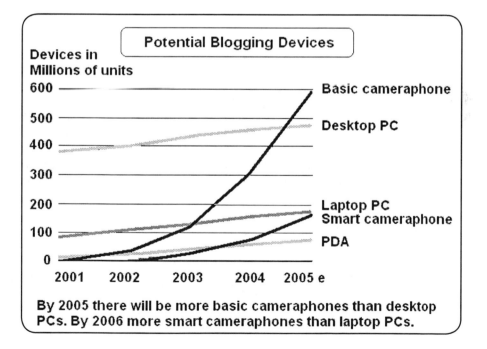

It may seem sometimes that this technology is in someone else's backyard. It may seem that it is only the geeks and technorati that would embrace such technology. However, the success of the Brighton Festival demonstrated that this was far from the truth. Focusing on the social aspect of moblogging, one can see that it is providing opportunities for communities to gather and share information and stories, in context that also is a "many-to-many" flow of information, point of view and comment. Pretty much like a real conversation – in its most simplistic terms.

D BLOGS AND TV

The story of American democracy over the past 50 years is the story of the growth of big media and the political control of it. Whether for a Republican or Democratic cause, television, the press and radio media have all been coerced knowingly or unknowingly into the services of political agendas. Cisco tells us that it took 13 years for television to make it into 50 million American homes while the internet penetration took only four years. *Wired* magazine wrote in September 2004 that the tipping point in behavourial change arrived at the World Trade Center attack of 9/11. Pre-9/11 the *Wired* article claims 3% of Americans used the internet for primary information, over 24 months later and post-Iraq that figure has risen to 77%.

This rise in online activity seeking "unfiltered" or less biased news and first-hand accounts speaks of a generation that distrusts big media, big business, their motives; a generation with an urgent desire for the truth. There is a saying that there are three sides to every story, your side, the other side and the truth. Blogs it seems offer at least for the moment the most direct access to truth or in reality a transparency of process. If the *New York Times* has to admit its journalists have made up stories, can we believe anything we read in the traditional media? But on a blog site we can immediately verify for ourselves what is the slant of coverage and evidence supported by any blogger. It is do-it-yourself truth-verification.

From the perspective of companies and their brands, it is this significant change in attitude by customers, who will actively seek out what is beneath the surface. This will force companies to re-examine how they market themselves.

Again we must emphasise how different this issue now is in a world of digitally empowered communities. It is not that one of your customers might discover a blatant error on your website – that could easily have happened five years ago as well. The point is that today your customer might be a blogger, and go post a comment to the most trusted blogsite where thousands of your customers regularly visit. The power of digitally enhanced word of mouth is enormous.

Tomi T Ahonen & Alan Moore

Consumers join communities

Customers just ain't what they used to be; they are forming online communities – and talking to each other behind the companies' backs. Some are even "broadcasting" their conversation over the internet – that is what blogs, in essence, are; conversations with a loud-hailer. A really loud megaphone. Marketing-resistant and information-rich, these folks are going online to find out about your products and offerings before they buy. More often than not, they go to a third party website or forum to see what people are saying about you. And they will do that because most likely your company's communication is little more than taglines and cheesy superlatives. As a result they will quite rightly see your corporate message as *noise* rather than *signal*, and simply go and ask someone else's opinion.

E BUSINESS AND BLOGS

By using blogs, many companies are finding that thoughtful but "unvarnished" communication can form the core of a trust-based strategy. The return is all too tangible when things go wrong and official press releases are generally seen as damage limitation exercises. If, however, you open a channel for communication with your customers during good times, they will be carrying your voice and be your advocates when you hit the bad times. This is when credibility generated by conversations with them is priceless. Evidence from the US shows that companies with strong customer advocacy are the ones with the strongest growth, and largest profits.

This can only work if a company has both the technical means in place to do so and the corporate culture to let employees say what they mean in an authentic voice rather than marketing-speak. Blogs have the ability to let you do that, without giving up control over your message. A blog can be a way to future-proof your company's profits by talking with your customers today.

Corporate Fear

The corporate world is known for its fear of being different. As Ron Denham is often quoted: "In a given organisation, job performance, whether excellent or incompetent, is overlooked providing you conform." We have a fear of being different. Fear of being creative. Fear of telling your boss your ideas. Fear of speaking up in meetings. Fear of going up to someone you don't know and introducing yourself. Fear of doing something that might destroy your career. And with new technology, of course there is the fear of it. Specifically we see a fear of blogging.

Branding and Blogs

Brands are promises that we have built in our minds over long periods of time. We associate a certain quality, performance, price, satisfaction etc with Mercedes Benz or Kelloggs Corn Flakes or Hewlett Packard, etc. Brands depend on us holding onto the image. Brands are potentially quite fragile. Blogs open up a huge risk to all brands, as they can so rapidly erode images and trust. Stowe Boyd of Get Real asks how blogging shifts the meaning, perception, and utility of a brand:

> *I maintain that a metaphorical shift of brand is taking place, analogous with the time shifting that real-time communication has engendered. Being able to touch people in real-time has changed everything in business conversation; similarly, moving the positioning of product or service from broadcast into many:many dialogue will force a reappraisal of brand. It will no longer be a promise, it will be an invitation.*
>
> www.corante.com/get real/archives/005247.html

Earlier brands could afford to wait for the initial reaction to bad news, and then decide if any reaction was necessary. That is no longer possible, the damage can be catastrophic in a matter of days.

First moblogging event held in Tokyo July 5, 2003

It is not all bad news with branding and blogs, however. Tobi Elkin of *The Mediapost* wrote an article on how marketers are starting to realise and use blogging or online publishing and conversations to engage with 18- 34-year-olds. One example is *Gawker Media* with 15 million page views per month. Elkin points out:

> *Gawker Media's portfolio consists of Gawker, Gizmodo, Fleshbot, Kinja, Wonkette, and Defamer. Currently the toast of the mediarati, Gawker Media has a target demographic aged 26 to 35, according to advertising data on its website, although founder and publisher Nick Denton says he's focused primarily on 18- to 34-year-olds. Either way, the influence of Gawker Media properties extends far beyond those groups. Wonkette's avid following includes Washington, D.C. power brokers, wily political operatives, and elected representatives and their staffs.*
>
> *Mediapost*, September 2004

Elkin also points out Nike's move to the custom blog *Gawker Media* has significantly moved the perception of blogs from geekdom to mainstream. Probably Jalopnik.com, a car blogsite which was until recently 100% sponsored by Audi, is doing the same thing. Dallas Mavericks' CEO, Mark Cuban, is also a blogger; his view is that through his blog he is able to get across his point of view and tell the real story behind the newspaper headlines. Sports journalists have limited time and space to write the full story.

> *Yes, celebrate every time your product gets written up by the New York*
> *Times (believe me, Buzz does, he calls me everytime he gets written up).*
> *But, use your blog to explain more. Will the New York Times explain all the*
> *new graphics that are available for the Maytag SkyBox? No, but their blog*
> *sure does!*
>
> http://www.blogmaverick.com

The real potential of blogging is to give branding a new meaning. Blogs can be the perfect tool for an "emergent brand", where the brand is a behaviour and an expression of an authentic identity to a degree much greater than current branding and marketing allows. Paradoxically, authenticity is very hard to get right and the entire practice of branding, marketing and PR has been the opposite – constructing an edifice, projecting an image on top of whatever was bubbling, and sometimes festering, beneath the high-gloss surface. Engagement was a no-no, hiding from a customer routine and style-over-substance has ruled the day.

Blogging only beginning

There is so much more that could be written about blogging. This book was not intended to be only about blogging, but the blogosphere is symptomatic of new community behaviour. There is, for example, tremendous potential in using blogging for internal communication and information flows. Blogs empower the individual employee and so go straight to the source of creativity within any business.

Communication failures, interminable email trails, and the cc and bcc maze can bog down the best projects. A blog, accessible to specified individuals and restricted from external/public view, can become the hub of information, ideas and expertise for individual teams or the entire company. Internal communication need not be a chore if it is based on individual contributions presented in a dynamic and collaborative format. A blog is also a searchable, structured and categorised record of the project during and after its completion.

The reader is hopefully convinced by our case examples that blogging is a serious phenomenon, and both a threat and an opportunity for business. It is also a new tool, and as such it will give rise to plenty of sillyness and umpteen examples of the bizarre that may cloud the judgement of some. Do not be misled by the trivial and focus on the relevant. The Big Blog Company's Adriana Cronin-Lucas often uses the printing press analogy in describing the ultimate social value of blogging:

> *Many books are trashy and worthless but that does not make printing press inconsequential. It's the same with blogging, even if 99% of blogs were boring journals, all it takes is one blog that shows the potential for the medium to be revolutionary. These are early days and we have not yet seen the full range of uses for a blog. Ultimately, blog is a tool, what makes is important is the use to which it is put by forward-looking individuals.*
>
> www.bigblogcompany.net

Eventually blogging will be as commonplace as email is today. There will be serious business use, there will be marketing use, there will be personal use and there will be abuse. The key is that all businesses need to learn to live in a world which blogs. In terms of learning to harness community power, bloggers are an ideal learning ground. They will be brutally truthful in their feedback.

A current example is the consumer uprising against USA mobile operator **Verizon**. Verizon was marketing the Motorola V710 mobile phone as having Bluetooth functionality, yet Verizon had disabled that feature. Customers started to complain and soon comments appeared in the blogosphere. By January 2005 it was obvious from the various blog postings that Verizon was not acting how its customers wanted, and a man in California proceeded to sue Verizon in a class-action suit. The blogs served both to prove Verizon's lack of desirable action, and to connect with other injured people and draw attention to the lawsuit.

Concluding blogging

Blogging is a rapidly growing part of the internet. For the businesses, brands, products and services, it is vital to understand that the blogosphere is currently the most potent threat. As far as communities go, in 2005 the bloggers are by far the most influential community, capable of launching immediate and extensive actions on behalf of, or against brands. Bloggers will not tolerate incompetence. But if you get on their better side, bloggers are also incredibly useful and honest in helping you redefine and refine your marketing activities. Learn to live with bloggers in harmony with your marketing, and you are halfway done in your corporate transition to the Connected Age. Do not for one moment dismiss the blogosphere as being something from the lunatic fringe; it is an emerging power. As the technology expert Chris Shipley wrote: "If you dismiss blogging as the blatherings of the internet elite, you will miss the most significant transformation in communications since the arrival of the web."

Case Study 6

Kryptonite Locks

The Kryptonite Lock PR disaster is an example of the power of blogs and what happens when a corporation is found out. A blogger posted a short video on his blog demonstrating how to open Kryptonite locks using a simple pen. One of the big bloggers, Rob Scobleizer at Microsoft, talks of the consequences of ignoring the blogosphere of influence. If someone asks whether blogging has business impacts, Scobleizer says: "Lately I've been answering with one word: Kryptonite."

Scobleizer advises us to Google "Kryptonite" and "Bic pen". The story that the Kryptonite Evolution 2000 U-Lock could opened by a Bic pen first was posted on engadget.com on September 14 2004. It related to someone demonstrating to a Texas police officer how he could open a Kryptonite lock. Engagdet.com even posted a film of the ease of opening their top-of-the range lock with a Bic pen.

Now if you do Google Kryptonite and Bic pen, there are 7,490 entries. The story ripped through the blogosphere and into the mainstream media, *Wired* magazine wrote an article on blogs entitled "the Pen is mighter than the U-Lock". Scobleizer in his blog post Fear of blogging says:

> *Here's what's going on: the word-of-mouth networks are becoming more efficient at a time when people trust large corporations less and less. The time it takes for an idea to be hatched, found by Slashdot, and then reported in the mainstream media, is now about five weeks. Next time around it will be even faster.*

In the end, Kryptonite had been forced to send out many thousands of replacement locks and offer up an apology on their website as they struggled to get these replacement locks out the door to many disgruntled customers. Go to the Kryptonite website today and you will be greeted by this notice

---

LOCK EXCHANGE PROGRAM UPDATE
December 14, 2004

We are happy to report that Kryptonite did begin this program in October and thousands of replacement locks have been sent out to customers in the last few weeks. Kryptonite continues to manufacture and ship new products to consumers on a weekly basis. The whole process of the Lock Exchange Program is a complex one with manufacturing and transportation all coming into play. We are building and air shipping the new locks to get them out to our customers as fast as possible.

For those of you who are still waiting to get your UPS postage paid label, here is an update:

Unfortunately, we have not yet been able to send UPS call tags to our lock exchange participants in Canada and Europe. We have been experiencing technical issues with the international software used to generate these call tags, but we hope to have the issues resolved within the next two weeks. Once we are able to do so, we will work to issue call tags rapidly, to make up for the time delay.

U-locks (bicycle and powersports), Padlocks, Cables and Evolution Disc Locks (New York Chain and New York Noose) – replacement locks are being manufactured at this time and will be shipped to consumers as they become available. Automobile locks – these locks are being manufactured now and will be shipped in January. DFS and KryptoDisco – these locks are being re-engineered now and will be available to consumers in March.

source: Kryptonite.com

   This story provides compelling evidence that corporations can no longer hide behind spin and hype. Unhappy customers have found their voice and their power. It clearly demonstrates the power of the blog, word of mouth and the dominance of communities over businesses and their brands.

Tomi T Ahonen & Alan Moore

"A pessimist sees the difficulty in every opportunity; an optimist sees the opportunity in every difficulty."

Sir Winston Churchill

VIII
Customers Changing
Brand polygamists or worse

Businesses models under threat, the unrelenting march of technology bringing with it the gales of creative destruction and discontinuous change. If that was not bad enough, consumers have escaped to become customers, "prosumers", informed and connected. Armed to the teeth with information, they see through your marketing strategies, go online and get it 20% cheaper elsewhere. That is right! Reach for the aspirin! Customers themselves are changing too. We will examine the general changes in customers as they become ever more digitally literate and aware of their options. We will also discuss the emergence of Generation-C, or the Connected Generation, the next evolution of the consumer, growing up in the children's rooms of our homes. Gen-C will be discussed in the next chapter. But let us start with mainstream customers today and how they are changing.

A THE NEWLY INDEPENDENT CUSTOMER

Early in the evolution of business, customers had equivalent power to the sellers. If we look at the street markets of old, the bazaars and so forth, a customer would learn to haggle, to compare prices of different vendors in a market and, arguably, if experienced, could hold similar power in the sales transaction as the seller. Gradually with industrialisation, standardisation and the emergence of the retail store model with suggested retail prices etc, the customer's power became eroded. Today we go into most stores and have a "take it or leave it" basis for the price. The company that makes the goods is not the company that sells the goods. The manufacturer will communicate with us via brochures, leaflets, advertisements, etc. Up to the end of the last decade this was seen as the natural state of things, a natural end-state for the evolution of business. In fact few doubted this state of affairs should not continue indefinitely.

Over long periods of time it seems that balances in nature swing from one side to another. Even this long trend of bringing ever more power to the business, at the expense of the customer, has now suddenly started to swing in the opposite direction. It was not because of, nor in the interests of business to promote this sudden shift. It has been initiated by the customers themselves. They are becoming empowered. Let us examine the elements that are enabling this shift, starting with the new independence of the customer. As consumers, we are suddenly very aware, knowledgable and empowered.

Self-actualisation

Generation after generation the populations of the world have reached ever higher levels of education. The wants and needs of consumers have also progressed up Maslow's hierarchy of needs. Today, older members of the working population increasingly seek opportunities to accomplish something. Just being employed, working for a paycheck and earning a pension is no longer enough. Younger parts of the working population start off in working life expecting to contribute to their own satisfaction by creating something, achieving something, discovering something.

These needs are visible in the various hobbies that people have, hobbies that two decades ago were the sole domain of professionals who spent a lifetime learning their craft. Today, parents make video movies with their children as actors. The movies feature professional edits, soundtracks, credits, etc. Amateur photographers edit pictures online and regularly create special effects that in the last century would have been near-impossible to achieve. Those who are musically inclined create their own music – or, as often is the case, sample music from existing sources and manipulate that digitally. Amateur journalists and wannabes publish web newsletters and blogs, etc. The list is nearly endless.

More cameraphones than laptop PCs and PDAs combined

The new awareness also reaches us as consumers. Consumers today are more aware of the options and sources of information available. As we saw earlier, already

60% of American car buyers will go to the web for information before the purchase. Consumers are increasingly taking the internet as a natural step in the decision-making process for any major purchase; to see what is available, what options exist, what price levels are reasonable, etc.

People don't want to be told

We as people do not like to be told what to do, what to want, what to think. Previously this was a necessary part of the business environment. The only way to learn of new offerings, goods and services, was through advertising. But we have been told what to do for so long, we are growing fed up with being told. The erosion of the power and respect of figures of authority, from the state, education and other formal institutions have all brought about the thinking among younger generations that they don't need to be told. That they can think for themselves.

We are in an age of the individual, the age of self-empowerment at every level of society, where people form and collect around their own ideologies. Roles within society have blurred as traditional boundaries of gender, class, ethnicity and geography have weakened. It means people today are made up of multiple identities, all of which contribute to how they see themselves. In this context marketing is no longer about changing people's minds. You need to seek to influence people at an attitudinal level. Seek to *influence* their behaviour not to change it wholesale from the outset.

Sceptical of marketing messages

In the past people trusted the media. If it was printed it had to be true. Even advertisements on TV and radio in the 1960s and 1970s were strongly believed. Gradually we have grown sceptical of all communications, and advertising definitely was the first to feel it. Today the presumption is that ad claims are exaggerated. In fact any messages from any interested group, such as politicians etc, are assumed to have a degree of "spin" and thus lack trustworthiness. With the recent scandals within various news organisations, even supposedly impartial news sources are losing their credibility.

Giving feedback to the channel

The current younger adults are also familiar with giving feedback and using rating systems. In previous generations it was the few truly activist types of personalities who went to the trouble of writing a letter of complaint to a company, or a letter to the editor of a newspaper, etc. As we saw earlier, already a third of Americans have participated in some rating systems. Electronic feedback and rating systems are much more timely and can deliver an instant acknowledgement of the comment.

This tendency to participate, evaluate and give feedback is one of the new elements of digitally aware consumers. It is an attribute of modern consumers that companies can work with, by proactively seeking the engagement of the consumers.

Varying feedback loops

The last decade has seen the progressive introduction of ever faster feedback methods. From the letter to the editor in the 1970s to the fax in the 1980s, to the email in the 1990s, today many TV programmes request feedback via SMS text messaging. As these messages are short, do not include a header that would need to be stripped, don't have attachments, and in 160 characters cannot have much beyond the main point, SMS text messaging is exceptionally well suited for broadcasting the feedback.

Many TV shows have introduced viewer comments in the form of a "news headline ticker" scrolling on the bottom of the screen. Viewers can send in comments, and a human editor selects which to pass onto the system for sharing. Feedback has become ever faster and now is in real-time. We will examine how powerful and immediate feedback loops are altering communications in later chapters of this book. Here we want to keep in mind that feedback is becoming a new source for content. Media outlets from TV news to tabloid newspapers are adding new content types based on viewer opinion.

Without a doubt the mobile phone and the internet have also empowered customers, they are more knowledgeable. They are more demanding and force companies to rethink what they do. For example, there is currently a big debate about what we eat, what goes into what we eat and where it comes from. The debate is fuelled by films like *Super Size Me* and the BBC's *Fat Nation*, as well as numerous articles and lobby groups. Cinema and broadcast are in this instance the catalyst. Then these debates go online and exponentially explode into communities of interest. Powerful enough to resonate through the vernacular of society, forcing people to stop and think about what they eat, and making McDonald's begin to rethink what it persuades its customers to consume. Fast food and supermarkets are aware that they must address the issue of people's growing paranoia about what goes into the food they eat.

Lifelong learning

We have become accustomed to the notion of lifelong learning. We understand that knowledge and information are the keys to future success. It is no longer the case that our learning stops at a particular life stage. We understand that to stop learning is to stop living, progressing and increasing our opportunities for a better life.

Tomi T Ahonen & Alan Moore

One way the digital future provides new opportunities for continuing education is in the UK. Teachers there are receiving their own dedicated professional TV channel. It is called **Teachers' TV** and it will provide continuous learning tools for keeping British teachers up-to-date with developments in their profession. *The Guardian* wrote:

> *The UK government has embarked on a unique experiment that will use*
> *digital television to enhance the continuing professional development of*
> *school teachers. British teachers will probably be the first profession to*
> *have a dedicated national television channel about their work. Teachers'*
> *TV aims to commission innovative programme formats aimed at helping*
> *teachers develop new insights into their practice, while offering practical*
> *suggestions for improvement. The channel will include a weekly news round*
> *up on developments in education.*
>
> *The Guardian*, November 3 2004

Receiving continuing education is nothing new. What is new is that it is done via a dedicated TV channel. The needs of modern people are very different from those of only a generation ago. Could our parents have ever dreamt of a TV channel dedicated to a profession?

B CRAVE ENTERTAINMENT

The consumer of today is increasingly demanding. It is no longer enough to be informed, the customer wants to be entertained. With audiences growing up with three-minute music videos on MTV and a fragmented media, there is today a poverty of attention. The competition to gain the interest of customers is intense and demanding.

Attention spans ever shorter

The attention spans of current consumers are ever shrinking. They are at the lowest point ever, and still growing shorter. The 1930s standardised the motion picture "story" to about two hours. Today, Hollywood movie lengths are about 1 hour 45 minutes on average. The 1960s brought TV drama as a mainstream story, with detective stories and westerns as well as soap operas. The average story shrunk to one hour. The 1970s brought us the sitcom (situation comedy) on TV, which condensed the typical story to 30 minutes. Our attention spans were being shrunk.

The dramatic change was in the 1980s when teenagers were exposed en masse to music videos, via MTV and its clones. Now, suddenly a story shrunk to the three-four minutes of the length of a typical hit song. TV advertisements followed these trends, with the one-minute ad shrinking to 30 second spots, and now many stations broadcasting even 15 second ads. An interesting phenomenon is that many popular music videos from Kylie Minogue to Eminem have found that even four minutes is way too long to remain on one theme, and videos started to have several subplots, or interruptions such as fake advertisements etc, interspliced to the short video clip.

Undeniably the storylines of content in popular culture have shrunk, which has shortened the attention spans of especially the younger audiences. No wonder teachers in schools complain that they cannot compete with the fast pace of MTV.

Need entertainment

Another key element of the modern society is that all of our information and education needs to be entertaining. It is no longer information, it is info-tainment, and not education, but edu-tainment. Digital tools, heavily produced content, with the entertainment element weaved into the news, information and education is the desirable way for modern customers. If you do not package your message the way your consumers want it, they will simply ignore it.

Entertainment = Experience = Engagement

A good example of edu-tainment is the docudrama, combining traditional pure facts-based documentary with the drama effects. The facts are there but brought to life in a more relevant, contextual and understandable way. *Walking with Dinosaurs* must be a landmark in creatively bringing massive skeletons to life from millions of years ago and creating a popular wave of interest that resulted in countless children's books, exhibitions and scores of other cultural and commercial activity. Author and film director Alan Rosenthal notes:

> *The docudrama wields more influence than the average documentary and reality-based stories taken from topical journalism are the most popular drama genre on U.S. and British television today.*
>   www.siu.edu/~siupress/titles/f98_titles/rosenthal_why.htm

Docudrama goes right back to the blockbuster history of the slave trade in the USA in the TV series *Roots*. Recent British popular TV shows include the *Last Fatal Days of Pompeii* and a history of *Battlefield Britain* which both used extensive re-enactments of the narrative to enhance the viewing experience. Broadcasters are adapting to customer tastes and docudramas fit that bill.

Back to books?

A great example of the power of cross-platform engagement is the BBC's *The Big Read* TV programme. It hunted for Britain's most popular book as part of a BBC initiative to encourage the nation to read and appreciate books. More than 140,000 people voted initially for the top 100 books, prompting sales of those books to soar by 1,100% throughout the summer. A BBC spokeswoman commented:

> *"Anything that encourages great literature is fantastic. Weekly book sales overall on The Big Read Top 21 have increased by 425% since the list was first announced. "More than 2,000 new reading groups have been formed, overall library lending has increased by 56% on the same period last year and 500,000 votes have been cast for the UK's favourite book."*
> Danielle Demetriou, *The Guardian*, 13 December 2003

Go to many schools in Britain today where microscopes are hooked up to TV projectors, the blackboard is vanishing and being replaced by a multimedia teaching experience.

Natural gamers

Yes, there are many differences between generations, but one of the key elements is the familiarity with video gaming. The generations can be rather well divided into those who grew up with gaming consoles, typically under age 35, and those who never had videogaming in their homes when they grew up.

The biggest single influencing technology for the previous generation was television. While TV is also of interest to younger generations, TV – especially how it was consumed in the past – is passive. Gaming is active, the gamer will enter the imaginary environment of the game, and take an active role in playing in it, with it, living it. Very similar to how older generations related to TV when they were young, young videogamers today will have dreams, even nightmares, based on the latest games they play. The game characters are introduced into the "regular play" just like previous generations brought favourite TV characters into their play.

Besides, playing games is more fun. And if we think about it, play is quite often how we learn. In their book *Got Game,* John C. Beck and Mitchell Wade show how growing up immersed in video games has profoundly shaped the attitudes and abilities of this new generation of 90 million and rising. *The Financial Times* reported:

> *Generation gaps are nothing new. But if John Beck and Mitchell Wade are right, those under the age of 34 think, learn and feel differently from everyone else. The root of this cognitive divide? Video games, since the 1980s a primary form of home entertainment for impressionable teens.*
>
> *The Financial Times* October 21 2004

In conjunction with mobile phone useage and the fixed internet, gaming has created a cognitive divide between baby boomers and the younger generations. For example, Americans now spend more on video games per year than going to the movies, which translates into three-quarters of US households with a male aged 8 to 34 owning a video game system. Sony's Playstation games console alone has a place in 25% of US households. According to *The Financial Times* in 2003 the games sector notched up global sales of $28bn. In the UK, between 30%-40% of the population now play games. Games are no longer "exotic" or "interesting" – they are an established feature of the media landscape.

One of the key elements of the gaming experience is that the player is in a principal dynamic role. Gamers have grown up learning not to be passive consumers of entertainment. And while many games are first played on Playstation and Xbox consoles or Nintendo Gameboy handheld devices, the next step for serious gaming is networked games. The fixed internet and the mobile phone are the domains of the future of gaming. There are lots of official sites and game sites which are becoming increasingly sophisticated and follow the principle of trailers just like those used in the release of films.

However, the internet really works as a place where fan-based gamer content is created. Fan sites, preview sites, cheat and hint sites, walk-throughs and review sites abound. The internet provides a way for fans and enthusiasts to produce and publish their content to an nth degree, and often this is better than official content.

C WANT TO PARTICIPATE

The modern customer is also actively interested in using the new digital tools and methods to create and customise content. That would then be shared with given friends, or in some cases even sold. As we saw earlier, this is a very new phenomenon as it was only the internet as a new digital platform that allowed an individual to produce mass-distributed content. And this became viable only towards the end of the last decade.

Tomi T Ahonen & Alan Moore

Generate own content

Consumers today are embracing digital production technologies and everywhere we see early examples of consumers generating their own content. Damien Rice recorded his award winning album *O* in his bedroom, Jonathan Caouette created a feature-length movie on his iMac using iMovie, for $218.32, which was good enough to be shown at the Sundance Film Festival. Software created by SixApart Moveable Type and Typepad has enabled the explosion of blogging so we can all become writers, journalists, crusaders for the truth, polemicists or debaters, if we want to be.

77% of Americans use Internet for primary news

There are several companies that allow us to create our own content. For example, xingtone.com is a company that lets us create our own ringtones. There is also noiseupthesuburbs.com, inviting an emerging generation of would-be musicians, from bedroom DJs and producers to pirate radio and independent label founders, to create music with their software.

Sony tells us to "Go Create" and we are in ever increasing numbers. The conceptual artist Joseph Beuys believed that everybody is a unique artist in their own right, that creativity is something we all possess. The falling costs of technology, the ease of use of computer hardware and software, camera-enabled phones, camcorders etc allow us to film our loved ones or make personal movies, documentaries, art films. This demonstrates how modern consumers have changed. Fact is today we are familiar with creating digital content.

Modern consumers are also learning to seek the professional media outlets to exploit amateur shots and videos. The evidence of Rodney King's beating, where the violence of Los Angeles police was shot on amateur video camera, helped publicise the idea that anyone can capture news. Today with the rapid sales of video-camera enabled cameraphones brings the prospect of everyman journalism to a global user base. Recent disasters such as the Indian Ocean tsunami of Christmas 2004 feature increasingly contributions by amateur videographers.

Part of this trend is the familiarity with modern digital tools, and a wide range of ready templates. Part is the ability to copy anything from sampling music sounds to copying digital images from websites. And the final part is the widespread penetration of such tools. First it was the separate dedicated digital cameras, videocams, laptop computers, etc. Today, of course, it is increasingly the smartphone that we carry on our person every day.

Sense of belonging

An elderly generation still remembers society as it had been for hundreds of years. There was the family community and perhaps the church community, and very closely held ties with small classroom size classmates, and later the bonds of friendship formed in long careers in the same jobs. Today, the nuclear family has evolved into a myriad of permutations, church attendances are down worldwide, schools have ever larger classroom sizes, families move frequently, creating disconnection points for children with their friends and, especially in our professional careers, typically today an employed person will change jobs numerous times in a career. All of this contributes to an increased sense of detachment, our sense of belonging to one place and one community is being eroded. Or, at the very least, life today is more multilayered and requiring different survival tactics.

We seek new ways to feel connected. Part is the virtual world, we connect increasingly with email and SMS text messaging, and very likely in the future ever more also with picture messaging. Many videogamers have found themselves addicted to some new videogame, staying up nights to master the latest release, etc. Others form dependencies with dating worlds, adult entertainment services and gambling offered on digital networks.

A very significant change in the young generation growing up is the association with digitally connected communities. Young people of today are actually less disconnected and less isolated than their preceding generations. The reason is the mobile phone. We will examine the new Generation-C in its own chapter next where we will explain this development in more detail.

D HOW TO GROUP CUSTOMERS

Regardless of how customers might evolve, to conduct business companies need to group their customers for marketing efforts. We cannot look at our customer database and decide that oh, Mr Smith of Elm Street, we haven't communicated with him for a while, let's design an ad campaign for him. Companies use the techniques of profiling, segmentation, clustering and bundling to achieve targeted marketing efforts. We discover a new end-user pattern or type, a-ha, the single divorced mother with school-age kids? Is that group large enough for our marketing? Yes? Let's design a version of our car for single mothers with kids. And so forth.

　　　　　　　　　　　　　　　　Tomi T Ahonen & Alan Moore

Companies from Mars, customers from Venus

Current modern marketing is premised upon driving customers to a financial transaction. Which is not the same as a focus on the needs and desires of the customer. The marketer's language is premised on the command and control desires and needs of the organisation. The notion that a brand wants to get close to a customer is not about helping the customer, it's about making the transaction, about *closing the deal*. As we have shown, this approach will become increasingly harder when the customer starts to be in control.

Today, practically all bigger business entities broadcast while customers hold conversations. If we again refer back to our struggling legacy companies they are still using models of marketing that presumed an industrial order of command and control. Don Peppers and Martha Rogers in their book *One to One Future* argue that:

> *It is impossible to talk about mass marketing without thinking of customers and marketers as adversaries... your customers know that their own interests are in direct conflict with yours.*
>
> Peppers & Rogers, *One to One Future*, 1996

There is virtually no overlap between business interests and goals, and those of the customer. Consider this table of how current big business identifies its needs and contrast that with what the current customer wants.

COMPANIES	CUSTOMERS
Growth	Hopes
Sales	Dreams
Profits	Desires
Products	Peace of mind
Economies of scale	Personalisation
Conformity	Family
Accounting	Trust
Supply chain	Communities
Engineering	Family
Product	Time
Promote	Discuss

The list is not by any means exhaustive and is intended more to start a discussion within the companies on how to better match customer interests and needs with those of the company. We will look at some of the ways innovative companies are actually achieving this in the Engagement chapter later in this book.

The age of perfect customer insight

We are also becoming accustomed to machine-generated personalisation. As consumers we are not at all impressed if a direct mailing addresses us by name. That a website knows who we are is no longer cool, it starts to introduce concerns about how much information the systems are collecting on us. Now the technology is becoming so automated and artificially intelligent that we are starting to see customisation to our personal preferences. We call up our mobile operator and it knows now to sell a single adult employed man a different service to a married wife with three teenage kids.

We feel that the future is geared to diminishing the differences between what users want from products and how closely those needs are met by the providers. Thus goods and services that enhance the life of the individual is the future. This related

Tomi T Ahonen & Alan Moore

cultural shift in how to get to that future has some bearing on how we consume media and how we receive marketing communications.

Today, people are constantly editing their lives. How much personalisation do we want? It is down to the individual. But all of the media are making it ever easier to register our preferences and start to receive tailored marketing messages. As Jeffrey Zaslow wrote in *The Wall Street Journal* in his article "Oh No! My TiVo Thinks I'm Gay":

> *A lot of gadgets and websites feature "personalization technologies"*
> *that profile consumers by tracking what they watch, listen or buy. Many*
> *consumers appreciate having computers delve into their hearts and heads.*
> *But some say it gives them the willies...*
>
> *The Wall Street Journal*, December 4th 2002

PVRs like TiVo in the USA and Sky+ in the UK have adopted techniques from the internet search technologies. This allows TV viewers to find and access content that they might like. Sky are currently advertising the benefits of their Sky box "in demand – on demand". The future of television has arrived.

We are witnessing the death of mass media as we have known it. The new consumer is not impressed by ever more channels, in fact it is a given that there will be more choice, equally there is another dilemma created by more choice, which is; how do I choose? And how do I find the best website/blogsite/message board/TV channel/magazine dedicated to my new-found passion? I go to Google and search, I ask my friends, I seek out the specialist magazine.

Splintered into ever smaller segments

As corporations use ever smarter systems to target marketing and create user profiles, some companies such as airlines, automobile manufacturers, telecoms operators, banks and credit card companies etc, already routinely handle thousands, even as many as ten thousand subsegments. The segmentation models grow into multidimensional ones, with deep insights for specific subsegments and clusters, and generalised summaries on the higher level segments.

---

90 Million play videogames worldwide

For example, Ford might consider a new segment of snowboarding young professionals in the countries with winters of much snow. A snowboarder might want

---

a wider "ski bag" in the car, to fit the snowboard rather than the narrow skis in the car. This car could have heated seats and other winter car features etc. The segment would be small and target cars to be sold in, for example, some Scandinavian country could be measured only in the hundreds or even less. When summarising the data for management, these car sales would be grouped with several other car types into, for example, the "hatchback" category of cars, separate from sedans and minivans, etc. Segmentation today can go very deep into specialist interests, and then again summarise up to the "top management level" of main classifications of the goods and services.

Beyond segment of one

The marketing industry has argued on behalf of the targeting to a segment of one for a decade now, as it became technically feasible via the fixed internet. We are actually now hearing some marketing people, especially those involved with the mobile telecoms space, talking of a segment of less than one. Or, more precisely, that most employed people display the behaviour of at least two, perhaps more, distinct personalities. We are one person at work, with our professional business colleague personality, and conduct communication behaviour in the style of that persona. We then transform, daily, to the domestic father or mother for the home and our family, where we behave very differently. For any company involved in the targeted marketing to such people, it is vital to know which persona is the one we intend to communicate with. Thus it becomes valid to discuss the concept of a segment of less than one.

In a practical world of segmentation, even the most advanced airlines, automobile manufacturers, credit card companies etc design service and product propositions for a population segmented into thousands, perhaps tens of thousands of segments. In a national population of the UK, Germany, France or Italy, for example, such segmentation still leaves average segment sizes from thousands to tens of thousands of individuals. This precision, while it may seem bewildering to those outside technical segmentation specialists, is hardly overkill. Naturally these companies keep the segmentation science and magic inside the confines of the customer insight teams and for the outside they deliver targeted offerings like a car for single women, or for outdoorsy hunting sportsmen, or safety-conscious first parents etc.

E   UNPLUGGED

Modern users of telecoms services have separated the notion of a fixed telecoms connection, and accessing telecoms services. This is at the heart of despair at fixed

       Tomi T Ahonen & Alan Moore

wireline telecoms operators. It used to be that the fixed telecoms wire that fed all households was the presumptive telecommunications connection. Not so for current users. Increasingly users are aware of alternate telecoms service mechanisms. We can have telephony services also on broadband internet, which may be on the old copper wire telecoms connection including ISDN lines, or on a high speed xDSL connection, or on a cable ("TV") connection, or wirelessly on a WiFi or WiMax or other wireless service, or via cellular or even possibly via satellite connection.

Even more revealingly, as the mobile phone is the only really vital and necessary telecommunications connection today, any other telecoms services are options to be considered. If our mobile service offers a compelling offering of internet access, for example, then there is hardly any need for a fixed wireline telephone connection to our households. In Scandinavia numbers are at about 40% of all households already that have abandoned the fixed telecoms line completely for alternate telecoms connections, that increasingly are wireless and/or cellular.

Reachability

The unanticipated and much greater effect of mobility and the personal nature of the cellular phone emerged gradually as users grew attached to their phone. It became obvious that very distinct from the fixed line phone, a cellular phone is distinctly *personal*. This personal association creates a very powerful attachment to the cellular phone, one very close to an addiction. No such attachment is observed with the fixed line phone, which is typically shared within a family or office environment. The European cellular phone companies were the first to observe the differences and have coined a name for the new concept, called "reachability." In its most basic form, reachability means that while on the fixed line phones you call a place, on a cellular phone you call a person. This is why a family home can easily get by with one or two fixed lines, but every family member wants his or her own cellular phone.

Reachability is the human need to feel connected. It is driven by a fear of being left out of something important because of having been beyond reach. Reachability does not imply any active measures to inform anybody of being online, connected or networked, but rather a passive continuous connectedness *in case* the important call arrives or event happens. Reachability is the single most addictive aspect of a cellular phone. It builds gradually and usually requires several repeated occurrences of having missed out on an important call because the phone was accidentally forgotten, turned off, or unintentionally in silent mode.

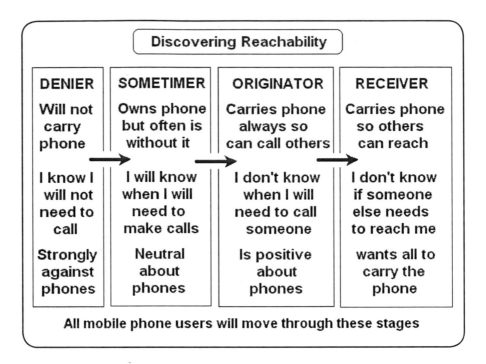

Discovering Reachability			
DENIER	**SOMETIMER**	**ORIGINATOR**	**RECEIVER**
Will not carry phone	Owns phone but often is without it	Carries phone always so can call others	Carries phone so others can reach
I know I will not need to call	I will know when I will need to make calls	I don't know when I will need to call someone	I don't know if someone else needs to reach me
Strongly against phones	Neutral about phones	Is positive about phones	wants all to carry the phone

All mobile phone users will move through these stages

Because of Reachability, cellular phone users want to check the phone first thing in the morning when they wake up, and last thing before they go to sleep. Users will check the phone several times during the day, and after any short instances of being beyond its ringing, such as taking a shower. Because of reachability the cellular phone is carried to most locations and events, even where actual talking may be near-impossible, such as a loud rock concert, disco, sporting event, etc. And after discovering reachability most users learn to never turn the phone off, and only control the level of connectedness by the sound on the ringing tone. The phone is kept turned on, but in silent mode, when more privacy is desired. In that way the phone will register the attempts of calls and numbers, as well as allow receipt of SMS messages, while respecting the privacy from the terror of the ringing of the phone.

F NEW CONCEPTS OF LOYALTY

The proliferation of choice, fierce competition between competing companies and then new entrants into an already competitive marketspace means that the vast array of choice means we will look elsewhere as we seek similar quality goods for less money. Equally, as we discussed earlier, trust in corporations and institutions overall means we are more promiscuous by default, unless we come across a brand that meaningfully resonates with our own belief systems. Such brands can achieve enormous loyalty but within a tightly defined market niche.

Brand-promiscuous

A critical other new phenomenon is that there is no longer a "brand monogamy" of consumers being loyal to only one brand in any given area or field. Modern consumers typically have a relationship with a couple of banks, a couple of telecoms operators, etc. The consumers are increasingly "brand-polygamists". This presents a problem for loyalty management with companies, as a consumer who is an active customer of your services may also be with a competitor. It becomes even more difficult to determine when a customer has mentally left your services and only maintains the remnants of a few services for whatever legacy reasons. Such customers are said to be "hiddenly churned" when the majority of current business, and all new business is actually with the competitor.

We are more aware of comparison services, rating systems and web search, allowing us to make a more informed decision. So, as an interested buyer in a product such as a car, the consumer might watch a TV show on cars like Top Gear, then go online have a look at a few sites and compare what others say about a product. The consumer might be persuaded to consider alternate brands than the initial preference, because others tell me in their own words that this marque is better than what had been the first choice. It is important to keep in mind that the modern consumer trusts the opinions of peer groups much more than marketing messages from brands delivered through advertising.

Neo-altruistic brands

Another variation in the branding game is the emergence of goods that have altruistic aspirations. **Cafédirect** is one of these, underpinned by motives beyond pure profit. Coffee production has widely been highly exploitative of the growers, whilst vast wealth has been created for those that sell on the coffee to the world market. Cafédirect products are sold through most of the major supermarkets in the UK. The company buys from 33 producer organisations in 11 countries, ensuring that over a quarter of a million growers receive a decent income from this trade. Cafédirect puts a percentage of its gross profits (8% in 2003) back into producer partners' organisations. As a customer you can decide whether you want to drink Cafédirect or Nescafé, whether Cafédirect's ethical position is important to you.

There are obviously many other examples. We mentioned already, for example, the Blackspot sneakers, made with environmentally sustainable materials and where the organisation is a non-profit making organisation. These consumers can choose to opt out of supporting big business.

Summing up consumers

We discussed how consumers are self-actualised and independent. We showed how active they are in feedback and that they want entertainment. We then showed what kind of issues companies face when attempting to place customers into segments for marketing purposes. The customer of today is very different from that of only a decade ago. Digital content, services, distribution methods are all taken for granted. Self-generated content is a significant element in the lives of modern consumers. How can you provide your goods and services to this kind of customer? That takes an active task of re-evaluating customers, reassigning priorities and responsibilities, and of revising your marketing to match the new realities. It is not easy, but it is necessary. If you don't do it, your competitors will. The priority is to readjust to the new reality of the new customer. As Louis Pasteur said about fortune: "Chance favours the prepared mind."

Case Study 7

Oh My News

Oh My News (ohmynews.com) is a revolutionary online newspaper in South Korea. Its claim to fame is its citizen reporters who contribute the vast majority of the total content of the newspaper. Oh My News is growing rapidly and is already considered one of the main newspapers of South Korea with over a million readers.

South Korea is the most digitally advanced country in the world today, where already close to 70% of all households subscribe to a broadband internet service, by far the highest penetration level in the world. The mobile phone penetration level is at an industrial world average of about 80% but again the penetration of advanced mobile phones is ahead of all other countries by a wide margin. As much as 80% of all mobile phones in South Korea are cameraphones with colour screens and an amazing 25% of all mobile phones are already third generation (3G) high speed data enabled. That is more than double that of the next best country, Japan.

Tomi T Ahonen & Alan Moore

Oh My News was launched as a newspaper to capture the interests of readers to contribute to a paper's content. The newspaper has recruited a vast community of contributors who write for the paper or submit pictures etc. Oh My News pays up to $20 per article − considering the Korean standard of living, this is a nice sum of money. The interesting thing is that for most of the citizen reporters, getting their name in the paper is the real reward for contributing. This feeds well into the development among modern consumers that they want to become self-actualised, not only succeed financially.

Oh My News is so popular that South Korea's new president Roh Moo-hyun granted his first interview to ohmynews.com after being inaugerated in February 2004. The Editor and founder of OhMyNews, Oh Yeon-ho, said:

> *"With Ohmynews, we wanted to say goodbye to 20th century journalism where people only saw things through the eyes of the mainstream, conservative media. Our main concept is every citizen can be a reporter. We put everything out there and people judge the truth for themselves."*
> www.collisiondetection.net/mt/archives/000365.html#000365

With its outspoken views Oh My News is challenging the traditionally conservative newsmedia in South Korea. Oh My News has a readership of 1.2 million per day, which makes it bigger than virtually every US newspaper, and has 26,300 citizens registered as regular reporters. It is seen as a model of a likely near future for much of the world's newspapers.

A small human observation however, we all seek recognition for the work we do. If we feel that we belong, it reinforces our sense of self. This is what Oh My News has been so successfully able to capture. One can see why Oh My News can make people feel they are part of something bigger and importantly they have a real channel to the wider world for their small voice.

"The more original the discovery, the more obvious it seems afterward."
Arthur Koestler

IX
Generation-C
The Connected Community

After Douglas Copeland introduced the idea of Generation X, we have seen and read of many other newer Generations; some are of more merit than others. With the shift to the Connected Age we are now seeing a birth of a legitimate new generation, one which we call Generation-C. Others have talked of other Generation-Cs. In our case we want to emphasise that the "C" in Gen-C stands for *Community*. Most of Gen-C are young, and they tend to be concentrated in the early-adopter mobile phone countries like Finland, Italy, Singapore etc. But Gen-C is appearing everywhere and, as they are the young, by the end of this decade Gen-C will be the most attractive market for practically all goods, services and brands.

A DEFINING GENERATION-C

Generation-C stands for the Community Generation. The defining and distinguishing characteristic for Gen-C is the *continuous* connection to and response to *digital communities*. This is very different from any other communities. Even a die-hard 40-year-old football fan of Chelsea may wear his colours every day and spend most of his free time with friends who are also fans. Yes, he is obviously a member of the Chelsea fan community. But when that Chelsea fan goes to visit his parents and suddenly gets into an argument, he is no longer a Chelsea community member. He probably will tell his Chelsea mates what happened, *afterwards*, next day at the pub. The difference is that a Gen-C member carries his/her community in the pocket and accesses that community at all times. Thus the young Gen-C member would share the anger and frustration of the argument with their parents, within the next few minutes, via a text message to close friends.

The community in your pocket

This illustrates the clearest outward sign of Gen-C. The only current tool that allows continuous connectedness at all hours and regardless of location, is the mobile phone. Thus one of the primary connection methods for Gen-C is the mobile phone. It is not necessarily the only digital network or means to connect with communities, as Gen-C tend to be very active on many communication networks. They easily use IM Instant Messaging, play networked videogames, actively surf the fixed internet, use email, and may well be involved in blogging. But these are ancilliary connection methods. The personal and primary connection tool for Gen-C is the mobile phone.

Generation-C is a very young generation today. But just being young is not enough to be a member of Gen-C. Gen-C is characterised by using *mobile phone communities*. Why is this distinction so relevant? Because as we explained in defining the transition from the Networked Age to the Connected Age, only communities on the mobile phone are truly immediate and completely personal.

Lets be very clear about this. On any other network the community needs to seek *access* to become connected at some time. For example, you might have access to your email right now, but not all members of your community are at their email devices at the same time. You may want to join in an IM Instant Messaging discussion, or to have a discussion in a chat room, but these can only take place if the other person is, by chance or plan, also connected now. All other digital networking technologies have availability issues, if not at your end, then at the other end. Only the mobile phone will allow connections at all times. Even if the other person is sleeping, at the moment of wake-up the mobile phone is there to show your text message, as the first greeting long before logging on to email or the internet.

Members of Generation-C will regularly, on a daily basis, consult with friends and colleagues from their various communities. To do so, they have to have continous access to their network. They must be "always on" and only the mobile phone allows this.

Being part of Generation-C

There are several signs of whether one is part of Gen-C. Obviously the first need is an addiction to the mobile phone. Is the mobile phone a critically vital tool always for you? Already in Asia, according to a Siemens study in December 2003 of mobile phone users in seven countries, over half of all Asians will return home to retrieve it if they left home without their mobile phone.

Tomi T Ahonen & Alan Moore

40% of households in Scandinavia have abandoned fixed telecoms

A second sign is the responsiveness to phone calls. Most older people tend to be troubled when their mobile phone rings, and feel the strong urge to answer the phone when it rings. Members of Gen-C do not feel obligated to answer a ringing phone, not even their own, and not even if it is their best friend calling. Gen-C can be not busy, see a good friend calling, and choose not to answer the phone at that time. Gen-C will manage the networks and communities, and return the attempt at contact when he/she feels like it.

A third sign is voicemail. If you leave voicemail messages, you are too old to be Gen-C. Gen-C will never remain on the line to listen to a voicemail announcement, and then leave a message. Gen-C will immediately hang up, and if necessary, will send an SMS text message instead.

Another test is the consumption of content or services on the mobile phone. Gen-C will know how to download content, be it a ringing tone or a logo or image, or news or entertainment clips etc.

Perhaps the most distinguishing test is how familiar one is with text messaging. Those in Gen-C will send several messages per day, and this can easily average over ten messages per day. How apt is the user in keying messages? Those truly of Gen-C can type out messages blind, *literally*. In other words they can type messages with the phone held out of sight, under the table, or behind their back, or with the phone in their pocket. They can take the phone from its locked position, seek the good friend's number from the phone book, and compose a long message, and complete the message and send it exactly as intended. Without error. And no, this is not using predictive text. Predictive is definitely the crutch for us older generations attempting to keep up with the young.

Text messaging has several other Gen-C signs. They can be carrying on a voice conversation, and send an SMS text message while carrying on the voice conversation. Gen-C is totally comfortable sending messages to someone in the same room. And all romances by members of Gen-C involve a daily SMS text message in both directions. If there is no message today, the romance is in trouble.

What age is Gen-C

Members of Gen-C are obviously mostly young. Gen-C started to form first in Scandinavia as ever younger teenagers received mobile phones in the late 1990s – today all over the age of 11 have mobile phones. Finland, both with the highest mobile phone penetrations of the time and the fastest adoption of SMS text messaging in 1998, 1999 and 2000, discovered the changes in behaviour. Sweden,

Norway, Denmark and Iceland followed, exhibiting similar patterns within a matter of months. Similar trends also in very short succession were seen in youth populations of Portugal, Italy, Hong Kong, Singapore, Taiwan, Israel, Austria. In these countries today Gen-C covers essentially the whole population between 12 years and 25 years of age.

In 2005 we find most countries where mobile phone penetrations are above 85% will have most of the population between 14 and 24 years of age exhibiting Gen-C behaviour and traits. This group of countries is most of Western Europe and Central Europe and many parts of advanced Asia. Even laggard countries like the USA, Canada and Australia have already a sizeable Gen-C population, that of most of the young population between the ages of 16 - 22. A rough estimate of the global size of Gen-C at the end of 2004 is about 30 million teenagers and young adults. That will double by the end of 2005.

Gen-C rapidly growing

In each country the Community Generation will continue to grow. In every case, once a member of society becomes part of Gen-C, there is no going back. The change is irreversible. Thus Gen-C will naturally grow with the ageing of the population. But there is also a curious "age creep" phenomenon. Gen-C tends to try to influence those slightly older than themselves, to bring them to the Connected Age. Thus young members of a team at the office will teach older ones how to use SMS text messaging etc. Students in school will bring the innovations to their teachers, starting with the younger and hipper of the teachers, and gradually moving up. Also in families, children will teach their parents. Age creep will not convert the whole population, but probably adds something like one year of age at the top limit, every two or three years, to the total population size of Gen-C in any given country.

We have said Gen-C will communicate with their peers with the mobile phone on a regular basis. What does this involve? To put it in practical terms, a Gen-C member will regularly seek immediate advice and answers via SMS text messages from friends in everyday situations. One of the early examples was attempts to cheat in school tests, which was one of the early catalysts for SMS text message adoption when the first Gen-C youths brought their mobile phones to school. The advice could be on where to go that afternoon after work or school, or for example advice on matters of the heart, problems with romance. Another is to use text messages to share a private joke, *while in the same room* with others. This is, for example, very common among Gen-C members when they go to meetings or seminars with their first jobs. Much like passing notes in class for previous generations, Gen-C will pass notes via the mobile phone, in real-time, both to participants present, and those who will enjoy the joke who are not present.

Tomi T Ahonen & Alan Moore

B GENERATION TEXT

A black and white delineation line between Gen-C and the rest of us is the communication vehicle of preference. Gen-C prefers to send text messages. They could call you, but they send a text. They could leave you a message on your voicemail, yet they hang up and send a text. You might send an email and receive a reply by text. They can be on a voice call with you and send you a text simultaneously. And, yes, they can send a text message to someone who is in the same room. All this on a shoestring budget, knowing full well that every text message costs.

Adults don't get it

Some of these messages are serious messages, but often it is the mischevious and frivolous messages that are sent this way. There is of course a counterculture for the young to have cryptic messages that adults are not even supposed to understand. Texting supports the need to be creative, to have entertainment – jokes – during the day. SMS is ultimate youth communication, fast, no grammar, limited characters, secretive, and one service which early on in every market the "adults simply do not get".

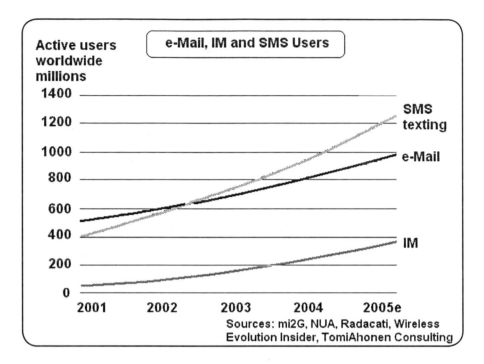

What may seem to many of us as the particularly strange behaviour of our own children, is in fact a universal trend all around the world. The young generations show a clear preference of SMS as their communication channel of choice. Several studies around the world show consistently that the young users prefer SMS to voice calls and prefer SMS to email. It is their private and secret communication tool that they can privately tap via their personal keyboards, without parents or siblings getting to listen in to a voice call or view an email. Even America is following the trend; at the end of 2004 already a third of Americans send text messages. The leaders there also are the young: members of Generation-C.

Less tobacco, less candy

Where is the money coming from? Obviously the heaviest spenders are teenagers. And while adults may think it is economically moronic to waste 10 cents per message on a text message when an internet email is free, teenagers are known for "being financially irresponsible" and preferring their own clannish communciation methods, and instant gratification, all of which feeds the traffic and spending on their own mobile phones.

In Finland teenagers are reported to spend 90% of their allowance on their mobile bill. And over half of this is on SMS. That money is not additional spend, it is obviously taken from the limited budget that teenagers have. So teenagers in Finland are spending less on clothes, the cinema, eating out at hamburger restaurants and pizza parlours. A study by Mobile Youth in the UK in April 2003 proved young people are spending less money on smoking due to the added spend on mobiles.

A study by the Mobile Data Association in the UK on disposable income of 16-24-year-olds in UK from August 2003 found that youth spend £400 per year on mobile phone and services, more than they spend on any other typical teen entertainment; ie, their music and stereos, TVs, video games and PCs, movies etc.

C PERSONAL ATTRIBUTES OF GEN-C

Generation-C is typical of its immediate older generation in being aware of digital devices and networks. The Community Generation, however, is much more deeply involved with the digital world. At the same time, over the past ten years, the digital world has evolved a lot to allow Gen-C to get more out of it, and to form a more intimate relationship with the digital and virtual worlds.

More aware

Generation-C members today are more aware, more critical, more knowledgable than ever before. Gen-Cs naturally understand that there are multiple overlapping networks co-existing, and that Gen-C members can usually select from a variety of networks to whichever suits their immediate needs and personal preferences the best. While the mobile phone may be the preferred means to communicate teenage love-notes with a current love interest, the same teenager might spend hours on the internet in chat rooms with other friends etc. They do not have a single network that they try to focus all activity, but rather are astute to distinguish between the relative merits of all available networks, and will very rapidly abandon one method for another, even in the middle of a communication, when a better network or means is possible.

Seek knowledge for themselves

Gen-C has grown up in a world of Google, and would never even consider using any non-digital research tools like a written encyclopedia in the family bookcase. Gen-C is quick to access blog sites and chat rooms to make independent discoveries of facts on issues that interest them. At some age this may be dinosaurs, at other ages it may be information on the pop music artists, or contraception, and then job search and career etc.

From 2004 over half of internet access devices are portable

Mobile phones are transforming from being merely a communication tool you carry to a fashion item that you wear. As we add functionality both to the mobile phone and its telecoms network it is easy to lose track of the ultimate utility of the phone. Howard Rheingold, the pioneer of virtual communities, never loses sight of the primary purpose of the mobile phone. Other uses are coming, such as shopping and consuming content, but the power of the mobile phone is communication. In enabling cooperation, as he says of mobile phones in his book *Smart Mobs*:

> *They amplify human talents for cooperation. They also change the way*
> *people shop, how they gather information on products they want to buy and*
> *where they decide to make that purchase.*
>
> Howard Rheingold, *Smart Mobs*, 2002

The Community Generation can be said to be very superficial, and to neglect "serious" and credible information sources on behalf of the first hits on Google and the most prevalent opinions found on the web. They also will steer towards the free sites rather than anything requiring subscription or payment, and this may limit access to some information sources or even colour their views. These are longer term trends that we cannot yet fully determine, but time will tell.

Very sceptical of marketing messages

Generation-C is not only as sceptical as its previous generations have been. For the first time this latest generation has the means to seek digital truth, on the web, via emails, in chat rooms, and especially on their own personal communication devices, the mobile phone. Gen-C is also very value-conscious. They understand what are typical price ranges for given goods, and make rapid comparisons of value across different options.

Generation-C is very selective. It knows that there are many channels, many rival brands, content, information etc. Generation-C will be fast to reject. If it's not for me, I turn it off. And growing up with MTV music videos and chat rooms, web pages and SMS text messages, Generation-C is used to content being of short duration and entertaining.

Tomi T Ahonen & Alan Moore

This generation is not only as digitally literate as its big brothers and aunts and uncles were, this generation for the first time lives in a life of multi-player digital games. Like many generations since, this generation too knows how to share music, video tapes (DVDs) and other content. But unlike previous generations, this new one has learned to use digital community power in sharing, with networked sharing systems like Napster, KaZaa, Grokster, etc.

Gamers

Another area which has had a significant effect on the emergence of Generation-C is videogaming. We have had videogames since Pong of the 1970s, but only the youngest generations have grown up with multi-player games. This again raises an awareness of communities and of how virtual worlds interact with people.

Videogaming moved from single play to networked play formats about ten years ago. It was first games that are called "first person shooter" games, such as *Wolfenstein*, *Doom*, *Quake* and *Half Life*, etc. The first networked games were available only on personal computers, and the early networks limited play to a few simultanous players. As we discussed earlier in this book, today there exist MMOGs, Massively Multiplayer Online Games, such as *EverQuest*, *Samurai Romanesque* and *Pocket Kingdom*, which can have hundreds of thousands of simultanous players. The gaming environment has totally evolved and has led to the creation of virtual communities within games, leagues, teams/tribes/clans etc. Today, game communities are some of the most evolved examples of self-defined communities online.

The other upshot of online gaming has been the creation of the user-generated levels for games. These are gaming fields, "cities" or "landscapes" or other places, locations or environments for that game, which are completely designed and built by a gamer. Many of the more advanced games today allow users to write modifications to the games so that they can create levels and place competitors into them, giving the game a new lease of life with new content. It is powerful as the position of control in the game production cycle is given to the audience rather than being dictated by the producer. This allows gamers to personalise their gaming environment and it is not uncommon to find, for example, that a gamer has created a game level that is a perfect virtual world copy of the school or shopping mall or office, so that the gamer can engage friends to shoot it out in a familiar place.

Just like a previous generation gained immensely over their elders in growing up with computers and thus not fearing them, the current Gen-C has grown up with virtual environments as a natural part of their lives. A gamer on *Tony Hawke* in France might skateboard in downtown Miami or a would-be driver in Singapore might race a Formula One car in Monaco. Kids have "experienced" the world in intensely more realistic ways than older generations that saw movies and TV shows from exotic locales. In their book *Got Game*, John Beck and Mitchell Wade undertook a study of 2,500 young business professionals. Their conclusion was:

> *"Growing up is simply different for gamers. They have replaced whatever traditional experiences they might have had as supporting players with a dramatic increase in experiencing the hero role."*
>
> Beck & Wade, *Got Game, 2004*

Games such as *Civilization*, *The Sims*, *Myst* and *Grand Theft Auto* are all popular examples of games requiring a great deal of strategic skill, building communities, cities and their infrastructure and fighting battles.

Teenagers in Finland spend 90% of allowance on mobile phone

The observation is that you do not come out of a computer game to put up with the sliced white bread of the average brand experience. Gamers have formulated into communities and are social within them. Furthermore, as we have demonstrated, gamers are used to co-creating their own entertainment and expect to play a hero role in their entertainment experiences. This has some interesting consequences for the joystick generation – as gaming contributes to and aggregates their sense of self-actualisation.

First generation to grow up with digital feedback channels

Earlier generations had to learn that their voice could matter, and that they had power in writing to politicians, corporations and other entities such as through email. Because of the feedback loops involved, a response might take a long time or it might never arrive. Gen-C is not accepting that. They know that SMS and IM are immediate contact methods. When they are offered a chance to interact via SMS or IM, Gen-C will expect an immediate response. Some communities and entities that have harnessed this have taught Gen-C that instant messaging formats can deliver – and should deliver – immediate comments. This reinforces the interest to participate, communicate, give feedback, and share the experience with friends.

A good example is the "Text a Celebrity" service from the Philippines, called **Star Text**, launched by the mobile operator Smart. The service has local culture celebrities like pop stars, TV actors etc agreeing to be available via text messaging to their fans for a given period of time. During those days or weeks, the stars agree to respond to every (legitimate) fan mail text message sent to them. The mobile

---

Tomi T Ahonen & Alan Moore

operator of course charges these as premium cost messages and shares part of the profits with the celebrities. The idea has been hugely popular in the Philippines and was rapidly copied around the world.

A similar application was then launched by political parties in Canada, sponsored by the Canadian Wireless Telecommunications Association, called **Youth Text**. Each Canadian political party agreed to respond to Youth Text messages and to reply within 48 hours. The purpose of the initiative was to get young people more active with politics, using the youth's preferred means of communication.

A lesson for business in general, and brands in particular, is that one-way flows of information look increasingly irrelevant to Gen-C. Advertising as image, command and control mechanisms that limit this generation are unappealing for a generation where content of one form or another plays a critical role in any of their experiences. Gen-C is the first generation for which two-way flows of information are the norm, not the exotic exception.

Smaller tribes

For many generations teenagers have exhibited "herd behaviour"; ie, they have copied each other. There has been an accepted way of dress, accepted brands of blue jeans or sneakers/trainers etc. Today's teenager herd is splitting into smaller herds than ever before. Now kids will find their own groupings and dress by their own "tribe", such as those who are into skateboarding, with a clear culture of behaviour, dress, music, drink etc. Thus even a classification of teenagers as a group is becoming useless; the kids need to be divided into ever smaller subgroups and microsegments. As American anthropologist Ted Polhemus and author of *Style Surfing: What to Wear in the Third Millenium* says:

> *What has caught my attention in particular is the fact that I think that fashion – in that strict sense of constant preoccupation with change and novelty and this year's colour replacing last year's colour and everybody falling into step behind these sort of dictates that the fashion journalists lay down – is going out of fashion. I think we are moving back to appreciate styles with its individual differences, with its capacity to express our social and cultural linkages between people, even across international boundaries*
> Ted Polhemus, *Style Surfing 1996*

Fashions may be useful for sociologists to track and analyse some very distinct behaviour patterns that are emerging. One of the most revealing areas is in how Gen-C approach dating. The behaviour is spectacularly different from that of older generations.

SMS and Dating

Dating is a good area to illustrate Gen-C behaviour as they use the power of SMS text messaging. In all countries of high SMS use the trend is clear – young men and women prefer to use SMS text messaging in starting up a romance. Men and women both like SMS as it is much less painful, allows time for consideration and is more gentle in handling rejection.

One Billion people are active users of SMS text messaging

It is now common for most single girls or women in countries of high mobile phone penetration to expect the man to start the courting for a potential relationship by an introductory SMS text message. This has replaced the traditional "pick-up line" in bars, clubs and discos. A woman will rather openly give the man her mobile phone number, and then expect the man to come up with a creative original romantic and humourous introductory message – all this in 160 characters of the standard SMS text message.

Why not a simple phone call?

The beauty of starting the courting process with a text message rather than in person or via a phone call, is that it is more gentle to both. A man can consider his approach and words carefully and write and rewrite the SMS before sending it, whereas many men stumble upon the early words spoken to the woman they are after.

Text messaging allows the girl more time to consider, she is not rushed, and this eliminates some of the hasty forced decisions that could be "no" rather than waiting, finding out about the man, considering, and agreeing. It also allows the girl to respond with a maybe, which for a man accustomed to receiving more rejections than acceptances for romantic advances, is a much better reply. Quite often the woman will then consult her girlfriends to consider the man.

This is idiomatic Gen-C behaviour – using the power of mobile telecoms to seek the assistance of the community. So far this is quite understandable, and we can well see older populations doing this as well. What makes Gen-C behaviour so distinguishing, is that the Gen-C girl will use that arrived romantic text message to share with her girl friends. She does that for several reasons; one, to find out if the message itself is an original, or perhaps the man had used it before, or worse, copied the message from a generic one. The girl will also share the message with her friends to find out if they know the man and if he has a reputation, good or bad.

Tomi T Ahonen & Alan Moore

Ease the pain

Even if the reply does arrive as a "no" to the man, it is seen as much less painful if the rejection is as a text message than said in person face to face, or on the phone. In survey after survey, from Finland to Singapore – young people both women and men – say they prefer to start a relationship this way.

As the romance picks up, the SMS messaging becomes intertwined into the relationship. 160 characters is a good medium to use for expressing an emotion, and creative romantics have managed short love poems in 160 characters. Romances soon develop a personal SMS language which may differ from all other previous romantic communications by either party with unique nicknames and recurring jokes and themes.

Memories in 160 characters

The reason this happens in SMS more than in other media is that the short communication is written and read, thus many funny things that might be said could be forgotten, but what was in writing tends to have more permanence. Many relationships which start with email courtship have such tendencies, but few relationships maintain a regular email communication pattern after face-to-face dating has begun. SMS messages are different in that SMS messages are sent all throughout the relationship, at least on a daily basis. Personal messages are stored and treasured.

Studies have shown that in relationships the partners measure each others' affection by receiving at least one message per day. If the other party does not show affection, something is wrong in the relationship. The use of SMS in relationships also extends to ending them – in the Philippines there has already been a court case based on whether a divorce announced by SMS was valid and binding. The court strongly disapproved of this new idea, but found the notification to have been valid and binding nonetheless.

D COMMUNITIES OF THE COMMUNITY GENERATION

As we have said it is the instinctive, continuous *access to communities* that distinguishes Gen-C from previous generations. While the cellular phone is important, this is not Generation-*Cellular* Phone. We also discussed the Connected Age, yet Gen-C is not Gen-*Connected*. It is "Community" as this is the exceptional difference for the generation. Now we will examine this phenomenon in more detail, with a few of the emerging behaviour patterns and types of communities that Gen-C is so comfortable with.

Change in behaviour

Generation-C is the first generation to live with their friends "in their pocket" – instantly available at all times. Again, it is important to highlight how different this is from any other communications. It is not the same if the friends are there to support you, on an instant messaging system, or via email, or in a chat room, or at home reachable via a fixed wireline telephone. That is not "always". If you do not have the ability to contact always, you will never discover the community support. If the other friends are not permanently connected, they will not be there to provide the support under all conditions. Only the mobile phone or, of course, other cellular network "always on" devices, such as the Blackberry, allow this.

Once a young person learns he/she is not alone, but can at all times contact friends, a much more interdependent relationship starts to build. Decisions are not made in isolation, even if late at night when a phone call would be frowned upon, Gen-C can contact each other silently via text messaging. Experiences are not felt alone, to be remembered with friends at McDonald's next day. No, experiences are immediately shared, when they happen. In Finland Professor Timo Kopomaa was the first to document this in his ground-breaking book *The City in Your Pocket* in 2000. Professor Kopomaa highlighted how differently young people behave when they have the power of the community in their pocket:

> *Nothing is agreed upon or fixed in precise terms, the spectrum of individual choice is kept as broad as possible. A certain ex tempore lifestyle becomes more widespread. Both shared and private decisions are expected to be taken rapidly, and schedules are not determined precisely, because they can be adjusted along the way.*
>
> Timo Kopomaa, *The City in Your Pocket, 2000*

This generation is used to sharing experiences and seeks the opinions of friends, via the mobile phone, at all times and in all situations. And, knowing that the friends are there, always, this generation can now actively seek their opinions and support at any time.

Sharing

Gen-C will be digitally literate and have multiple technical means to capture and generate content for themselves. They are also very apt at sharing, so they will borrow the friend's scanner, the big brother's digital camera and the uncle's faster computer or the aunt's CD burning drive to achieve what they want to do. They will also make do with their own equipment to a surprising degree. Even if their own

Tomi T Ahonen & Alan Moore

cameraphone has very limited resolution, they will be frequently using it to capture significant events and memories, such as the big skateboarding meet, or the birthday party at Pizza Hut, or the partying that happened with graduation, etc.

Gen-C is also very used to sharing, especially using various peer-to-peer networks; ie, Napster, KaZaa etc. They will make good use of digital memories, so a grainy image of a friend very drunk at a party a few years ago may suddenly emerge as part of a birthday card etc. Gen-C is very aware of the costs of sharing, so they will happily store digital memories on mobile phones, iPods, personal computers, network hard drives etc, and share them when they can do it at no cost, rather than use some of the expensive networking technologies. Then again, Gen-C tend to be young, and thus arguably "irresponsible" with their money. They can easily spend all of the disposable income on the virtual world and feel no remorse about it.

One in four on internet are active IM Instant Messaging users

The Generation-C members have instinctively learned to use the power of the network, their own community of support, in any situations that may arise. And with that connectedness being delivered most often via the mobile phone, this strengthens both the addiction to the mobile phone and also the ties between the connected community versus other friends who are not in that inner circle.

E ARE NOT LIKE THEIR PARENTS

Members of Gen-C relate to mobile phones and in fact all networks in a different way to previous generations. The network is there not to interrupt me, it is there to serve me. The network will not control me; I control the interaction on the network. Let us start with the ringing of the phone.

Why didn't you answer the phone?

A most revealing change in Gen-C behaviour when compared to older generations is the reaction to a ringing phone. When the telephone network was the only connection, it was also given a very high degree of importance. Older generations were taught to keep phone conversations short just in case there is an important phone call coming in. When the technology allowed it in the 1980s, most of society bought telephone answering machines to ensure that the important calls were not missed. During these times if a marketing call was made, be it a market research call on a consumer survey or opinion poll, or perhaps a sales call, such calls were readily accepted, even welcomed, by many. Today, of course, even for market research polls and interviews, more than ten calls need to be made for every one interview achieved.

When the telephone line was the only connection, it was also considered always worth answering. There could be very important information at the other end. Thus again older generations would even answer other people's phones if visiting their home or office. We were taught to identify ourselves when answering the phone, as telephones were shared instruments whether at home or the office. But most importantly, a ringing phone had to be answered.

Gen-C behaves totally differently. It is completely normal to them, to be at home or at work, at their phone, with no distraction such as a meeting, to see who is calling, know who it is, and still not answer it. This drives the older generations like our parents totally livid. You were at the phone, had the time, saw it was me calling, and didn't answer the phone? But this illustrates the difference between the attitudes to communications by Generation-C and older generations. Gen-C know there are many networks, many reasons for calling, and that a phone call is *not* the most urgent contact. If that person really wants me to urgently talk, he will next send a text message. If it was just a social call, he will not send a message.

No, Gen-C will happily see his best friend calling, and not be involved in anything particularly important, and not answer. He will return the call perhaps an hour later, when feeling like it. The best friend will understand. A call is an interruption, and Gen-C feels it is perfectly acceptable to reject the interruption.

I see you

Gen-C also knows about mobile phones and displaying the phone number. So Gen-C is quite accustomed to skip the "Hi, this is Jim, is it Joe?" or "Hi, this is Joe speaking" kind of introductions to phone conversations. Gen-C doesn't have time to waste, and this is utterly unnecessary. The caller knows that nobody other than the mobile phone owner will answer the phone. And the receiver of the call will see who calls. So Joe will answer directly: "Hi, Jim, what's up?"

Generate own content

Gen-C is used to creating its own content using various digital means, both by sampling and copying from existing sources, and using the wide range of digital cameras, scanners, built-in microphones, etc. The generation is also very familiar with editing tools on the computer and will easily use these to edit, improve and crop content to suit their tastes.

Tomi T Ahonen & Alan Moore

My identity

Gen-C is also associating own identity factors with the mobile phone. As the mobile phone is so critical to community contacts, it is even more important as a personal status symbol. For the youth, what used to be associations with being cool, adult, sophisticated – that were attributes strongly promoted, for example, to associate with cigarette smoking in the 1960s and the youth strongly still associate with cars today – are increasingly associated with the mobile phone.

What phone one has, what covers on the phone, what ringing tone, what games, screen savers etc, will all help the Gen-C communicate to peers and to others a sense of who that person wants to be.

Who may use the phone

Again, it is interesting to see how differently Gen-C, especially younger people, use their phones with accepted inner circle friends, and others. For example parents, little and big brothers and sisters, favourite uncles etc, will not be allowed to scroll through saved messages etc. Even if it is a new phone, which the youth may be very eager to show off, such as its new camera feature or latest game, that youngster will not want the other to dig through messages and calling histories etc. to find out what personal communication that young person has been up to.

But see the same Gen-C youngster with his or her best friends at a McDonald's or Pizza Hut. They will all happily put their phones in the middle of the table, and all will reach out for each others' phones, play the latest games, read through *all latest messages*, comment on them, etc. Again Gen-C has learned to use the community, and the most important community for a Gen-C is much more valued and trusted – on a daily basis – than family.

Even adult age mobile phone users have soon developed a personal intimacy with the content on the phone so intense that in most relationships and marriages, if one partner tries to read what the other has stored on the phone, it results in a fight. The phone is that personal.

My phone my money

For the Gen-C the first financial instrument is not the credit card, a checking account or a debit card with a bank. It is the mobile phone. This generation assumes it can pay for anything with the mobile phone. In fact where the phone account is a "post-pay" or contract account, it is usually the first tool of credit that Gen-C is exposed to. They may make a hamburger payment on the mobile phone simply because their cash is low, and they know the phone bill will not become due until the end of the month: very short-term credit.

Gen-C will not be surprised that parking can be paid by mobile phone, such as in Croatia, or that public transportation such as buses, trams and underground trains can be paid by mobile phone, as in Helsinki, Finland. They would expect to meet most vending machines with a mobile phone operation code from Poland to Singapore to Japan. Gen-C is not surprised that Austrian train tickets can be paid by mobile phone, nor that Norwegian ski lifts accept payments by mobile phone, nor that Korean car drivers can pay for petrol by mobile phone.

Still not convinced?

Members of Gen-C are remarkably different from older generations in how they approach digital networks of any kind, and in particular in how they use their mobile phones. We saw in this chapter many examples of what Generation-C will do. For those readers who may think that the examples are beyond belief we ask that you pose the example to an elderly teenager friend, say between the ages of 16-19, and ask is that behaviour feasible. You may be surprised to find that most teenagers in that age group will immediately identify all of the behaviour examples in this chapter, and find them totally natural to themselves and their peers. Only do not project your own behaviour and values to this group. You are mature. They are not. They are young. As the American comedian George Carlin said: "Age is a very high price to pay for maturity."

Case Study 8

Star Text

Mass audiences all around the world are increasingly interested in celebrities. There seems to be an ever-increasing range of celebrity from movie stars and chart-topping musicians, to TV show hosts, soap opera actors to even reality TV participants on shows such as the Big Brother house, Survivor Island, Pop Idol, the Bacherlor, the Apprentice etc. There is also a vast interest by common people to access their stars. Some attend various events where they can meet their stars. Stars try to capitalise on their – often short-term – fame by rushing out books etc.

Few stars are able to establish a real fanbase and get hardcore fans to pay to sign up. Mostly pop musicians have been able to do so, and increasingly also sports clubs. There are ways to capitalise on various merchandis-

---

Tomi T Ahonen & Alan Moore

ing from T-shirts and posters to DVDs, subscription websites etc.

A recent potent innovation to capitalise on celebrity was released in the Philippines in 2003. The mobile operator Smart introduced what it calls "Star Text". With Star Text there are celebrities from the Philippines market who agree for a limited time to respond to any contacts, via SMS text messaging.

The text messages that fans send to the celebrities are, of course, charged at premium SMS rates, typically about five times the regular rate of text messaging. Fans are very happy to be able to communicate directly with their stars, and this premium is not seen as prohibitively expensive. In contrast to a letter sent to a fan club, this text message is guaranteed a response.

The incentive to the celebrities to participate is that they get a cut of the premium payments – they get paid essentially for every response they make. They would have no such incentive in traditional "snail mail" nor with email based responses. As being one of the featured celebrities on Star Text is a short-term limited time by which any one star is on the system, the stars will not be overly burdened, and also the stars can limit the "exposure" their persona gets in the media. Yet they get invaluable direct feedback from their devoted fans; a direct dialogue with them.

Of course the service has limitations. There are filters to eliminate rude messages and stars will not reply to inappropriate messages that will simply be rejected by the system. The stars will naturally not respond to the messages using the clumsy text input of a mobile phone, but rather will have a comfortable personal computer keyboard and screen by which to rapidly respond. The system will have many automated standard response templates like "thank you for writing" etc, but the star will typically include one or two lines of real responses to each fan.

In the Philippines the most popular star so far, according to the International Herald Tribune on February 14 2004, was the local soap opera star and TV host, Kris Aquino. The same concept is since being introduced in markets all around the world from South Africa to Canada.

They beauty of using premium SMS is that the total fan mail can be capped, limited, to be reasonably able to be handled by the star. If using traditional email, some stars might get an overwhelming amount of mail simply because it is free. Equally the payment shared from the service is a good enticement to bring stars into the system. They get paid to participate, they are "professional entertainers" and must generate income from their profession. Of course the mobile operator Smart here gets a lot of premium traffic and reaches parts of the population who might otherwise not be eager to communicate via SMS.

"Television is democracy at its ugliest."
Paddy Chayefsky

X
Advertising in Crisis
If we say it just one more time?

Procter & Gamble bankrolled commercial television worldwide for 30 years. When Chief Marketing Officer Jim Stengel says that television spot advertising had stopped working circa 1987, and when the company announces a significant shift in its marketing strategy and advertising budgets, it is clear that the fate of the 30-second TV spot is being reappraised. This chapter examines how marketing messages are doing amidst all the changes. Needless to say, when the messengers, the medium and the receivers of communications are all changing, so too must there be changes to the message itself. We will examine the health of the advertising industry overall through the example of the biggest, brightest and most lucrative part, TV advertising.

A INDUSTRY IN CRISIS

Most analysts of the advertising and marketing world agree that the old rules and principles are no longer valid. In all media, from TV and radio broadcasting to the print media, billboards, even internet advertising, the same trends appear. More ads, less attention, less efficiency. The argument rages; what are the causes and what might solve the problems.

Consumed by advertising

It is a daily bombardment of interruptive advertising communication. Depending on which analyst report you read it is anything between 1,500 to 4,000 interruptions per day. At the same time audiences have splintered into ever-decreasing fragments. To reach them today takes enormous financial spend. Jim Stengel explains: "In 1965, 80% of adults in the US could be reached with three 60-second TV spots. In 2002, it required 117 prime time commercials to produce the same result."

We are seeing the combined efforts of sensory overload of competing marketing messages with ever smaller accessible audiences. This leads inescapably to the diminishing efficiency of the individual advertisements in a specific medium in any given campaign. Every ad we launch into the competing marketplace of ideas brings an ever diminishing return. In response all advertisers create ever more ads. This further erodes the effectiveness for all. It is a vicious cycle with no end in sight. Simply and undeniably the overall effectiveness of traditional interruptive communications is diminishing. In a recent *Wired* magazine article, "The Decline of Brands", the author James Surowiecki said:

> *The world, it seems, is disappearing beneath a deluge of logos. In the past decade, corporations looking to navigate an ever more competitive marketplace have embraced the gospel of branding with newfound fervor.*
> *Wired* November 2004

Yet this is at a time when customers are looking for and demanding greater quantities and manifestations of value. With the advent of internet search, consumers have changed from being passive, who once would have been motivated by image advertising, to an ever more discerning and proactive audience. They are becoming more elusive for advertising campaigns and naturally more distrustful of superficial claims.

Let's use Apple as an example. Apple's iTunes, iPod, retail stores, iMac, iChat, iLife, iMovie, Garageband, Final Cut Pro, Apple's web presence, Apple's advertising; all, separately and together reinforce the greater sense of added value. Are its sensorial flagship stores purely retail, or are they advertisements; are they educational or are they spaces for entertainment? This is what modern marketing is all about and Apple, via its iPod, has successfully entered into the vernacular of everyday life. All the customer experiences are an enhanced experience. It is what we call "Value-Plus" (Value+). Yes, Apple is tiny, it is a flyweight punching it out with the computer heavyweights. But, for any brand struggling with growth and diminishing returns, Apple is a lesson on how innovation, great design, great retail, great advertising, great packaging and great products all aggregate to deliver for the customer and the company itself. Apple engages its audience in every media channel. In many ways it is common sense,

Tomi T Ahonen & Alan Moore

you can make it a dull experience or you can make it a great experience; you can make it an uninspiring product or you make it an aspirational product. You can think in silos or you can think holistically – do customers think in silos?

Fast forward past ads

The home video recorder was the first mass market gadget that allowed fast-forwarding past advertisements. Today, PVRs (Personal Video Recorders) like TiVo in the USA and Sky+ in the UK, are allowing real-time pausing and rewinding of audio-visual content. The boxes allow easy avoidance of advertisements. In fact avoiding ads is one of the oft-stated reasons why PVRs are bought.

Mark Gimien, writing in the October 4 2004 issue of *New York Magazine*, delivers a critique about the state of advertising and how it is struggling to adapt to the well-documented waves of change that are currently in motion.

> *Ad agencies are currently overwhelmed with the suspicion that the language of contemporary ads – the catchy tagline, the celebrity put in a funny situation, the twist ending, even the TV commercial itself – doesn't work like it used to. Ad agency executives saw numbers that claimed to show that young beer-and-car-buying men were deserting television for the pleasures of PlayStation and online porn. They looked at Google, a company that became the star of the internet while selling "ads" that consisted of nothing but three lines of text. They all got TiVo, and started talking about how they could TiVo the shows and TiVo past the commercials. And they sighed over the teenage kids, who just didn't seem to care anymore about perfectly good, clever, glossy TV commercials. "How am I supposed to communicate with someone who is used to writing 'I wnt2cu'?" asks noted (veteran) adman Jerry Della Femina.*
>
> *New York Magazine* Oct 4, 2004

That is precisely the point. We cannot try to advertise to the new generation using techniques of mass media persuasion in the early 21st century. Such activities will at best be ignored, at worst work against brands, condemning them to the unacceptable category, as old-fashioned, unreasonable, preachy and irrelevant. Yes, today we have to embrace the vocabulary and media of our customers and find ways for brands to become meaningful in their lives. And that is not by interruptive advertising. As Adriana Cronin-Lukas of the Big Blog Company says: "This is the end of the age of sledgehammer advertising." Today, we have to engage our target audiences. That is becoming increasingly difficult and requires very different skills and tools from those that worked in the past.

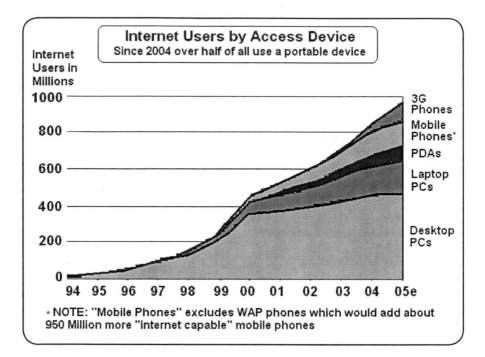

Engaging audiences is a total turnaround on the philosophy of who has access to the truth. The change in mindset in the marketing industry is to be no less severe. Brands – and the agencies supporting their advertising and marketing – have to evolve from one-way marketing communications beginning from the "pulpit" of TV ads, to interactive engagement methods.

Think Apple, think different.

Viewer numbers in real time

Audience ratings are a critical element of the value proposition of the deliverables on TV advertising. Nielsen ratings have been the basis of these measurements for as long as there was advertising on TV. Today several new technologies are encroaching on this space. Online TV ratings sites have appeared to offer instant ad campaign results such as the website by TV planning agency Guerillascope. It offers instant access to real-time TV viewing figures.

Another example comes from New Zealand where mobile phone-based viewer responses were generated using **Power points** – a game to solicit SMS text mes-

Tomi T Ahonen & Alan Moore

sages from viewers whenever they saw a specific logo on the screen. The local TV station was able to generate real-time viewer information not only on actual viewer numbers, but most revealingly the actual viewing patterns of a given viewer over a night of programming. If 25% of the audience watches the show at 8pm, and 27% of the audience views the show at 8.30pm, how many of those are the same viewers, or how many have changed? Now this kind of information is becoming available.

Customers less loyal

Consumers are becoming increasingly disloyal to brands. With more digital platforms and the extensions of brands into new spaces, more competitors emerge and competitive media appear for many services. Companies are losing what they often held as their right to sell to their customers exclusively. Customers leave, or are openly "promiscuous" by consuming goods and services of competing brands.

A study by a retail-industry tracking firm NPD Group revealed loyalty levels as they relate to brands. They discovered that nearly 50% of those who described themselves as "highly loyal" to a brand were no longer loyal a year later. And even bigger brand names did not seem to have much success either in keeping their customers. Another study found that just 4% of consumers would be willing to stick with a brand if its competitors offered better value for the same price. It means that 96% of your customers can be captured by a brave competitor which decides to build a better value proposition! Consumers are continually looking for a better deal, opening the door for companies to introduce a raft of new products.

Need to be entertaining

TV advertising is caught in the overall societal trend for everything to be more entertaining. So if interruptive TV advertising fails to deliver on "entertainment", "information" or "price value", it is likely that your audience will be doing something else, none of which helps advertising deliver its message. The audience can be chatting amongst themselves about their day, picking up a magazine that they had already dipped into during a previous commercial break, or doing household tasks like cleaning or ironing, or doing office work. If more a couch potato, the viewer can spend all of the ad break just mindlessly channel-hopping out of habit. Some even have their computer next to the TV, and go internet surfing during ad breaks.

What the advertiser wants is for the viewer to stay on that channel and watch the advertisers' messages, actively paying attention to it. That is not easy. Or better yet, to cause some discussion based on the ad with the viewers in the room. Or if the viewer is watching alone for them to actually pick up the phone and call a friend about the ad. How many ads do that anymore today? Zero. A provocative statement, yes, but we would argue it is true.

B TV ADVERTISING CHANGING

The most expensive television advertising spot in the world is the first 60 seconds of half-time at the SuperBowl. The broadcast of that expensive advertisement also co-incides with the single biggest flush of water down the US sewerage system, argues Stuart Crainer in the *New Zealand Marketing Magazine* of April 2004. Nobody is watching the ads, because they have been drinking Budweisers for the last 90 minutes. It is a mass exodus to the bathroom. Media buyers on the other hand will sell the SuperBowl on the basis that it reaches gazillions of people. Make no mistake, the game does. The TV programme reaches the millions of viewers. But the ads do not.

> ## We get up to 4000 interruptions by advertisements per day

We are seeing a shift away from being defined by the brands we consume to being defined by the brands we do *not consume* and advertising and media companies are contributing to this shift. The old image-based advertising model, the one that took us from 1950s washing powder commercials right up to classics like the Guinness beer's *Surfer* of 2000, has gone.

False sense of security

While many see a brave new marketing world where words like "relationship" have replaced "advertiser" and "consumer", in the mind of the customer the new advertising world looks pretty much the same as the old world. An advertising message in the form of a TV commercial is tasked with creating awareness in the (largely mistaken) belief that at some point down the line, our attention will translate into a positive action – usually, that someone goes out and buys the product. Rather than sending an ad message to the consumer, we use the ad message to build a relationship. Problem solved? No. Advertising is not repaired. Why then, do businesses, their brands and advertising agencies still persist?

They are bound to follow that path, even if it becomes less useful, as nobody, they argue, can show an alternate path. Let us refine the message; do it even better, maybe that can bring back the good old days. As an industry, the advertising world is trying to sell horse-buggies to customers who have driven a car. Even if we were great salespeople – and we are not – it would not work. But still we persist.

And that is the point. It is not because the advertising is good or bad, it is because we have become too familiar with the process of being advertised to. Advertising in

---

Tomi T Ahonen & Alan Moore

the main does not move us, and in the rare occasions that we are moved, we are not attributing this emotional response to the brand – we are attributing it to the adver-tisement. We have disconnected the ad from the brand. So, when we are moved by the ad (albeit occasionally) it no longer connects back to the brand. Why should it? We know that is how we are meant to respond.

Involvement

The problem is that the modern customer wants to become involved in the market-ing process. As we saw in the Society chapter, we are looking for experiences. We want a relationship with brands that are involving and that reward us for the time we spend interacting with them. We still know that we are being sold to, we do not mind because the reward is greater than the sacrifice. We have moved on beyond simple, naive trust. We have stopped believing in brands that just dangle an image in front of us then expect us to buy it. Marketing still works, it just works far more effectively when it involves the participation of its customers.

Viewers disappearing, money too

John Ranelagh, a founding commissioning editor of British broadcaster Channel 4 and a former commissioner of the UK regulator ITC (now Ofcom), has said that evidence shows that broadcast has lost young males to computer games.

In 2003 Frank Rose claimed that The **Coca-Cola** Company had cut its TV ad spend by 10%. But where did that money go? For 2005 Coke is adding $400m to its marketing budget. Where is that money going? Coca-Cola is one of the pioneers of marketing and undeniably one of the world's best at understanding new marketing methods. David Raines, the Coke VP who allocates ad spend, was quoted as saying: "The bottom line is, ad dollars will follow the consumer."

Some of the new opportunities for Coca-Cola ad dollars are product placement into movies such as *Matrix Reloaded*. Coke is sponsoring Atari's *Enter the Matrix* video game. Last year Coke launched its biggest mobile initiative in Spain and in the UK selling music downloads, much like Apple does with iTunes. Mycokemusic. com is already one of the most used sites for downloading MP3 files in the UK and Spanish markets. Coca-Cola is shifting its marketing spend to movies, video games, music and the mobile phone. That is where the young Coke-drinker is today, not in front of the TV.

Last year the total US advertising spend was flat at 20%, while global TV advertis-ing spend fell by the biggest percentage ever. Rishad Tobaccowala, president of new media at StarCom Media, projects that in the US $3bn could migrate to other media channels within the next three years. That is a reduction of 15% of current spending.

All around the world advertising budgets for traditional TV are diminishing. Mitsubishi in the US cut $120m from its autumn 2004 TV ad spend because it believed there was a better way to spend the money. At the same time companies such as Anheuser Busch, Ford, General Motors and McDonald's have all migrated significant TV ad spend away from TV advertising.

Death of mass media?

What is happening to the money? Businesses still need to spend their marketing budgets. In the USA some people argued that product placement would address some of the need. The argument is that by placing your product into movies, TV shows etc, like the Aston Martin cars and Philips electric razors into the latest James Bond movie, could fill the gap. Adam Gerber, director of media strategy at MediaVest, explained very clearly that this is a fallacy. His comment was printed in *Media Daily News*: "You can't squeeze a 60 billion dollar marketplace into product placement. People will turn their sets off."

> ## 50% of "highly loyal" customers switched within one year

And they most certainly will, if the type of product placement described by *Fast Company* magazine August 2004 is anything to go by. Linda Tischler, writing in an article entitled "The Good Brand", talked to John Hayes, CMO for American Express, who had been sponsoring a TV programme called *The Restaurant*:

> *We need to be where people are and involved in things they value, Hayes says. But, as with any new venture, he concedes there are still a few kinks to be worked out. AmEx's presence on The Restaurant was, he admits, occasionally ham-handed, as chef Rocco paused, midcrisis, to extol the virtues of the company's small-business service.*
>
> *Fast Company Magazine August 2004*

American Express is a good example of the above debate. In 1994 American Express spent 80% of its marketing budget on TV; by 2003, that number had fallen to 35%. The change, driven by the audiences migrating to DVDs, the internet, cable (HBO), video games and PVRs combined with the emergence of an ever wider range of marketing communication vehicles and media.

C TV AD ECONOMICS

The TV advertising industry has always been strongly stacked in favour of the broadcaster. If your brand wanted to advertise your product or service on TV, you would go to your media agency. They would suggest a series of ads within the ad breaks of appropriate TV shows. The aim is to gain a large viewership or what the industry calls to get most "eyeballs".

Heads I win, tails you lose

The broadcaster buys programming from independent TV producers, from syndication, or commissions it from the TV channel's own production teams. A small TV station might only do the local news, a major organisation like the NBC or HBO would make significant revenues from selling the rights to their own shows. The advertising money is used to pay for the TV content. While some shows turn out to be hits, other shows crash and burn, over the span of a season of programming the TV broadcasters have generally always won. What they charge advertisers ends up more than paying for the programming and the remainder is then distributed in the form of bonuses, dividends etc.

Traditionally, the broadcaster is the gatekeeper. True to form, broadcasters like to keep advertisers and content producers very far from each other. The TV station has maintained supreme control of the whole equation. In this way the broadcasters have been able to profit from the big hits that invariably come along every so often.

The model once seemed robust and iron clad. Advertisers knew TV was the favoured channel, so what if it was a bit on the expensive side? The TV show producers were paid. The broadcasters made money. Everybody was happy. Except that we now have disruption from all sides of the TV broadcasting picture. We have video on demand, cable and satellite TV, internet TV, TiVo, and even TV on the mobile phone. Suddenly we have intense competition and all players are reconsidering their positions. Margins are being squeezed. The advertising-based TV model is crumbling beneath our very eyes, as Mike Ritson of the London Business School says:

> *A commercial break is not a time when we watch ads. It is not even a time when we avoid advertising. To infer avoidance one must first infer attention, and attention was rarely continued over the momentary bridge between a programme finishing and a commercial break starting...*
> *viewers are talking, reading and snogging.*
> http://www.mediatel.co.uk/newsline/2003/02feb/04/ads.cfm

Not only are the TV production and broadcasting industries feeling the disruptive effects. So too is the advertising industry. Companies from ad production to media planning and distribution agencies have all suddenly felt the threat of their steady money streams disappearing. The pressure reflects in the creative work, initiating a downward spiral. Less money means less talent, less effort, worse ads, which in return mean less effectiveness, further diminishing revenues etc.

New income for TV

Rival business models are viable to sustain the TV industry. Subscription TV already generates more revenues in the UK than TV advertising. On some content delivery channels, including the pay TV channels or 2.5G and 3G mobile phone services, advertising is the jam, above and beyond mainstream revenues. Mobile telecoms has introduced totally new income streams, in particular from premium SMS text messaging. Shows like the *Big Brother* house generate one-quarter of the total revenues from the shared benefit of premium priced SMS text messages. *Who Wants to Be a Millionaire?* has financed the show and all of its money awards from premium calling to its phone numbers by would-be contestants. At the extreme, shows like the Finnish model of SMS to TV chat, and various SMS to TV games will fully fund the programming costs of such simple – and viewer generated – programming.

Suddenly content providers have access to direct revenue streams. Voting and other mobile phone participation can deliver direct income. The increasing popularity of product placement is another option. Advertisers themselves also see alternate means as preferable when the mainstream TV advertising is underperforming. What is the role of the major TV broadcast brands? Suddenly they seem bloated, and ripe for some disintermediation.

New value chains

This goes to the nub of the issue that the money is starting to flow in different ways and directions, not only from advertiser via broadcaster to producer. Advertisers are under pressure to deliver ROI (Return On Investment), to be more effective with their marketing communications because of the increasing sophistication of their customers. The unbundling of the mass media and the proliferation of more direct digital channels to their customers means advertisers have to seek different solutions. In fact they are compelled to find new solutions. This process is unstoppable.

Viewer groups have splintered. TV content has spread to multiple digital channels. Some still function on advertising but many do not. As TV advertising diminishes in its significance, so too is a paid-for audience an ever less viable marketing communications channel. It is yet another battleground in the digital convergence and diver-

Tomi T Ahonen & Alan Moore

gence arena. Who gets to control the access, the billing and the content? It is not who has the biggest audience or the best-rated TV shows. Now it is ever more important to become a preferred partner in a content-partnership system. The best at partnering will win. This is not a core competence of traditional TV broadcasters, who can provide the best and user experience and who can make it the simplest to use?

The issue is now; it is not tomorrow, or next year. The issue for brands is how then do you spend your marketing budget? How do you reach your customers? How do you differentiate in a crowded marketplace? How do you create pull to your brand? Part of the answer is to create scaleable creative assets that can travel across channels, across national boundaries, across stakeholders, that will drive business results; reducing costs, delivering sales, and creating greater customer advocacy. A new form of marketing that activates customer communities. It is not advertising as we know it.

D CALL FOR CREATIVITY

Now brands need to work harder to engage their audience. Working harder means deploying communication platforms upon which existing channels of communication can be based. It means short-circuiting the waiting game for the right content to come along and creating it yourself. It means using this content to work as a media platform for new and more direct communication techniques. It means ownership of an activity, which can be used as a tradeable commodity, either in direct media purchase or to generate future revenue.

Joey Reiman, CEO of Brighthouse, says: "Advertising agencies have become an antiquated broker business, selling space to clients with creativity thrown in for free." Reiman argues we live in a world which is ad rich and idea poor. Ads create transactions; ideas create transformations. Ads reflect our culture; ideas imagine our future:

> *The old model of advertising and branding was to improve public perception.*
> *The new model demands companies improve public life. To survive,*
> *advertising agencies must start nurturing ideas, not just managing clients.*
> *Business Results* newsletter, Autumn 2004

Some use the term "Advertising Funded Programming". This is a clumsy and inappropriate phrase. Most of the current programming on our TV screens, after all, with the possible exception of public service broadcasters, is funded by some kind of advertiser function. More clever, harder-working communication does not mean "duping" the consumer with hidden implicit brand messages and product placement. And woe betide those that decide to go down that route. We show later in this book how quickly and decisively communities will punish brands that overpromise and underdeliver.

Only 4% of customers will stay loyal if rival similar service cheaper

---

Unfortunately, the very essence of interruptive advertising is so deeply ingrained to be about driving consumers to the point of transaction, that really the very concept of embedding experience into what advertising does is anathema. Today, the best traditional advertising can offer is heavy handed-product placement, or sponsorship. What is certain is that to fix the problem, we do not need more of the same old advertising; what we need is to put our efforts into new directions.

From push to pull

We combine the diminishing effectiveness of interruptive advertising with the growing trend of consumer activity, proactive consumers or "prosumers." We arrive at the inevitable crossroads for the marketing profession. We find ourselves at the opportunity of engagement marketing. From interruption to activation; from *push* to *pull*. As an industry the advertising and marketing business must wake up to this ultimate end-game, and start to take their customers, the branded companies, products and services that advertise, to this new status.

It will be a difficult journey, but one that is necessary for any companies that can survive. The opportunity to build customer desire by interruption is closing, engagement is the only viable way for the future, and for any growth along the way. This is echoed by Glen L. Urban, Professor at the Sloan School of Management:

> *Evidence is building that the paradigm of marketing is changing from the push strategies so well suited to the past 50 years of mass media to trust-based strategies that are essential in a time of information and empowerment.*

Glen L. Urban,
The Trust Imperative Sloan School of Management MIT March 2003

This new world is about opportunity, it is there to be harnessed, culturally, technologically, financially. But it requires a different approach. To succeed in a digitally connected business environment, any entity attempting to persuade – be it a business trying to sell or a government attempting to serve, etc – must learn to

---

Tomi T Ahonen & Alan Moore

engage the intended audience. There are more brands in the "brand hospital" than businesses care to admit. And throwing more money at the problem, using the same old methods in an attempt to create higher shareholder return, will simply not help. We have come a long way from the corner store.

New technologies, media fragmentation, effects such as information overload and changing consumer attitudes have all combined to undermine the economics and logic of modern marketing. It is not just that different parts, such as advertising, are less effective. The system as a whole has become dysfunctional. In its broadest sense, encompassing all go-to-market activities, marketing now accounts for 50% of all economic activity. But is it really worth paying for? Where is the return? Brands can no longer be created in isolation: they must be forged collaboratively between businesses and customers who engage with each other.

Orange Wednesdays

British mobile operator Orange has been developing services with a community dimension. One of the successful campaigns has been with the biggest cinema chain in the UK, UCG, under the concept of "Orange Wednesdays". Any movie-goer who pays for a movie ticket on a Wednesday with an Orange branded mobile phone will get two tickets for that show. This is to encourage Orange customers to bring their friends to the movies. In the fiercely contested UK mobile phone market – where already about 20% of the population has two subscriptions – this appeals particularly to the 16-24-year-olds who are regular movie-goers. Orange still runs the ads in the cinema. It has a captive audience. The communication is relevant, is specific and offers the added value. This advertising is not wasted. But what Orange is not doing is trying to shoehorn their entire unique sales proposition into a 30- or 60-second TV spot.

Integrated marketing communications

After a brand or company has started on a path for engagement marketing, the next step is to synchronise all of its legacy marketing tools and ensure that the intended marketing messages and any engagement are deployed in a consistent manner through all tools. The current thinking typically isolates ten different communication tools available to the marketer.

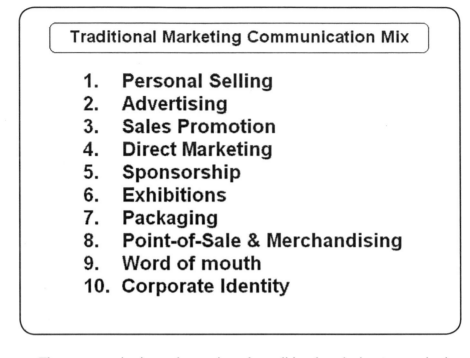

These communication tools constitute the traditional marketing communication mix. Each element of the communication mix should integrate with other tools of the communication mix so that a unified message is consistently reinforced. This new direction for marketing is referred to as integrated marketing communication (IMC).

Marketing communication has many faces – sponsorship, direct marketing or database marketing, TV ads, billboards next to the road, radio ads, magazines, trade publications, newspapers with articles and adverts. To stay ahead and make an impact we need to innovate. However, innovation is not marketing gimmickry. It is about something very different.

The above ten points all deal really with "interruptive" communications, which are financially costly and increasingly less effective. The real challenge is to adjust to these major changes and to generate a multiple effect for both businesses and consumers. This multiple effect is based upon *the notion that consumers can become partners in the co-creation of experiences*. In an entertainment context, Red Bull's FlugTag, held in the summer of 2004 in London's Hyde Park, was a brilliant demonstration of "experience co-creation", which was then broadcast on terrestrial television. BMW offers custom cars, delivered in 12 days, where a choice of 26 wheel designs and 123 console options are available on the Z3 Roadster. Dell's individualised built-to-order computers have generated phenomenal success for the company, where value is co-created.

Ending advertising

We have looked at how advertising is in crisis. We used TV advertising as the example as it is the biggest and most prestigious. Make no mistake, the same issues confront radio, print, billboards etc. The mighty $350bn advertising industry is on its knees. Ads cost ever more to produce, to place, and deliver to an ever smaller audience in an ever more congested environment of advertising message overload. Change is traumatic. It is disruptive. Yet it can be invigorating, especially for a creative talent that thrives on competition, as many in the advertising industry are. Every disruption provides an opportunity for those who can instinctively sense a business opportunity and are creative enough to break free of the old mindsets. Marketing and advertising people tend to be this way and should be the first to get the gist of the enormous opportunity outlined in this book. Cory Treffiletti said it well in his article in *Media Post* in January 2005: "It's a great time to be in advertising, and a scary one if you don't think about the future."

Case Study 9

Tango soft drinks

Perhaps one of the earliest examples of engagement marketing was the re-launching of the soft drink Tango in the UK by advertising agency Howell Henry Chaldecott Lury in the early 90s. The media world was still pretty simplistic back then and the campaign was initially driven by some highly creative TV advertising. The Tango campaign was a project that used non-traditional areas of marketing communication that provided the brand with a real sense of personality forging it into a national icon, and driving its business success.

Talk to people about Tango today, they remember the Orange man, the Gotan doll and the ambushing of the Conservative Party on national television. Tango was transformed from being a lame second division brand you might find in a fish and chip shop to being one of the leading youth icons in the UK.

In Britain of the late 1990s Tango operated in a market dominated by Coca-Cola, the number one brand in the world. Coca-Cola's marketing power, derived from their flagship brand, enabled the company to also dominate the fruit drinks sector in all the countries in which they operate. Tango was the domestic UK fruit-flavoured drink brand of modest marketshare.

Tango innovated in non-traditional media – for example, the sponsorship of *The Word* a highly successful young adult TV show on Channel 4. Promotional activities played a big part in Tango's history. They were a way of not only driving product sales but of encouraging consumers to interact with the brand and reaffirm their relationship with it.

Megaphones and Gotan (anagram of Tango) Dolls build on a history of telephone numbers (Apple campaign) and are physical manifestations of the brand's offbeat view of the world. The Gotan Doll promotion was the first ever use of premium rate phone lines for funds transfer in a self-liquidating promotion. 200,000 Gotan Dolls sold in eight weeks. Tango's Megaphone Promotion generated 200,000 phone calls and over 100,000 megaphones were despatched. Financially, it delivered significant contribution to Tango's bottom line through sales of megaphones and premium call lines. The launch of apple Tango with a direct response mechanism via telephones, generated 1.3 million phone calls and a 35% increase in overall sales in the first year.

The ambushing of the Conservative Party Leadership Election Result on Parliament Green with Tango advertising characters was the first example of ambush marketing on live national TV; it created the first website to embody brand personality rather than just information. It transformed advertising and integrated marketing. The point is the brand was dynamic, and behaved "rebelliously" in many different media formats. Axel Chaldecott later stated: "Tango was the first FMCG brand to involve its customers in the brand experience beyond the moment of consumption."

When the transformation began, Tango's share was 75% of Coke's leading brand Lilt. Four years later, Tango's share was 150% of Coke's entire fruit portfolio (Lilt, Sprite, Sunkist and Fanta), the only occasion in any country when Coke's portfolio has been overhauled by a rival's fruit brand. This share increase was achieved at a 13% price *premium* to main brand Coca-Cola.

In its heyday – Tango contributed a record profit back to the parent business. Tango, during that period, dramatically expanded the industry's understanding of what was possible in marketing communications.

Tomi T Ahonen & Alan Moore

"Progress in industry depends very largely on the enterprise of deep
thinking men, who are ahead of the times in their ideas."
Sir William Ellis

XI
Branding Losing its Power
Is anyone listening?

"You talkin' to me? You talkin' to me?" We all remember Robert de Niro in the movie *Taxi Driver*. That same *You talkin' to me?* is also the title used most appropriately in a report by the British Chartered Institute of Marketing on how customers consider traditional marketing communications as increasingly intrusive. As we saw in the previous chapter, the business world is perplexed in that traditional advertising seems not to be working. In fact traditional brand and marketing communications overall seems to have caught the flu. This chapter examines marketing more broadly. We look at marketing economics effectiveness and why it is in such a state of flux. We focus in this chapter on the recent darling of the marketing profession: branding.

A BRANDING IN CRISIS

Brand is an overused word. It is fascinating that the brand can contribute so much to a company's stock and yet can be so underutilised, even damaged by everyday marketing activities of the company. An established brand is one of the most valuable assets for a business and still brands are more vulnerable today than ever before. The obsession with conventional brand and marketing practice is in fact exposing the Achilles heel for many companies.

Growth of branding

Brands are usually the most public and visible part of a business. Brands are by definition the user interface for a business. Branding grew to become the mantra for marketing towards the end of the last century. It was the holy grail for business success. If Perrier could sell *water* at premium prices even in markets such as Switzerland and Sweden, where tap water is as clean as it gets, surely branding could help any business with goods and services that delivered more tangible benefits to their users.

Branding evolved from the need to create simple differentiation in products and services. Once Surf or Omo or Palmolive or whatever brand it was, was faced with equitable competition it needed to move from "I must have clean clothes" to "I must have the *cleanest* clothes".

So branding became the necessary tool to increase the perceived value of services and goods and to help you choose. Marketing and branding help big companies grow bigger. Big companies need big revenues, they are hungry mouths to feed. In a command and control society, branding had its heyday in the last 20 years feeding that hungry engine. A trusting public liberated economically, socially etc embraced brands as emblems of their changing habits and lifestyles. Businesses realised that brands were important and indeed valuable enough to put them on the balance sheet.

Context and Meaning

Most people do not describe things generically, they tend to talk about their products through the brands involved. It is not my blue jeans or running shoes; it is my Levis and my Adidas. People often define themselves through brands. This process is the key to becoming a successful brand, as it is about the context that a brand has in someone's life and is a signifier to greater or lesser levels of meaning. Take Apple, for example. Today Apple has high levels of context and meaning.

Apple is successful, we suggest because the iPod revolutionised the way we consumed music and created meaning and context by delivering a great user experience. 20 years ago it was the Sony Walkman. Successful branding is inextricably linked to the product benefit, not stretching the product truth to such an extent it becomes valueless.

An empowered consumer

The primary reason that makes brands so fragile today is the emancipation of the consumer to the empowered customer. Brands today are in a very different position to that

Tomi T Ahonen & Alan Moore

of 10 years ago. People have an overwhelming sense of being colonised, of businesses being economical with the truth – think pensions, the financial services industries, Enron, Worldcom and Arthur Anderson. Consumers feel as though they are being coerced by big brands and their marketing activities. Customers have learned to be more discerning and less trusting. The burgeoning growth of blogs, websites, activitst organisations, niche magazines in conjunction with the established organisations such as JD Power, are guiding customer decisions of what and what not to buy. Today, these are all challenging the hegemony of brands over customers.

The customer has increased demands for quality. The customer comes armed to the teeth with information, knowing what is a fair price level and what he/she can expect to be discounted. Don't want to play ball, fine I'll go next door or I will buy it via the internet. Go to Epinions and you will see a community rating everything from well-being medicines to the latest movies. This means brands will rise and fall, it makes it easier for new brands to enter the fray, but then they have to work very hard to survive.

Being big and being a powerful global brand used to be a haven from the competition. That is no longer true. Brands are not for life. Tom Peters goes so far as to say brands should emerge as shooting stars, deliver a fantastic experience, but then die away to make room for the new growth. We do not go quite that far, we think there is room for longevity with brands, but brands do have to change to the new socio-economic environment. Today, successful businesses and their brands must build win-win situations with its customers.

Need to work harder

What brands can do is make their business *strategies* and *communication* work harder. Brands can take advantage of new digital opportunities. For example, a brand can expand and become a media owner, and then use that media to communicate with their consumers. Not as a broadcaster with the same message to all, but an activating engagement marketer, inviting and promoting customer interaction. New digital delivery channels allow bi-directional communications. The brand does not have to do it all itself, new digital delivery channels allow end-user created content. In fact end-users enjoy interacting with the brands of their choice.

> **In UK already 20% of population has two mobile phones**

The opportunity is not limited to the glitzy and sexy of the global products and services opportunities. Not only for Jaguar cars, Chanel perfumes or Nokia mobile phones. New opportunities exist for all brands, no matter how mundane, or whether they are business-to-customer or business-to-business facing. For those enlightened brands that "get it", this means sitting down and thinking about what it is that makes them special and thinking about how to deliver increased value to their audience and customers. But to illustrate our point, let's pick something less glamorous. In fact, one can hardly think of something less sexy and inherently less-interesting than house-cleaning. Yet the British reality TV programme *How Clean is Your House?* is a big hit. Alan Mitchell references this when discussing a recent Procter & Gamble initiative in *Marketing Week*:

> *It is easy to be sceptical about the appeal of such a venture, but it is well to remember that Channel 4 has had a hit with the reality TV show How Clean is Your House?, which features two women going around cleaning up filthy homes. The show's website even offers to text house cleaning tips to people's mobiles. These days, even the most mundane household chores can be turned into mass entertainment.*
>
> *Marketing Week*, 11 November 2004

Branded content could be a programme created by a brand based upon a brand proposition designed to deliver a key demographic, a digital channel, TV or radio distributed via digital satellite or an ADSL link. The programme could be delivered in store or at home, a quiz played via mobile phones in a closed loop within a cinema chain, a movie, an album, or a magazine. It may only be a small percentage of the overall content market, but it's all going to be growing percentage from now on. That's the point. Learn the new rules because the old ones are becoming increasingly outmoded.

It's been a long goodbye to our old traditionally slow media world, and it's been a very quick hello, marriage and honeymoon with our new always-on-mobile, interconnected media world with teched-up, informed customers, who want to participate and engage. If only you know how to press the right buttons.

B   BRANDING CHANGING TOO

Brands proliferate. In addition to new brands appearing, existing brands have expanded their reach into new markets – further cluttering the brand offerings – and brands have multiplied with sub-branding and co-branding. There has been a massive explosion of branded consumer messages. Since 1991, the number of brands in grocery stores in the US has tripled and the average American sees 60% more advertising than 15 years ago. Similar statistics are observed throughout the world. At this point a customer will stand still, throw up their hands and say, how do I choose? Why is brand X different to brand Y?

Brand extensions

Under pressure to financially outperform the market competition, yet locked into the past by brand history or brand legacy, many companies compound the brand pervasiveness by making line extensions of their brand(s). Research conducted by two INSEAD professors, Chan Kim and Renée Mauborgone, found that while 86% of the business launches were line extensions – that is, "me too's" or incremental value improvements that sought a larger share in the existing market space – they explained only 62% of total revenues and a mere 39% of total profits. The remaining 14% of the business launches – the true value innovations that created new market space – explained 38% of total revenues and 61% of total profits. They also found that line extensions were usually the results of competitive improvements that aimed at building advantages over the competition or countering recent strategic moves of rivals. Brand extensions have also featured in several famous failures such as the Ferrari Laptop and the Hooters airline.

Coca-Cola Music

We all love Coke, it is just that we do not quite love it as we used to, or at least we are not drinking it as much as we once were. Coke has also been struggling with the issue that its caffeinated high-sugar drinks are becoming less popular. Together with its main rival Pepsi, Coke has seen the main product lose market share to diet cola drinks, to various healthier drinks from real juices to juice mixtures, and even the increasing success of bottled water products.

Perhaps in recognition that TV is no longer the way to talk to a youth audience, Coke has ventured into mobile telephony in Spain, teaming up with mobile services provider Buongiorno and launched its brand to the mobile music space on Spain's largest telecoms operator, Telefonica. The service is an attempt to follow Apple's lead of creating new marketspace beyond its traditional – in Coke's case drinks – market, and appealing to young customers using their preferred media. New Media Age writes:

> *(Coca-Cola has selected...) Spain as the launchpad for a branded mobile internet community. The company's Mobile Community features mobile services and content ranging from chat forums to voucher redemption. Coca-Cola has tied with mobile services from Buongiorno in order to extend its online Coca- Cola movement concept to mobile. The service is intitially available, via i-mode or WAP, on Telefonica's content service MoviStar e-mocion. Content will include ringtones, logos, competitions, news and chat. Customers will also be able to redeem vouchers from on-pack product promotions in order to purchase any content.*
>
> *New Media Age*, 18 June 2004

Why is Coke now shifting to mobile phones? When we bear in mind that there are more mobile phones in the world than there are TV sets, this shift suddenly makes perfect sense. It is even more obvious when we bear in mind that the younger generations have a significantly stronger bond with the mobile phone than they do with the TV set.

C LOST AT SEA WITHOUT A COMPASS

So what replaces the old with the new? Brands know there are new trends and new media, new channels and new ways to connect, but which to pursue and how? Is it product placement and infomercials, or is it web search ads, own broadcast channels, or something else entirely? What is the future?

What is my message?

Brands seem to be perennially repositioning themselves, minor adjustments, a new tag line, a variation on the colour scheme or a new visual facelift. John Hegarty, Chairman of BBH, discusses two leading UK retail brands that are struggling to reconnect with their audience:

> *Boots may be our trusted high street chemist but its advertising has continually failed to capture the value of that positioning and communicate its value in a way which creates capital, despite being so highly trusted. In its latest work, it's throwing snowballs at carol singers. I'll leave you to fathom that one out. And of course there's poor old M&S. Having decided it needs to actually soil its hands with advertising, waking up to the fact that it can be quite advantageous to hold a dialogue with your consumers and perhaps persuade a few new ones to try you out, it employs a fat lady running up hill, naked, shouting "I'm normal" as the possible answer. The sign-off line was just as baffling: "Exclusive for Everyone". I'm not sure how you can be exclusive for everyone. It smacks of desperation not confidence. The company is now telling us "It's your M&S". Another change in strategic direction? No wonder the investors are getting nervous.*
> *The Guardian,* November 29 2004

Comparison of Fixed and Mobile Internet 2005

ISSUE	FIXED INTERNET	MOBILE INTERNET
Devices in use	Less PCs and PDAs	More browser phones
Cost of device	More	Less
Sell annually	Less	More
Content	Mostly free	Always costs
User preference	Wants free	Willing to pay
Billing	Difficult	Is built-in
Micropayments	Very Difficult	Easy
Paid content	Is problem	Is built-in
Messaging	E-Mail	SMS text messaging
Users	Less	More
Cost	Almost free	10 cents per message
Preference	By older population	By the young

Hegarty's polemic is that interruptive advertising communication is an investment that pays back dividends. He argues for clear strategic positioning that can be creatively leveraged in advertising. And he is right. "It's true," he says, "it pays to watch the ads." However, the issue here is whether image advertising works anymore. Absolutely! The point is that today a brand must create dialogue with its customers. The new issue is how to do that. We agree with Hegarty, what is Marks & Spencer advertising exactly? How does "Your M&S", translate into an added-value experience, especially when they are endorsed by supermodel Helena Christensen. How does that differentiate the brand? How does that drive into everything M&S does, how is that a tangible benefit when you go into the store? Customers will scan these ads, blink, filter and move on. Unless the brand strategy delivers on the promise, it is just advertising – background noise in an already noisy street.

Brands have the opportunity today to be more dynamic, to engage their audiences in meaningful ways as we have demonstrated time and again in our examples and cases in this book. We would point the reader in the direction of the Apple store, or the Guinness visitor centre, or suggest retailers look at the customer behaviour that underpins and surrounds eBay and Amazon or the customer advocacy that drives the clothing brand howies and think, why did and does that work?

Gone in 30 seconds

In every industry the trends are the same. Marketing costs more and delivers less. *The Financial Times* ran an interesting overview of Hollywood mathematics for the year 2003. The average cost of making a new Hollywood movie went up 8.6% in 2003. The average cost of marketing a new Hollywood movie went up 28% in 2003. Yet audience numbers *fell* by 4% in 2003. This is yet another indicator that marketing is not delivering the same "bang for buck" that it used to do. The business world is spending ever more on a "match what the competition is doing" contest of marketing, advertising and branding, to ever diminishing returns.

The most revealing insight being whispered in Hollywood is the sudden effect of community swarms, the **word-of-mouth** now "cell-cast" via the cellular phone. The success – or more precisely the lack thereof in 2003 – of what were strongly promoted as Hollywood blockbusters, of movies such as Hulk, Charlie's Angels 2 and Gigli, was attributed to movie-goers specifically bad-mouthing the movies via SMS text messaging. This "word-of-text" instant review spread bad news about new movies faster than any previous method of community action. We are on the verge of something dramatic and new. Yes, communities can dominate over brand messages, even when multimillion dollar marketing spends by Hollywood are involved.

Again, it cannot be repeated enough that the young users are willing to *spend their own money* to spread the bad word. Email would be free. Instant messaging would be free. But the young users have grown to treat any valuable community messages as worthy of paying on average 10 cents per message, and spreading in such a way the word. The old rules of a passive receptive audience are irrevocably broken, when those consumers are now willing to pay their own money for spreading the bad news. You cannot ignore these new powerful communities.

Marketing must change to meet the new world

With all the prevalent converging trends, traditional marketing strategy and communications is delivering diminishing returns. Today, marketing communications requires a holistic approach. Marketing communications requires companies to understand we need to move from a cookie-cutter approach and push-only one-way communications, to an age of consent and engagement. We need to engage communities and allow our target audiences to interact with us. Businesses need to co-create their branding, advertising and marketing communications, with their audiences to work in this new century.

If we look at the first newspaper advertising in the 1800s with the magical promises of instant cure medicines and amazing machinery, to our discerning eyes the ads are clearly full of unreasonable claims. Yet back then, those ads delivered a lot of business. Consumers were naive. In the same way later in this 21st century students of marketing will look at the last century in amazement that interruptive communications was able to deliver any relevant marketing success, that marketing often seemed divorced from the business model. Alan Mitchell said: "If marketing was a thing in its own right, would anyone want to buy it?" It is a point well made. We set the new standard to be successful marketing when it integrates so well with the product/service experience that one cannot separate the two.

> **Only 14% of launches are true innovations; rest are brand extensions**

But that means we need to move from trying to drive customers to the point of purchase and into something more seductive, more compelling, more valuable. It is possible, but you need to have a cause, a mission, a belief that you want to passionately share with your customers.

Brand and marketing strategy can help companies grow and differentiate in a crowded marketplace. But we do not need more of the same; we need a "version 2.0". In this century we will go from "just in case" to "just in time", from blanket bombing to precision. Precise initiatives delivered only to our intended target audiences. From shouting to discussing, from monologue to dialogue, from interruption to engagement. A different language?

D THE TRUTH, YOU CAN'T HANDLE THE TRUTH

Is the industry finally waking up to the fact that it is not an incremental adjustment required, it is radical revision to the whole way advertising, branding and marketing is done? Not just to understand the technical and other trends affecting the industry, but to recognise the effects they have on our target audiences. Our audiences are evolving, and we can only be effective if we understand that. It is like playing a game where the rules are changed in the middle of the game and the goalposts keep moving. But it still is a game, and there will be winners in the end. Those, however, will not be the ones best at playing by the old rules. The winners will be those who are most adaptive to change, to capitalise on the emerging opportunities. Tom Peters writes in his book, *Re-Imagine*:

> *We must learn to add value through creativity... by inventing ...*
> *Extraordinary Experiences... which provide scintillating "solutions"*
> *to customers' oft unexpressed desires and dreams. Out: Tangibles.*
> *In: Intangibles.*
>   Tom Peters *Re-Imagine* 2004

The point is to move from innovating within the confines of a product or service, to innovating in the business model. This problem is now the reality for all businesses in all sectors of industry. Everyone in marketing should have woken up to it a long time ago.

The old ways are very deeply entrenched. As Fallon's Lawrence Green is quoted as saying, in an article in the *Financial Times* 26 August 2004: "The ad industry has a terrible reliance on billings. It's our crack cocaine." Most ad agencies look at any project and think that the TV advertising will be the main element, and all thinking then revolves around the budget, schedules and creative staff availability for the TV ad project. Yet Peter Miiles of SubTV points out an obvious but oft skirted truth, "Young people have better things to do than sit in front of the TV." The old advertising agency model is old and becoming obsolete, the interruptive marketing model isn't just unwell, it's dead.

Marketers worth their salt must recognise this and act decisively, help our clients become relevant again. Post-Big Brother, it is obvious that people want to interact with brands, co-create them. The message could not be simpler. Engage or die.

Brands, who has the control?

Brands are not in control as they once were. Brands are starting to recognise that they have to put the customer at the beginning of the value chain and not at the end. Customers, as we have already said, are more promiscuous with brand loyalties; customers have awoken to the power of community information sharing. I will tell everybody about my experiences, and next time I need to make a decision, I will consult the community to see if anyone has had any relevant experiences with my intended brands.

TV ads influenced only 17% of American car buyers

We trust the community more than advertising and branding promises. Community opinion actually trumps the brand message. We would argue that communities dominate brands.

Companies need to recognise that the value of their product or service is increasingly in the role it plays in consumers' lives. It is in the everyday that real value is found. Companies that are, for example, information rich, have an asset which they could redeploy to their customers in more meaningful ways. Be that retailers, financial services, travel companies, media etc. It is more of a question of sitting down and thinking through what this value is that can truly differentiate. Alan Mitchell writes in his book *Right Side Up*:

Tomi T Ahonen & Alan Moore

The information age won't reach its full potential just because of a few inventions like the internet. It needs to create a new and different system capable of unleashing the win-win potential inherent in plummeting trans- action costs, ever richer content and new flows of information. And to do so it needs its own web of institutions, practices and concepts: joint-info-stock companies or consumer agents, relationships and communities, consumers as information investors and co-producers seeking value "in my life" – and buyer-centric marketing.

Alan Mitchell *Right Side Up 2002*

Conventional marketing and advertising is the silent movies of the 21st century. The proletarian nature of the internet, blogging, moblogging, the mobile phone, in- teractive TV, media choice and the PVR, the rich flows of information and the reach of that information, have all contributed to bringing an era to an end. The message couldn't be simpler for any business. Engage your communities of interest, as com- munities will support you or they will destroy you.

Where is the real influence?

We have shown how the efficiency of traditional advertising and branding is di- minishing. We have argued already on behalf of community influence, and our next chapters will make this point in more detail. Perhaps the most startling facts arise when consumers are interviewed directly on what influences them.

In a US study in October 2003 management consultants Cap Gemini Ernst & Young interviewed American car buyers. They found that only 17% of the 700 US consumers surveyed said TV ads influenced their car-buying decisions. Ads on in- ternet search engines influenced 26%. Nearly half, or 48%, said a direct mail offer from a car dealer would influence their purchases. The most influential measure was word of mouth, cited by 71%. Yet, today, the cost of running a TV ad campaign will be many times that of activating the friendly users and interested community. As American businessmen like to say, this is a no-brainer. It costs the least while delivers the most? There is no issue to consider.

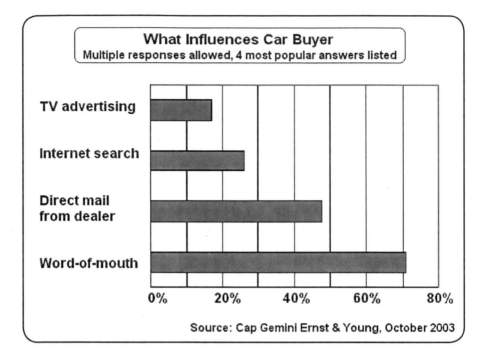

Brands need to create bigger, richer narratives – rather than just trying to amplify their message through mass media. We have got used to two-way flows of information. We would argue that the so-called "pyramid diagram," where TV and print advertising is on top, needs now to be reversed 180 degrees. Certainly the Cap Gemini Ernst & Young study supports this position. Our money and effort should go where it has the biggest influence. Word of mouth is the most important thing to activate. TV advertising, apparently, is delivering *the least* for us. Yet how much of your marketing effort goes into building compelling word of mouth?

Co-creation

Businesses need to harness communities and learn to co-create with their customers. By co-creating experiences, companies can get better data for segmentation and provide more accurate segmentation models. they are in a position to help persuade customers to change their own minds, but also to learn and so it becomes more intimate and valuable as an experience for both parties. John Moore, writing on his blog, believes brands should be more organism than machine:

Tomi T Ahonen & Alan Moore

Brands Emerge Similarly, I've said before that I think it helps to think of brands as emergent. Not things that unfold according to the master plan, but that emerge as a result of all the encounters between people who belong, with varying degrees of enthusiasm or loathing, to the community around a brand. That doesn't mean, that there is no role at all for strategy and planning but to my mind it should shift attention towards responding rapidly to what's going on at the chalkface (I hate that word "touchpoints"). Because your brand is not created in the boardroom or marketing department, it's being created by us ordinary folks who stack your shelves or pick our cornflakes off them.

http://www.johnniemoore.com/blog

Therefore, brands will need to become ever more organic. To adjust not only by strategic direction from top management, but by increasingly accepting input from the customer community. To develop together, to use co-creation methods for success.

Do you want to compete on price?

One of the possible strategic options is to focus on being the price leader. We see price disruption in many industries such as the discount airlines or the service providers and virtual operators in telecoms, etc. If you are really serious about successfully competing with price as the value proposition, then you have to re-engineer your whole organisation to deliver that. Price leadership requires enormous scale to be sustainable. Yes, Ikea can do it. Dell can do it. But most players in the market cannot compete on those kinds of levels of pure price leadership.

If not price leadership, then other marketing methods must be embraced, and some other value proposition must be generated. That, of course, takes much more work on the creative marketing side of product design, channel management, branding, promotion and advertising, sales etc, than merely setting prices lower. For most businesses in the world being the price leader is not a sustainable market proposition.

Mobile telecoms should know. Mobile phone calls used to be a remarkably profitable business all around the world. In Finland mobile voice call prices have dropped from 24 Euro cents per minute in 2002 to 1 Euro cent in 2005. Hong Kong already offers mobile phone minutes at one fifth of one cent. Where do you go from here? How do you grow? What is your strategy that will deliver long term growth? Or, as Phillip Kotler asked, are you a 1P marketer?

Brand needs to add value

In the modern digital and connected economy there is no sustainable competitive advantage. Everything can be copied. Competitors will appear to every profitable opportunity. Any competitive advantage will disapper over time. Bruce Mau in his book *Lifestyle* wrote about sustainable competitive advantage:

> *"Except where innovation or style are proprietary, there is no sustainable advantage in the product itself. The only way to build real equity is to add value. The product – the object or service attached to the transaction – is not the brand at all; the brand has become culture and intelligence."*
>
> Bruce Mau, *Lifestyle* 2000

Importantly, in moving into this space, brands must learn the fine balancing act of acting commercially and socially; where the customer identifies that the brand/business is supplying something to them of real value. Brands need to occupy a place in the fabric of people's lives. They have to live in conversation, they have to communicate through the vernacular of society, they have to resonate within the mainstream. This was echoed by Mitchell, Bauer, Hausruckinger in their book *The New Bottom Line*. The authors explained how the greatest opportunities for growth for companies fell outside the classic marketing battlegrounds based around product, quality and price. The *New Bottom Line* shows that new marketing falls into the space between the rational and the emotional:

> *Many marketers have nodded towards these emotional needs in their marketing communications... but so far few companies have actually attempted to build businesses that address these needs as the central core of their value offer.*
>
> Mitchell, Bauer, Hausruckinger *The New Bottom Line* 2003

It requires a rethink for some companies how they market themselves and to question how they differentiate themselves. It also offers a great opportunity if businesses are prepared to think a little harder about their marketing strategies. "Adding or creating value", whatever that may be, will be the mantra for the next few years.

Summing up branding

Brands need to rethink what, how and why they do what they do. As professional marketing and branding knowhow has spread to cover the globe, all businesses and many other organisations now use branding. The copycat process has diluted branding power in most cases to near zero. Branding can have a new birth, but that requires a radical rethink. No longer one centrally planned master-plan for brand image marketing, what we need is to embrace the consumer, activate and engage. As Martin Raymond wrote in *The Tomorrow People*: "Future-faced brands are not brands that are omnipotent, or consistent in the traditional sense that brands are consistent or standardised across all territories, but rather that they accommodate the personal, the individual."

Case Study 10

Thomas Cook TV

The travel industry has been facing a severe cost squeeze from no-frills airlines and internet bookings. Many traditional travel agencies have been squeezed out of the business altogether. Thomas Cook, a major travel agency in Britain, has decided to innovate by combining TV and travel, through its Thomas Cook TV programming.

Thomas Cook TV runs several hours on the free-to-air digital offering Freeview in the UK and features short films of interesting holiday destinations. The show is very typical of travel TV shows with exotic locations, lots of views of sunny beaches and skiing resorts, etc. Naturally the TV show is intended to support the sales of travel destinations served by Thomas Cook so the countries and hotels and resorts featured are all selected from those that Thomas Cook currently offers in its catalogue of holidays.

The TV channel costs £2.5m ($4.6m) to run and shifts £150m ($240m) of inventory per year. Simply in terms of a brand extension, the channel is a good investment for the Thomas Cook company and profitable.

A deeper analysis of Thomas Cook TV viewers and shoppers is most revealing. 92% of individuals purchasing from Thomas Cook TV and broadband have never bought a Thomas Cook holiday before. The TV channel is not cannibalising sales from stores, it is accessing a whole new segment of travellers who never visit the stores. Thomas Cook has been able to tap into a previously unavailable market.

As Thomas Cook offers immediate ability to book vacations and frequently advertises its phone numbers etc, the audience is strongly a captive one. For viewers who see an attractive location at a good price, there is little incentive to do an exhaustive internet search to try to find a comparative or cheaper holiday, in particular as Thomas Cook TV has already shown you the exact hotel you will be getting, etc. In effect Thomas Cook has removed itself from the cut-throat holiday sales price squeeze, and built itself a monopoly of offerings that match its TV show.

Return on Investment (ROI) is at the core of such transitions and expansions of the brand into new digital delivery platforms. ROI is at the basis of digital content and marketing strategy, taking content from retail TV to broadcast TV to web to mobile to DVD/video, joining up from one to the other to drive sales. Thomas Cook TV is branding and sales as entertainment, its holiday inventory management is plugged directly into the programme so editorial can be rotated quickly to ensure efficient management of inventory.

Holidays, as we all know, are about inspiration and also we require a guarantee that there will be no nasty surprises whilst we are away. Through the format of TV broadcast and broadband, Thomas Cook TV can amplify those two key ingredients. The audio-visual experience allows us to explore and to be inspired, the presenters tell us how well looked after they were. Their personal story is not seen as a corporate message but as a personal recommendation. We trust them as individuals to give us their truth. This could never be achieved within the pages of a holiday catalogue, where tone of voice becomes perceived as marketing speak. Can we trust them? Are all the pictures taken at the one true beauty angle? Will there be enough room?

Thomas Cook has taken full advantage of the new digital economics and made it work in spectacular fashion as a very efficient marketing tool. It also has created a new channel and marketspace to sell its holidays.

Tomi T Ahonen & Alan Moore

XII
Emergence of the Community
Trust your friend

From the Zapatistas of Mexico, to the running street battles of Seattle, to the massive increase of bookclubs across the UK, online and off-line communities are forming and becoming increasingly visible and effective. The emergence and the notion of the community as a counterforce in business is not new in many ways, but it has evolved recently into something far more potent. All through its history mankind has, of course, lived in communities. First the caveman had his family and tribe, then gradually emerged the nation-states and with industrialisation mankind found several different communities. Up to the end of the 20th century, communities were dormant as a force to consider in business. Yes, there were isolated incidences of consumer reaction to an oil spill or child slavery labour etc, but for the most part individual consumers did not instinctively group together to form a power of the masses. Not until the Connected Age, where we have authorities on social contagion, social network theory, the tipping point theory. The list is endless – the point is they are right.

A CONNECTED AGE

We discussed the change from the Networked Age to the Connected Age in the Introduction chapter. It is an important theme to our book and for this chapter we need to return to that theme. The Networked Age was a good term for the last decade, as it did describe how we as humans approached "the network" – ie, the internet. We logged on, we accessed our email and we surfed seeking information. The Networked Age was the dawn of how humans could build virtual communities, and is a necessary step on our evolution to the Connected Age. Much of what most readers will consider the digital world and digital convergence will consist of that networked model. It is imperative to understand that all the effects of the Networked Age are but the prelude to the period of the Connected Age.

Half step into the Community

The Connected Age is like the Industrial Revolution before electricity. The first steam-powered machines were central engines, like a big heart in a factory, and all devices were then connected by pulleys and belts and other mechanical means to such engines. The first factories, such as for clothing, worked like this. There was one central engine, and it *physically* powered all sewing machines of the factory. The whole design, from the engine power to the power transmission to individual sewing stations, had to be carefully planned and built.

The factory and its working stations were very precisely tied to explicit locations. There was not much room for variation or expansion in this model. It was much better than no engine at all, but it wasn't until the advent of electricity that it became possible to have an omnipresent power source – the electrical grid – and free machines and workers to perform differing deeds in differing locations. Much more importantly for any growing business, it allowed a smooth expansion of capacity by just plugging in more devices to the electrical outlets and paying a bit more in the electricity bill.

The analogy to the fixed internet is that while readers may think the internet has created immense changes to their business, it is like the first mechanical machines for the industrial age. Yes, major change. But very modest changes when compared with the much greater change that came through electricity-based machine power. Any changes you have witnessed due to the fixed internet will become dramatically more pronounced via the mobile internet during the next ten years.

Much like our ability to connect to "the network" – whether by *accessing* our email, *accessing* our voicemail, or *accessing* the internet – there was a two-step process. Something might have happened in the virtual world – like us receiving an email – and we had to check in periodically to see what if anything was going on. The connectedness was by necessity limited to telephone outlets; our internet and voicemail were accessed through the telephone network, which in the middle of the last decade was a fixed wireline network everywhere, even in Finland. But like the advent of electricity, now telecommunications is omnipresent, wirelessly, through the cellular or mobile telecoms network. Now human networks can grow and move as the need emerges.

Most importantly, the newest technologies are all built on an always-on principle. The power and speed of SMS text messaging is not with the sender; though yes,
we like it that we have the sending machine in our pocket all the time. The true factor of speed is that *every recipient* also carries the same device on their person, and
are able to receive text messages even when voice calls are not practical. SMS text
messaging has shrunk the *receiving* side of human communications. That is why a
new telecommunications term, "reachability" has been coined.

Addictiveness of connectedness

When we consider Generation-C and other connected people living with electronic
communities, it is possible to connect with traditional electronic media, particularly the fixed internet, email and chat, but the real power of communities arrives
only through connectedness. We achieve connectedness through the mobile phone.
Rather than our internet access which is mostly locked to a place such as our desk
at our office, one room in our home, or the computer lab in the school, the mobile
phone is on our person, with us at all times.

Item	Networked Age	Connected Age
Time	1992 - 2004	2002 - 2014?
Platform	PC/PDA	Mobile phone
Network	One grand net	Multiple overlapping webs
Availability	Place-centric	Everywhere
Connection	Fixed phone line	Cellular network
Use	Plan next use	Spontaneous
Services	e-Mail, voicemail	SMS, IM, blogging
Voice calls	prefer fixed line	prefer mobile phone
Commerce	Reject: hippie-like	Commercial: business-like
Content owners	Beggars	Make money
Key	Access	Reachability
Need	Acquiring	Sharing
Content	Pull (I seek)	Push (system offers)
Authoring	Docs, web pages	images, sounds, blogs
Privacy/ownership	Semi-private	Personal and unique
Addiction	Some service(s)	To device
Global lead	USA	Scandinavia

Rather than an actually or potentially shared device, such as the personal computer often is at home, and may be at work where a secretary or colleague or boss might suddenly borrow your computer, or walk in and see what is on your screen, the mobile phone is always personal and private. Most of all the other networked systems require logging on, we have to set aside time to access our network, our internet, our email, our chat. But the mobile phone is always connected. Thus while yes, all the other means were going in the right direction for the digital community mindset, they were only a half-step. The full step is the Connected Age.

Now sharing information is power

The Connected Age brings with it a new paradigm also for the role of information and power. All through the centuries and up to the Networked Age, information and power had held the relationship that those in power held onto information, keeping it to themselves. Withholding information maintained and built power. During the Networked Age and always before, it was that those who had information held power. Withholding information was the key to power. This is how bureaucrats built their empires from Roman times to today.

The Connected Age reverses this equation of power. We all know that any information in a mainstream digital format conforms to the thought that information is very different from cash. With cash if I give one dollar to you, I don't have it anymore. But with valuable information (in digital form), if I give it to you, I still have it myself. While you have become richer for the added knowledge, I am no poorer for telling you. Now, when everybody is always connected, it means that information will reach everybody who wants it, eventually. That is why the equation changes and those who understand the change and learn to live in it will prosper.

Those who have mentally arrived at the Connected Age, understand this principle fundamentally, even subconsciously. The impact is that people of the Connected Age rush to share information. They intrinsically understand how important speed is in the spread of information. We have seen evidence of this throughout this book, but nowhere as strongly as in the Blogging chapter.

With the emphasis shifting from withholding information to sharing, the most rewarded contributors are those who are fastest at sharing. They get a reputation for information communicators, those who always know. They will invariably be rewarded by their contact network, where others will send information to them, in return. This enriches those who know how to share. Equally anyone who is found to be hoarding information, withholding it, is punished. In a very real sense it means that in the Connected Age, *sharing* information is power.

Tomi T Ahonen & Alan Moore

B SMART MOBS

The person who discovered the notion and concept of "smart mobs" or "swarming" was Howard Rheingold. He wrote about it in his landmark book of 2002. Rheingold, a pioneer of virtual communities, indentified that via the internet and digital technology per se, people's behaviour was changing. Up to then, if you wanted to meet someone, it had to be in a specific location. You agreed on the location beforehand. Swarming is the exact opposite. You know you will meet at an approximate time, but the final destination is set by the community at the last moment. Earlier young people would sit at home on a Saturday waiting for the calls to discuss what to do. Now they go out, and catch up with friends later on, via their mobile phones.

As the internet and mobile communications merge, as cellular phones increasingly become something that a teenager gets before the driver's licence, and as they shrink from a tool you carry to a fashion item that you wear, Rheingold sees a profound shift in society. *(Cellular phones...) amplify human talents for cooperation,* he says:

> *Smart mobs emerge when communication and computing technologies*
> *amplify human talents for cooperation. The impacts of smart mob*
> *technology already appear to be both beneficial and destructive, used*
> *by some of its earliest adopters to support democracy and by others to*
> *coordinate terrorist attacks. The technologies that are beginning to make*
> *smart mobs possible are mobile communication devices and pervasive*
> *computing – inexpensive microprocessors embedded in everyday objects*
> *and environments. Already, governments have fallen, youth subcultures*
> *have blossomed from Asia to Scandinavia, new industries have been born*
> *and older industries have launched furious counterattacks.*
>
> Howard Rheingold, *Smartmobs, 2002*

The key to the power of mobiles is that they liberate people from their desktop telephones and computers, moving the action out to that much larger portion of life that encompasses wherever and whenever humans roam. Social swarming, Rheingold argues, involves sharing your life with others in real-time. It means pulsing to the rhythm of life with one's community of friends. It means a non-stop emotional connection to one's swarm.

Always spontaneous

Since Rheingold's book, the wide range of potential connecting devices has converged into the cellular phone. The preferred method of coordinating is the SMS

---

text message, as it is non-intrusive, immediate and private. Only being connected via the mobile phone allows last-minute changes to our daily schedules. It starts with the occasional "I am running 15 minutes late" type of SMS text messages and voice calls from mobile phones. There is almost no point in attempting a "15 minutes late" message via email as, more often than not, our recepient will not even be at his/her email within the next 15 minutes.

Soon that kind of last-minute behaviour transforms into the pattern of "let's not decide yet" kind of behaviour. We agree to meet for beers after work, but let's not pick a place and time until later today. Since every one of us has a mobile phone, it will be easy to decide later. The first one to leave the office picks the place and the others will appear there. It is what makes life exciting, the sudden decision to do something unplanned, a mini adventure in our daily lives.

Flash mobbing

A new type of behaviour capturing this mentality has been coined as "flash mobbing" and it is happening with greater frequency. Perhaps the first such event happened in Finland when local pop band Nylon Beat released its newest hit song not as a CD or MP3 file or for radio airplay, but as a ringing tone in 2000. The band then had its fans all converge on a hill in Helsinki where fans were to play the song together. To the cacophonic sound of plink-plonk of the early ringing tones on mostly Nokia phones, the event collected thousands to celebrate their favourite band.

Word-of-Mouth influenced 71% of American car buyers

This incident could be dismissed as an isolated example. In fact it was just the very tip of the iceberg about to hit the Titanic of group behaviour. Now mobile phones are becoming the tool of choice for any group behaviour needing urgency, and being adopted in all countries with high mobile phone penetrations. Just consider these two recent examples that have taken place in London in 2004. What was called the "Pillow Fight" took place outside St. Paul's Cathedral on 6 October 2004. *The Evening Standard* reported:

> *They came in their hundreds, with pillows stuffed in plastic bags. Then, at the appointed hour, they drew weapons and battle was joined. What ensued yesterday was one of the biggest pillow fights ever seen. An email did the rounds to those in the know inviting them to attend and then, at 5.40pm, a whistle blew, Hannah Ford, 35, a project manager, said: "It was mayhem.*

Tomi T Ahonen & Alan Moore

*There wasn't any shouting just this padding sound. People were laughing
their heads off." Minutes later, the madness ended as suddenly as it began
and the crowd disappeared.*

The Evening Standard, 7 October 2004

500 people turned up to this event to join in the pillow fight of their lives.
Another London flashmobbing occasion happened at Paddington Station. The BBC
joined the throng of flashmobbers in the Flashmob Opera, broadcast live on BBC3.
A full orchestra of 65, with three opera singers and a choir of over 40 entertained
commuters for an hour.

Let us not forget the famous flashmob of iPod crazies dancing silently together
listening to their own music on a main street station. The interesting thing about the
mobile and the mobile internet in this instance is that it can connect communities of
interest together and mobilise them very quickly. The outcome for these people is
"an enhanced experience" to be shared and treasured.

Now, for any brand out there wanting to connect with its target audience in this
fragmented media world, these are thoughts worth thinking about. How to capitalise
on these cultural/technological changes?

Another vivid example of the power of swarming comes from birdwatching in
Finland. There are 27 birdwatcher clubs and societies across Finland. The Twitchers
Union has developed a text messaging system to alert members when a rare species
is discovered. Members can select messages by species or geographical location.
For example, 5,000 birdwatchers recently gathered in Viikki within 60 minutes of a
sighting of a male grey-headed woodpecker.

Simultaneous parallel networks

A key element of the currently connected society is that its participants have learned
to navigate multiple, partially overlapping, networks. The current digitally aware
society is not easily manipulated. One wants a direct call, another hates the call but
prefers listening to voicemail, a third will want the contact via email, a fourth via
SMS text messaging. Even more, we may have different preferences by the time of
day, or type of communication, or the person contacting us.

Similar to the multiple connectedness with networks, we also have grown very
adept at maintaining multiple communities. We have our family, our work colleagues,
but also friends sharing a hobby, like buddies with whom to go watch football, or
play golf, or bowling or play poker or bridge or whatever. We will very likely assign
different communities amidst our work colleagues, especially if working for a larger
organisation. There may be those who are in the same department, but others only
partially overlapping who work on a favourite project, and yet others who may be

distant and perhaps disliked, etc. Different communities, and different preferences for each. Before the mobile phone we did not have a strong selection of options to differentiate between our communities. Now we can even program our phone to ring in different ways depending on which person calls etc.

Virtual schizophrenics

The changes with technology have enabled us to adopt multiple personalities, depending on our situation and what type of life experience we are seeking. We can go dating safe in the knowledge that we can mask our identity, if we need to. Or that we can be a motorcycling, jazz playing judge and will want to share these experiences with very separate communities, perhaps every day, all the while still being very much the family man. Equally we are becoming closer as generations where a father of 40 will pretty much listen to the same music his 15-year-old daughter does.

Information society

American economist Jeremy Rifkin believes we are moving from an era of industrial to cultural capitalism as he writes in his book *Age of Success* in 2000 "Cultural production is increasingly becoming the dominant form of economic activity" and "securing access to the many cultural resources and experiences that nurture one's psychological existence becomes just as important as holding property."

Within this context your cultural capital becomes important, if not critical, and your network becomes vital to your success. Look at the business networking site Linkedin, where you can visually see how connected someone is. Where you can invite people into your network and where as a consequence the more connected you are the more powerful you are. Similar digital societies are forming around former university students, job-seekers like Monster.com etc. Before we did not have the ability to seek communities of strangers who share our interest. Today it is commonplace. This is a profound societal shift and signals the emergence of the community.

C   THE FOUR C'S

As part of our research and exploring how the combinations of business, the media, culture, customer behaviour and technology are creating such dramatic change, we arrived at a concept that Axel Chaldecott and Alan Moore have described as the Four Cs. These are: **Commerce, Culture, Community** and **Connectivity**.

Our theory is that the once separate provinces of innovation and technology, business and economic activity, culture and communities are pulling and converging into one another, in increasingly intimate and more powerful combinations. In fact we believe they are inseparable. Understanding the Four Cs means that one can start to realise more differentiated routes to market, more compelling ways to engage one's customers and deliver organic growth.

Commerce

The driving engine for most human activity is the desire for gain. Commerce is based on this principle. Businesses expect to make a profit, and in the long run to bring greater economic value to their owners. Commerce had evolved over the millennia mostly independent of Culture, Connectivity and Community. Commerce existed in a mostly one-directional relationship with its customers. The power of commercial enterprises grew greatly with industrialisation at the expense of the opposite number, Community. Now community, connectivity and culture are embedded into commerce in a multitude of ways. They offer gateways to commercial success if addressed properly within the context of that particular business.

Community

Communities are beginning to materialise as an economic and socio-economic force. Only over the past 10 years or so have we witnessed the rise of community. It has been a move back to localism, to friends and colleagues as frameworks for authoritative advice, and the age of the Do-It-Yourself demographic where communities can and will rapidly form around a collective agenda.

> **Hong Kong mobile phone one minute costs one fifth of a cent**

As political and religious institutions become less dominant, as society becomes less rigid, we seek other bodies to belong to. These communities are more vibrant, more vocal, more dynamic, more connected, and are often collected around a single issue. These communities can be global, national and local. Communities are widely varied, ranging from book clubs, anti-petrol price rise demonstrators and the truth detectors of the blogosphere to the 26,000 online news contributors to the Korean paper Oh My News. These communities will counteract and balance against the interests of pure Commerce or become drivers of it.

Technology via the internet or the mobile phone makes these communities highly informed. These communities feed off information, analyse that information – from collective points of view – and determine action. Communities also redistribute refined information to their network.

Commerce and Community moving closer

Our recent past has been 200 years of an industrial age, mindset and order. This is no longer true, and we are emerging into a knowledge and service driven economy. Many industries have become highly saturated and differentiation is becoming increasingly difficult. On top of that industries have fragmented – creating even greater competition.

Businesses have several communities that they can co-operate with; their own business community – we are already seeing the rise of joint business ventures – and societal communities. Generating win-win initiatives is the way forward for companies if they want to grow and survive. Business success requires greater agility, and greater quantities of creativity. It requires commerce to understand the importance of the rise of social networks as the efficacy of its traditional business model comes under threat.

Commerce via various channels has converged with culture, in a realisation that we just don't shop the way we used to. Customers can no longer be identified by consumption alone. This process is turning retailing into a part of the entertainment industry, the entertainment industry into retailing. Commerce has to understand the other of the Four Cs if what it makes and what it produces is to have any chance of success in the market place. eBay has demonstrated the powerful business model of connecting many to many as opposed to one to many. They generated a powerful trading community in the process.

Culture

There was a time when culture was considered a semi-autonomous and fringe element of the economy. During the Middle Ages there were a few artists who sculpted and painted, often paid for by the church or royalty. Before newspapers there was little mainstream literature or media. Today, culture has become a major element of the global economy, from TV and radio, to movies, music, print media, books, videogames etc. Culture still has attributes to it that are businesslike (a newspaper has to sell copies, a TV show has to generate an audience to sell advertisements) but Culture also still has elements that are Community-directed. Many artists are "struggling" and holding onto a second job simply for the love of their artform, wanting to make a small contribution to culture, even if their dancing or acting or writing or music career will never hit the big time and provide a full-time employment.

Tomi T Ahonen & Alan Moore

Connectivity

300 years ago people were connected almost exclusively to those people they met on a daily basis. The family, the people at work, and perhaps the people on Sunday at church. A formal postal system started to expand connectivity beyond these contacts and the rolling out of steamship and railroad connections two centuries ago allowed people to maintain connections to friends and family even in other countries. But it was not until the widespread adoption of the telephone that enabled connectivity on a global level. And only with the advent of the internet did it become practical for the average person to regularly communicate with friends on other continents.

Culture and Connectivity coming closer

Culture is significant as a catalyst for connectivity. We want to talk about what we saw on TV, what we read in the newspaper, what we heard on the radio. Connectivity is significant in the spread of culture. Printing presses allowed book authors and press columnists to spread their thoughts. Radio broadcasting, motion pictures and music recordings from about a century ago dramatically expanded the ability for culture to be spread. Television 50 years later further enhanced the reach of culture. Many might argue that there is a dilution of talent, that as we get ever more channels, the quality of culture diminishes to the point of approaching zero – witness current quality of "reality shows" on TV. Still, when considering in contrast, Connectivity and Culture support each other, act as opposites.

As culture converges into the marketplace, the concept of rigid institutions, industry sectors ring-fenced from each other becomes seemingly antiquated. Our age is one in which science, economics and politics challenge the notion of fixed categories, perceived oppositions, and impermeable boundaries. Successful brands and business ideas have to become part of popular culture and live within the daily vernacular, and be identified as bringing something positive into public consciousness, rather than something that does not contribute a positive effect.

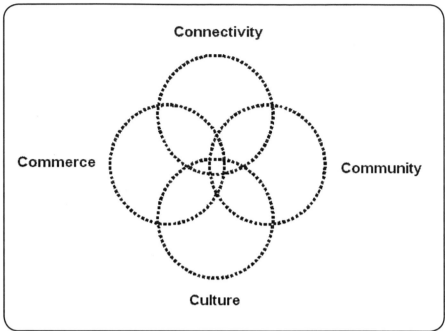

Convergence in the 4 C's

Culture can gain from – and many purists might argue is damaged by – Commerce. Commerce certainly can gain from Culture as we see from the various popular culture icons being recruited to endorse various products and services. Commerce can gain dramatically from Connectivity as it broadens the reach of Commerce. Because of Connectivity we can buy electical goods made in Korea etc. Obviously many Connectivity organisations benefit from Commerce; the global telecommunications industry alone delivers close to 4% of the global GDP.

Communities can gain from Culture, bringing purpose and enlightenment to Communities. Culture can gain from Communities by expanding the reach of Culture. Technology is changing the capability as to how, what, where and with whom we consume culture. We are able to gather and find the things that are important to us in ways never before possible. This is part changes culture and gives greater importance to community and the connectivity of those communities.

Tomi T Ahonen & Alan Moore

The heart of the 4C's

At the very centre of the "flower" model as we call it, is its heart, where Commerce, Culture, Community and Connectivity meet. Connectivity provides companies for the very first time the opportunity to generate two-way flows of information, feedback and engagement. Connectivity provides the opportunity for brands to create powerful pull mechanisms to their offerings and for customers to self-segment themselves.

Connectivity enables via the internet and the mobile phone to identify who are prolific connectors and networks that could be key distribution point to viral contagion and sharing of word of mouth messaging. Connectivity alone is not enough, there must be good content (Culture) and a population of interest (Community). If this can be combined with a genuine business enterprise (Commerce) the sweet spot is achieved.

In this book we have illustrated pioneering examples of where this convergence of the Four Cs is happening. The community of amateur journalists on the Oh My News service in Korea is one such example. The 26,000 members of the amateur journalists use connectivity to create culture, and are paid for their contribution, hence commerce.

D POWER OF COMMUNITY

We have already seen the surprisingly activating power of flash mobbing. In earlier chapters we have seen how brands suffer when a community decide to act against them, from the failure of some Hollywood movies to the crippling of the bicycle locks company Kryptonite. Make no mistake of the sheer power of community power. A vivid illustration of the clout of mobile phone based communities was seen in the Philippines, when the Philippines Government was peacefully overthrown by a Smart Mob of enormous size. Joseph Estrada was forced from office in 2001 after charges of corruption were brought against him. During the four days of the uprising, leading to Estrada's removal from office, SMS text messaging was used to coordinate protests, keep protesters abreast of events as they unfolded, and to mobilise citizens to march, to bring food, and to keep vigil.

Bigger is Better

A benefit of networks was discovered by Robert Metcalfe, the founder of 3Com. His law said that the utility of the network increases by the square of the people connected. Thus if we have a communication network that connects four people, and we double that number to eight, the utility – our benefit from that network – did not double, it quadrupled. Because of this, many formal, official networks and communities are attempting to achieve benefits of scale.

As the natural tendency for digital networks is to grow with time, there is a significant first-mover advantage to building communities. The community that achieves critical mass early will have an incredible size benefit over all rivals. For example Monster.com or eBay have tremendous competitive advantages over other job search or auction sites, simply because more of the potential interested parties are already there. Being second largest is almost certain to be a bad business proposition. Once the leadership position is achieved in any given community setting, it becomes a strongly virtuous cycle. Any new member wants to first join the big community, then consider possibly joining other communities. Thus the first big community has almost an "unfair" advantage in sustaining its size advantage. And as long as the size leader retains his size advantage and does not offend the community, it can relatively easily hold onto its market dominant position.

Dating communities

Dating is one of the early community groups that is appearing on the internet and the mobile phone. Dating is very personal and full of frustration and disappointment. The digital communities that allow engaging in dating activities from the living room provide a new and often less painful way to pursue a new romantic partner. And using dating services is addictive.

20% of British singles use internet for dating

The British online dating industry is worth £11m per year. Research from Bath University found that a third of all internet users turn to the web to establish some sort of relationship and 20% of the 11 million singles in the UK today have used some type of dating agency. Meanwhile across the pond, Match.com's vice president of romance, Trish McDermott, claims that "in the US, the single scene is the internet".

Testing new products and services

A friendly user community is an excellent location for testing new services and goods to launch. This idea is now becoming the norm for testing new telecoms services, as telecoms operators are learning to utilise the power of network effects

---

Tomi T Ahonen & Alan Moore

and learning about such pivotal influencing members of communities, such as the concept of the "Alpha User".

Connectors and Evangelists

In *Alternative Marketing Vehicles* "The Future of Marketing 'To One'" an article on the Nielsen website explains that viral marketing relies on the influence of "Connectors", that special category of people who have mastered what sociologists call the weak tie or social acquaintance. The larger their network of social acquaintances, the more power "Connectors" wield in society, and the better positioned they are to trigger trends. For example, Malcolm Gladwell's seminal book, *The Tipping Point: How little things can make a big difference,* shows how this works through the example of Hush Puppies, all driven by what Gladwell describes as "the power of context".

Hush Puppies were a small company, selling some 430,000 pairs of shoes per year. They had not changed their marketing activity for some time when without warning sales orders started to rise, and rise dramatically. Within the space of two years Hush Puppies were in every mall in America. The reason: a bunch of preppy kids in New York had decided Hush Puppies were cool. They had created the virus that spread, which became a tipping point, then everyone thought "those shoes look cool". Viral. Simple, except it is not.

Marketers have given these customers or definitions of closely similar groups as influentials, carriers, trendsetters and evangelists. In the digitally connected space, we can go even further and identify the single key "Connector" of every distinct virtual community. This best possible connector person, one for every distinct community, is the Alpha User.

Introducing Alpha User

Alpha Users were first isolated by Finnish customer analytics specialist firm Xtract Ltd, and were discussed for the first time in Ahonen, Kasper and Melkko's book *3G Marketing* in 2004. As mobile network operators in the most advanced mobile markets started to explore the deeper insights into the new virtual communities, they discovered tools to isolate distinct communities from the literally tens of thousands of communities in any given mobile telecoms network of millions of users. Each community will have its dominant influencing members, who coordinate communications within the community. Applying theories of how diseases spread, telecoms communication analytics soon discovered the ability to track the communications of every distinct virtual community to a single users who most often initiates communications. This powerful influencing person is called the Alpha User.

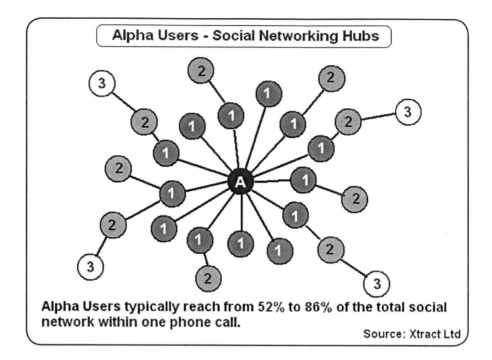

Alpha Users - Social Networking Hubs

Alpha Users typically reach from 52% to 86% of the total social network within one phone call.

Source: Xtract Ltd

The Alpha User is naturally a very efficient communicator and active within that community. The user is also one of the most aware of electronic communication methods for that community. So, while not necessarily a "telecoms nerd" in a tech-nology-geeky way, that Alpha User is usually one of the most telecoms technology-aware within that community. For an Apple iPod user group it will definitely be very much the techno-geek gadget freak. But even the bridge club of 60-year-old ladies will have its Alpha User, who probably has only recently discovered SMS text mes-saging and by most definitions could be classified a technology laggard. Still, for her community, she is the telecoms technology pioneer, their own communications guru. And her bridge-playing lady friends will listen to her opinions about the next mobile phone or subscription, just as much as the iPod user group's active members will listen to the opinions of its Alpha User.

Alpha User is not same as Early Adopter

Most students of marketing are familiar with the Early Adopter concept first in-troduced by Rogers and Shumaker in their book *Communication of Innovations* in 1971. Until the advent of the Alpha User, Early Adopters were the best possible target audience for any innovative technology. The problem with Early Adopters is that they include many kinds of people in their social networks and communication skills. One could argue that the majority of Early Adopters are poor communicators. They prefer to play with the high-tech gadgets and do not socialise well.

The Alpha User is identified by his *communication pattern* and influence within any given community. Some Alpha Users are also Early Adopters. But even a group of Early Adopters – such as a community of iPod or Blackberry users or bloggers in 2005, will have one Alpha User. And any community where nobody is an Early Adopter by technology-orientation, will still have an Alpha User who can be identified again by the communication patterns and influence within the society. Thus the Alpha User is actually a class of people where there is no connection to the older notion of the Early Adopter. Before today, the Early Adopter was the best target that marketing people could identify.

Today we have the Alpha User, a much more potent target for marketing activity, and not related to Early Adopters. Some Early Adopters are Alpha Users. Most Early Adopters are not Alpha Users. And there are many Alpha Users who are not Early Adopters. Yet for the market launch of any goods or service, the Alpha User is the optimal introduction target.

Managing communities

A final point to make, but one that will increasingly become relevant, is that we are learning to manage our communities. We can tune in and tune out of life experiences and take a selected community or friends with us, as it happens to suit our mood. We have the possibility to graze in very different ways. We are actively aware of our choice to enter or exit a community at will.

Concluding Communities

This chapter has looked at the emergence of the community and explained the stage of where we are in community power evolution through the concept of the Connected Age versus the earlier Networked Age. We have explored different forms of Communities and discussed swarming and reachability. We established the new role of communities in the overall economy through our "flower model" of the Four Cs. Finally we gave several examples of how to commercially capitalise on this new power and define the Alpha User. Underneath it all is the enabling technology, digital communication networks. John Grant, in his book *After Image*, put it clearly: "Networks help feed the systems and processes which make value creation possible. They feed in knowledge, fuel innovation and create the context for valuable relationships."

Case Study 11

howies

Sometimes you stand still, look up and wonder why is it that I am standing in a river which is flowing in the opposite direction to the direction I want to go in? Why is it that the world of business and commerce seems disconnected from everything else in life? Where is the meaning in what I do? Why is it that I cannot connect business with other issue important to me?

These are the questions that became the motivation for howies, a clothing company that has set its course and agenda based upon ethical guidelines and a point of view about leading a more balanced life. The concerns of howies are the concerns of its owners Dave Hieatt and his wife Clare. These concerns encompass producing their goods ethically using environmentally friendly production processes. Their beliefs about the environment, pollution, organic farming, food safety, self-development, corporations and sharing knowledge are at the very essence of their brand. You wear a howies T-shirt or a pair of jeans; you are giving voice to a shared and common belief about the world. As Dave Hieatt says on the howies website:

> *Why are we in business? For us it is not as simple to make a profit.*
> *Like any company we require a profit to stay in business. But it is*
> *not the reason we are in business. The thing that has not changed*
> *from day one is the desire to make people think about the world we*
> *live in. This is, and always will be, why we are in business.*
>
> www.howies.co.uk

The brand is activist and politicised. Their hope is that in combining their causes inextricably with their clothing brand they might change people's attitudes and behaviours about the environment, what you eat, how you approach your life, about how you do business. For example, go to page 97 of the howies Winter/Autumn catalogue. And you will read the following:

> *A recipe for disaster*
> *Firstly, add four pinches of insecticide. Two pinches of fungicide.*
> *And two measures of herbicide. After picking, store in conditions*
> *that reduce the oxygen from 21% to 3% and replace with the*

Tomi T Ahonen & Alan Moore

*corresponding amount of CO2. This is perfect for stopping the
ageing process so the salad still appears fresh, but it can't stop the
goodness being lost with each day that passes. Keep in this state
for anything up to a month. Then take some chlorine, 50mg per litre
should do it, a measure the equivalent of 20 times the strength of
your local swimming pool. And gently rinse. Then simply bag, ready
for sale. Supermarkets now wash your hands of that.*

howies Winter/Autumn 2004 catalogue

Not only is there a powerful personal polemic against big supermarkets
and the safety of mass food production. We also get information where we
can get organic food locally via various websites. The same catalogue continues with statistics about overeating, and provides advice about friendships
and experience. It includes a wonderfully real example of people defining
themselves through their experiences of snowboarding in Japan.

howies has a belief system that is connected directly to the business; it's
about thinking long-term, it's about friendships – "we do not answer to the
city, we answer to our friends" – it's about standing your ground. Standing
your ground is part of what makes howies special, why its very specific
modus operandi about how it wants to make its clothes, how it wants to grow,
what it wants to talk about etc, creates very powerful advocates of the howies
brand who are prepared to go to quite extraordinary lengths to help the brand
on its crusade.

On April 14 2003, howies received a letter from the lawyers representing Levi Strauss & Co. Levis were of the opinion that howies had infringed
their copyright and demanded immediate cessation of the sale of any gar-
ments that infringed that copyright. Apparently only Levis can have tabs on
clothing.

What followed was what howies called "Operation tickle". howies introduced a colour-blind test for people buying their jeans. Just to make sure
they could tell the difference between grey (howies) and Levis (red). howies
also introduced a spelling test. Asking their customers to spell corporation,
oppression, Machiavellian etc and naturally they had to spell Levis and howies as well. If people failed the spell test, howies refused to sell them the
jeans. howies sent out howies tabs to disgruntled Levis owners who could
replace the Levis tab with theirs.

howies instigated a massive campaign of disruptive public relations. In
the end the lawyers acting on behalf of Levis asked for a private meeting to

stop all the publicity. The fans and friends of howies combined together and as a community gave their time, their brains and brawn to face up to a giant corporation. As Hieatt says on the website

> *Thanks to the radio stations, the newspapers, the TV news channels, the magazines, the websites, the chat rooms, the free legal advice and you guys and gals out there who told all your mates who told their mates.*
> *Guess no one likes a bully.*
>
> www.howies.co.uk

howies had been able to build a loyal and activist customer community. So powerful that it could engage the community to act against a powerful global brand, Levis, and win. This is a small indication of how much power communities can deliver.

Tomi T Ahonen & Alan Moore

*"The highest and best form of efficiency is the
spontaneous cooperation of free people."*
Woodrow Wilson

XIII
Communities Dominate Brands
Companies from Mars, Customers from Venus

In the book so far we have shown how digitally converging technology is altering society, businesses and consumers. We have seen the decline of the efficacy of branding and advertising. We have seen how a new Generation-C is becoming more literate in the digital world than traditional marketing experts are. And we have seen individual examples of the sheer power of communities, from exhibiting brand loyalty, to killing the success of movies, to literally toppling governments. While branding and advertising are in decline in the balance of marketing communications, community power is on the increase. This chapter will examine that dynamic of the power of the community more deeply, ranging from bloggers to the mobile phone connected Gen-C. We arrive at the inevitable conclusion that today the power of communities actually dominates over the power of brands.

A SLOW DEATH OF BRANDING AND ADVERTISING

We saw in the Branding chapter earlier that marketing communications in general, and advertising and branding in particular, are already experiencing challenges to their power from the convergence of market and environmental forces. Now as we introduce the counterbalancing force of communities, we arrive at the biggest problem for the future of branding. It is that the communities of interest have changed the relationship between brands and their customers forever. Doc Searls on his blog

"Branding is dead", wrote on 20 October 2004:

> *Blogging is all about ECO-logy. Branding is all about EGO-logy. The two*
> *are not compatible. Which is why brand-wimpy Microsoft has hundreds of*
> *bloggers [a well-known fact], and why you can get fired for blogging at*
> *uber-brand Apple [so I've been told]. Apple like the conversation they're*
> *currently having. They don't want it to change, internally or externally.*
> *They want to control the means of conversation. I've seen branding work.*
> *I've seen blogging work. My conclusion? Branding is dead. Holy Shit.*
> *Branding. Is. Dead. We just thought just marketing and advertising were*
> *dead. Nope. Branding kicked the bucket, too. Dead, dead, and dead. Holy*
> *shit.*
>   http://doc.weblogs.com/2004/10/20#nowItsOfficial

It is fair to say that if not quite as dead as Doc Searls writes, branding is indeed in the brand hospital, everyone is doing tests, everyone is an expert and everyone has a different opinion. But branding as it was is struggling for a relevant role. Many legacy brands are struggling with an identity crisis, wrought by the new digital economics.

Advertising has been able in the past to change the behaviour of people and to persuade them to think about the world in a different way. Branding changed human perception on an industrial scale. Bill Bernbach's DDB's "Think Small" campaign, which sold a little unknown German car called a "Beetle" to a gasoline guzzling V8-loving USA four decades ago was nothing less than spectacular. But that was at a time when choice was limited, when big media was still big media. When industrialization was in many ways at its zenith and we were more trusting.

> ## Virtual Tourist website has 400,000 members sharing info

Marketing today is perceived as *marketing interruptus,* and advertising is now perceived as invasive. Undesirable, that is no longer acceptable. Markets are conversations, and those conversation flows can come from the CEO, from the employees to customers to suppliers. Microsoft, even if some call them wimpy, have some 650 bloggers, Jonathan Schwartz COO of Sun Microsystems blogs. The vice chairman of General Motors blogs. Companies are beginning to wake up to the fact that two-way flows of information, feedback and comment, are to become a very necessary part of marketing relationships and communications. No longer can corporations set the agenda and coerce their customers as before. The interruptive and disruptive role of advertising is particularly annoying to consumers. A Yankelovich study reports that:

> *Intrusiveness has always been the one thing that consumers dislike the most about marketing and advertising. The greater percentage of consumers mentioning this dislike in 2004 arises from the exponentially greater degree of clutter and intrusiveness true of the marketplace today. Negative opinions and concerns about intrusiveness give rise to consumer resistance to marketing. And this resistance reduces the effectiveness of marketing and adds to the cost of doing business. The fervour with which consumers are resisting marketing suggests that the impact on marketing productivity is considerable.*
>
> Yankelovich Partners *Marketing Resistence Survey* April 2004

We seek the truth in increasingly greater numbers and go online in search of it. This capability is the fundamental reason why big media control of information is now challenged. Let us remind ourselves that the recent case of the humbling of veteran CBS News anchorman Dan Rather by the blogosphere profoundly makes the point. He resigned shortly afterwards. And in an article in *The Economist* entitled "Dropping the Anchorman". the New Media as it is called is described as too voracious for any institution to control them. In 2002 the bloggers kept the heat on the Republicans' then Senate leader, Trent Lott, for racist remarks that the *New York Times* originally buried. He resigned.

B COMMUNITIES SELF-GENERATING

Today, we have been cast free from geography, from the institutions of state and from class. Young people are becoming effectively curators of their own cultural frameworks, they are focused on the consumption of culture. And to do this successfully they must have access to networks and communities. In many ways, it is the communities that we choose to belong to that define us. And these communities are becoming ever more powerful.

People prefer opinions of community

Which is more believeable? A press release from, say, Ford Motor Company, or a few blog entries from the people who designed the new Ford Mustang's powertrain. The Ford blog is a good and, we would argue, reliable indicator of what is to come. Here are people who obviously love what they do, who have been empowered to share their interest, and who then do so passionately but with full facts. If you are leaning towards a Ford automobile, would this group of Ford employees be some of the most trusted contacts you would ever want to communicate with?

One of the pioneers of new community-generated content comes from South Korea, where a citizen-generated online newspaper **Oh My News** is revolutionising the local newspaper industry. The online newspaper has 26,000 what they call "citizen reporters." These reporters send in stories and pictures which make up 80% of all content. The bloggers get paid and also get to see their name in print.

• In Holland a 24/7 news site **NU.nl** encourages the general public to send in their pictures of breaking events; they get paid if their images are published.

• For the traveller there is **Lonely Planet Thorn Tree,** an online bulletin board with over 5,000 posts a day (Lonely Planet also receives around 1,000 emails and letters a week from customers, helping them to constantly fine-tune their content), claims trendwatching.

• And finally **Virtual Tourist** where 400,000 members from over 219 countries share insights and experiences to help each other travel smarter, from finding the best place to get great airfares, accommodations or car rentals, to solid insider advice on what to see and do. In their own words: "VirtualTourist members are a friendly and helpful bunch and it's a snap to use the collective experience and brain power of our members to get the help you need."

Trust word of mouth

The very underlying premise in this shift in the balance of power from the brands to the communities is that we trust community opinions more than messages of corporations. In fact, we will take a total stranger's opinion, on a community we trust, as more valid than the press release statement of a known executive of a corporation we deal with. This is worth repeating. The voice of a stranger on a community we trust is more trustworthy. That is how powerful communities are. That is why the shift is now happening. Remember the statistic from the Cap Gemini Ernst & Young study we quoted in the Branding chapter – the most influential measure is word of mouth while the least influential is TV advertising. Yet TV advertising takes nearly half of all advertising and branding dollars worldwide.

It is vitally important for all marketers, and in fact all involved in any business anywhere, to understand that now, in the beginning of 2005, we have for the first time identified compelling evidence to draw an overall conclusion of what ails marketing, branding and advertising.

Tomi T Ahonen & Alan Moore

Communities have emerged and in the role of marketing communications they perform a critical *counterbalance* against any one way marketing messages. It is possible to engage the communities, to harness their power, to influence them and to use them. This requires a deeper and more sophisticated approach to marketing communications. But the need to adjust is vital. Corporations that ignore this seismic shift in communications dynamics will die. Only corporations that achieve success in community communications can succeed. This is truly the dawn of a new era in marketing communications.

Community rapidly learning

A key element of virtual communities is that they can immediately implement what they think of. Any innovation within a community can be decided upon by the community and then implemented.

Very importantly for the businesses and brands that sit at the other end of the power struggle, communities are not only fast at mutation from ideas within, they are also remarkably fast at learning from the outside. As communities are connected – by some number of degrees of separation – to every other community, soon a good idea in one country is copied in another. The contagion effect is remarkably fast. For example, in the World Trade Center terrorist attacks, SMS text messages were for a while the only way of communicating in that disaster as other telecoms networks shut down, and text messaging was often the first connection that was re-established once networks started to come back online.

By the time of the big East Coast electicity power grid breakdown in the summer of 2003, and then at the Boxing Day tsumami disaster in the Indian Ocean of 2004, people who were caught up in those events were ever more aware of the ability to attempt connection and access to news and help, via their mobile phones. Communities learn and improve.

C FROM SERMON TO DISCUSSION

As interruptive and preaching styles of advertising, marketing and branding are becoming irrelevant in corporate communication, the only viable alternative is to activate the target audience into a dialogue.

Pulpit preaching is dead

We believe that one-way, controlled marketing communications is arriving at its end-game. Traditional marketing and branding has until now been about coercion, and driving people to the point of transaction at which point the value is released. This meant that at the point of exchange the marketer's job was done. There is no value, no cultural capital in image advertising; we have moved beyond that. Mobile phones, the internet, MP3 players, the changing cultural fabric of our lives, the splintering of delivery channels, all together mean that brands are no longer in the driving seat. As Mike Bayler writes in his book *Promiscuous Customers*, customer value is equal to meaning.

One can see that companies that only want to broadcast their marketing message propaganda, and produce marketing communications which is about their agenda not their customers' agenda, will not survive the next 10 years. Their customers will be busy connecting, talking, sharing information and experiences. Those competitors who learn to live in a world of engagement will thrive. They will take over from those brands who only close their ears and only preach their own message.

From monologue to dialogue

The *Cluetrain Manifesto* authors Doc Searls and David Weinberger have urged companies to regard markets as conversations. The central message is that far from aiding such exchanges between companies and customers, formulaic corporate PR is an obstruction to the process in an era in which sophisticated, internet-savvy and information-rich customers regard slick marketing-speak as something to be filtered out.

The *Cluetrain Manifesto* authors point out that the internet has restored the original conversational dynamic of the marketplace, where individuals exchange information in their authentic voices. They herald the end of "business-as-usual", describing how the internet has changed information asymmetries forever. "Business-as-usual" is characterised as top-down control of employees by a depersonalised corporation and a barrier erected between customers and its employees, who are the natural communicators of the company's authentic voice. In the traditional model, marketing and public relations are one-way channels through which customers are bombarded with messages. Top-down, cookie cutter, depersonalised marketing has become a barrier to effective communication, the opposite of a conduit to valuable customer relationships.

We, of course, need to refine and add to that, that people connected via the internet are only of the Networked Age, that of the last decade. As we clearly stated in the Generation-C and Community chapters, any power that can be imagined from an internet-connected community, is greatly amplified by users connected by the mobile phone. This includes both reach of users and the immediate ability to activate. In other words, any lessons learned from internet networked communities will become even more pronounced and powerful in the connected communities of the

Tomi T Ahonen & Alan Moore

mobile phone generations.

Companies that do not join the conversation will soon have no customers to talk to. Connectedness enables customers to talk about the company amongst themselves, bypassing corporate messages, if they wish to. Allowing employees, the true repository of the company's value, to join these conversations and communicate directly with customers enhances the company's credibility and increases its presence in the marketplace.

Interactive communications, especially using weblogs and mobile phones, offer a way for companies to reclaim a place in the marketplace conversations using their employees' credible voices. The company can build a community around its brand(s), products and services and provide an informal focus for customer loyalty. The communication has to be individualistic, customised and scalable. It originates in individual conversations and is a ground-up, grassroots phenomenon. Customer connectedness is changing the modern corporation.

We are at the end of the command and control business world. We are at the beginning of the coordinate and cultivate business world. We are in fact experiencing:

- movement toward human freedom in business that may be as fundamental as democracy was in government 200 years ago
- lower transaction costs and globalisation that combine to create enormously efficient and dynamic markets
- large corporations allowing 100% of the workforce to represent them in the marketplace (eg Sun Microsystems and Ford allowing any employee to blog on the company's site)
- large online sites that can be described as communities with an individual mayor heading up each one (eg eBay is the community of 40 million people and Meg Whitman is the mayor).

Cannot ignore community

One of the most critical failures of modern corporations is to ignore its existing communities. We have two widely reported examples from leading high technology companies. Nokia stated boldly that it intended to enter the gaming platform industry and to expand the potential gaming user space, and gain millions of users with its first launched gaming phone, the **N-Gage**. Nokia spent enormous amounts of marketing funds and resources in the global launch of N-Gage and had a lot of visibility. Nokia seemed to be the perfectly poised player to succeed with this strategy, as at the time its mobile phone market share, at near 40%, was almost triple its nearest rival, Motorola, and Nokia had been the innovator to bring gaming to mobile phones with the original "Snake" game, arguably the world's most played video game. Its brand was the technology brand of preference for the youth of the time.

Nokia's first generation N-Gage device sold less than half a million units world-wide and was not moving off the shelves even with massive subsidies. What went wrong? The ironic truth is that Nokia had recruited early adopter types of test-ers for its near-final product. Those had repeatedly voiced the same complaints, that changing games was too cumbersome (needing the removal of the battery), the voice calling position for the phone was bad, etc. Nokia ignored these complaints and launched N-Gage knowing it was not meeting its core target users' desires. The first generation flopped. How much was Nokia's credibility damaged in the gaming community with an approach that demonstrated the brand was not listening? Only time will tell. Nokia took a year to fix the problems, and suddenly the second gen-eration sold in a few months the same amount as the first product sold in a year.

Another widely reported example is Hutchison, the Hong Kong based multi-national telecoms operator using the brand "**Three**" in most European markets, on the new 3G third generation mobile phone services. Three in the UK went out of its way to recruit prospective early adopter types to act as its pretesters and evangelists, during 2002. They had thousands of prospective Early Adopter types signed up via email. Those were hoping to receive contacts from Three about the launch of the service, any early handset details etc, as Three was approaching its launch date in March of 2003.

Again, a totally wasted opportunity. As 3G telecoms expert Steve Jones, lectur-ing at Oxford University's 3G business course, explained: those recruited prospec-tive evangelists were *never contacted* by Three. They were simply ignored. What happened was that these, who if they had heard of 3G technology in the UK dur-ing 2002 had to be "techno-geeks" of the most involved kind, then informally got together on various discussion boards at The 3G Portal, Ecademy, and other such technology discussion sites, and complained about their early Three UK marketing experiences. Here was a community ready to be harvested, but it was ignored. It turned out to be a very vocal *opponent* of Three UK.

D COMMUNICATION MODEL REVISED

The emergence of the community is a new force that was not covered in the traditional model of communications. The traditional communication model is widely accepted and is the foundation of all media businesses and the basis of advertising and branding. We now are in the position to make the first major addition of a new element to the basic model, and to dramatically alter the communication patterns that the model explains.

Tomi T Ahonen & Alan Moore

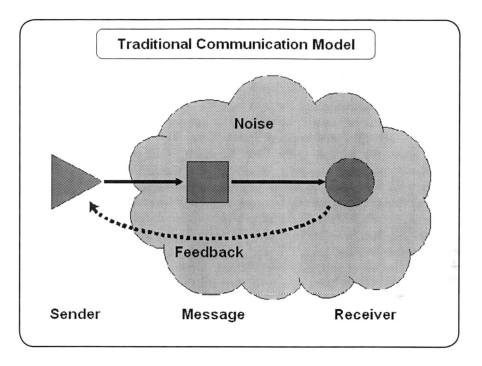

Traditional communication model

The traditional communication model describes how the media and all businesses and most other entities communicate with their target audiences. At its core the model has four elements, a sender (company/brand) a message (an advertisement) a media channel (TV, print media, etc) and a receiver (the target customer). Typically most of the time the communication is depicted as an arrow going from the sender to the receiver, with perhaps a thin dotted line showing the possibility of a feedback loop back from the recepient to the sender. Very importantly, the message, media and receiver are usually depicted to be inside a cloud of noise; all the distractions of other messages plus the various daily clutter than will hinder the clear reception of our intended message.

There have been numerous developments of the basic model to explain various different media channels; about effectiveness or the lack thereof of conflicting messages from any one brand; about the effects of sub-branding and co-branding etc. Still the basics of the model have a company sending its message on a one-directional path through a media or several media to the intended target audience.

Communities are the counterforce

Many researchers have felt the basic model was out of balance. The sender has enormous power and, as the feedback loop is most ineffective, the model seemed to be unstable. Furthermore, if that communication model truly depicted reality, our advertising and branding today could not be in the crisis it is in. Something had happened that was not captured in the model.

Now we can offer communities as the new counterforce. We place the communities as a group that partially overlaps the receiver(s). While an individual customer usually will not bother to react to the sender, a community can and increasingly will. Now the feedback loop can be as strong as the message sending arrow. It is important to note that the communities are not created by the companies and brands, but rather they are self-forming. Furthermore, that for any given end-receiver of a message, there can be several communities with partially overlapping membership of our target customers.

Where individual customers would rarely if ever communicate amidst themselves, the members of a community will specifically discuss our brand with themselves. Suddenly customers have allies. They are no longer isolated.

Act as filtering element

The communities emerge in the traditional communication model as a filtering element, between the message and the receiver. We must keep in mind that for any brand-interested communities, such as an iPod users community, the opinion of community members of that specialist group is given a much higher degree of confidence and respect than the marketing communications coming from the brand itself. If there is any conflict, a member of the community will trust the opinion of another member rather than the message from your brand.

The community is actually an intelligent filter. The community might not like your message, and substitute another message – such as its own, or a message from one of your competitors – in place of your message. The community will increasingly evaluate, analyse and comment on your message, further colouring and altering the message before it reaches the intended audience.

Preferred channel becomes feedback loop

Also, differing from before, now the customers are empowered to communicate and encouraged to give feedback. They use the preferred means of communication for that community, be it instant messaging, email, blogging, chat rooms or text messages, and share comments amidst themselves. The customer that is active in one of the communities is no longer a passive recipient of your marketing messages. The customer is already active in the discussions about you between other members of the community. That community has established communication tools that are digital. They will form the natural feedback loop in the model. Now the feedback line is no longer a dotted line.

It is important also to note that all brand-interested communities have already started to attempt contacts with the brands involved, but mostly this is still informal and random contacts. For example, a community of chat room participants around Canon brand digital cameras might come across a question by one of the members that nobody knows the answer to. They can then say, let's try to ask Canon itself. And someone perhaps knows of a colleague who works for the Canon organisation, and then sends an email to that friend, etc. As soon as brands learn to engage, the first steps are to open up communication channels with the designated community contact persons who already are attempting to do that on behalf of the community.

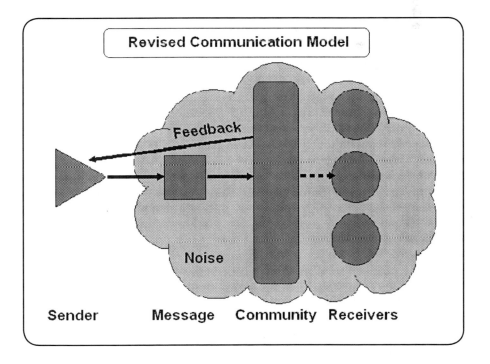

Balance achieved

The communication model has two end-points. The sender/company/brand and the receiver/customer. The brand has its message that it wants to communicate. The customer has its community that it uses to defend its interests. The message can now go in both directions. The community will prefer any messages that are delivered on a communication channel such as blogging rather than a mass media channel such as TV advertising. The brand will prefer to have the community in a positive mindset rather than neutral or even hostile. Thus the brands will migrate their community-oriented communications rapidly to the preferred media of any given community.

We have seen the roles of the community and the channel and how they appear in the communication model. As to the role of engagement marketing, that is actually the *altering* of the message and its media. Rather than *sending* a *message* to the receiver, the brand now *invites participation* in dialogue. Engagement changes the type of message/media that is initiated by the brand. Thus engagement appears as an alternate to sending a marketing communication message. Rather than interruptive advertising, we engage our target customers. We do so through their communities. In fact, a smart brand will promote the recruitment of communities, to enable random unconnected customers to join in brand-interested communities, to empower the customers and to support the communities. This is engagement at the very heart and soul of it.

Communities become the dominant elements to any communication. Communities filter, amplify and counter messages they receive. Communities can endorse a message and add to its credibility, or actively destroy the level of trust for that message. The community can even act as a substituting agent, discontinuing your message and substituting that of an alternate communicator, perhaps a message from your competitor. At least for the near-term, meaning this decade, the community element has the greatest influence in the communication model.

Imagine snowboard advertising

Up to today, corporations targeted their marketing by the process of segmentation. And most of the segmentation was based on demographics. So a snowboard manufacturer might think that one of its target groups is the university student population in winter countries, in an age group of 20-25.

A snowboard manufacturer would then research that population and find that they read the university paper, which usually has inexpensive ad rates. They could also target the students by posting billboards near the university and, for example, advertising on the campus radio. Today, communities will often be totally independent from what the companies had defined as their target segments.

Let us assume that there is a university ski club that is the snowboarding community for a snowboarding university student. Typically, that kind of club allows family members of students to also join in their activities. Thus the 28-year-old advertising executive big brother of a biology student can also be an active member of this community. He will never read the campus newspaper or see the billboards or hear the ads on the campus radio. If the snowboard manufacturer specifically sought out and engaged the ski club, it would have a much more meaningful dialogue with the actual active members of the club, with no waste of ads to students who do not snowboard, and reaching all actual members of the club, even those who are not students.

Where the ski club is not a media outlet, it will not have set processes for market messages. This is both good and bad. It means more work for the brand. But it also mostly means that the money spent will be much more cost-effective to the real benefits of the end-users belonging to the club. After contact has been made and the brand engages the community with the preferred digital communication tool(s) of that community, an open channel will be formed between the brand and the most powerful influencer of its customers, the user community.

E   POWER OF CO-CREATION

A *Harvard Business Review* article entitled "Customer-Centered Brand Management" published on 14 September 2004 looks at how the relationship between businesses, their brands and their customers can become more mutually beneficial if a "co-creation" principle can be established. C.K. Prahalad and Venkatram Ramaswamy in their article "The Co-Creation Principle" wrote:

> *Companies spent the 20th century managing efficiencies. They must*
> *spend the 21st century managing experiences. Because companies have*
> *historically controlled all business activities involved in the creation of*
> *the things they sell, it is their view of value that is dominant. Indeed, the*
> *consumer typically has little or no influence on value created until the point*
> *of exchange when ownership of the product is typically transferred to the*
> *consumer from the firm. This is true whether the consumer is a company*
> *or an individual. Now consumers are challenging this corporate logic of*
> *value creation. Spurred by the consumer-centric culture of the internet*
> *– with its emphasis on interactivity, speed, individuality, and openness – the*
> *consumer's influence on value creation has never been greater, and it is*
> *spreading to all points in the value chain.*
>   www.strategy-business.com/press/article/18458?pg=0

We believe that customers have their own "Profit & Loss" account upon which they judge these experiences. Here the profits and losses are taken in a broad sense, beyond strictly financial instruments. Customers will consider the time and effort involved, and non-monetary gains and costs as well. "Was that experience worth it or not?" should be the question customers ask themselves.

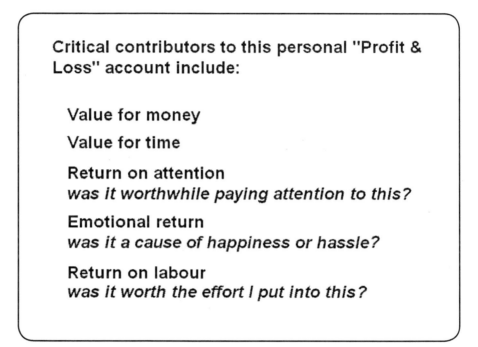

Critical contributors to this personal "Profit & Loss" account include:

Value for money

Value for time

Return on attention
was it worthwhile paying attention to this?

Emotional return
was it a cause of happiness or hassle?

Return on labour
was it worth the effort I put into this?

We would argue value for money as a yardstick simply isn't adequate in the 21st century. So a question companies should ask themselves is: "Do we see the world through a compartmentalised brand/business unit lens or through a customer lens?" The answer to that question will determine your near future.

Viral marketing

It is interesting, that the word viral has moved increasingly centre stage over the last two years. In the previous chapter we already discussed the role of evangelists and the recently discovered Alpha User in the spread of messages through a community.

Tomi T Ahonen & Alan Moore

Some companies are getting smart, getting creative and though some are industrial giants, they have humanised their marketing activity. Ford Motor Co is one such example. Ford marketed their hi-tech hybrid eco-friendly SUV (Sports Utility Vehicle) the **Ford Escape** with a word of mouth campaign last autumn. It was a carefully studied and planned campaign. According to Ford research the target audience watched 14% less television than the average consumer.

Ford developed a website crammed with information about the car, about ecology and the technology of the car. It offered a mileage calculator that demonstrated how fuel-efficient the car was. Surrounding this site were very smartly targeted press ads, and a roadshow that was to go to nine key cities in the US. Ford sought the advocacy of its customers who would then evangelise about the car and virally spread the word through their communities better than any TV spot could.

This is sophisticated viral marketing but why not? It is also in line with the Ford **Mustang Blog** for those that enthuse about their Mustangs – why give up the right as a company to participate in the dialogue? Why give it up to a magazine or some other third party? Fans would rather hear it from the horse's mouth. Somehow we have managed to create a language and jargon for marketing, pseudo-research, etc, which forgets the point that we are all people.

Viral marketing makes sense as it can talk to a community of interest that is interested in what you have to say. The key question is that you really have to do your homework first – and be clear about what buttons you are pressing, to anticipate the mood of your audience, and to invite them in such a way that excites them.

This is exactly what Ford was seeking to do. Their method is what one would describe as social contagion. Driven by relevant content, put into context, that pulls its audience and potential customers, that then creates word of mouth and a viral spreading of that information digitally, which ultimately becomes buzz or PR – friendly articles and columns – with credibility. Your customers have seeded and marketed your product for you. They are happy to do it for you too, as long as your product is worth talking about.

F   HARNESSING COMMUNITY POWER

We are witnessing individual examples all around the world of communities starting to wake up to their power. One of the early examples is the Mozilla Foundation. This not-for-profit organisation is developing the **Firefox** browser as a rival to Microsoft's internet Explorer. The Mozilla Foundation's marketing director, Rob Davis, is understandably short of funds due to the very nature of a not-for-profit organisation. He appealed to the grass-roots to help with funding the marketing of the browser. Mr Davis was hoping for 2,500 donors. What he got was 10,000 who have donated a quarter of a million dollars. The community effort is very potent; already seven million people have downloaded the Firefox browser and were waiting for the next release in November 2004.

Adam Morgan writing in *Eating the Big Fish* tells the story of rap artist **Run DMC** and their song "My Adidas". Fandom as we know generates powerful loyalty. Run DMC were at the time talking to Adidas about sponsorship of the group. Adidas were unconvinced, so the hip hop band invited them to a gig. In the middle of their song "My Adidas", one of the singers yells out, "Show me your Adidas" and 20,000 pairs of Adidas sneakers were hoisted into the air. The guys from Adidas reached for the cheque books.

This is a wonderful demonstration of communities adopting things as their own. When Run DMC wrote "My Adidas" there obviously was no commercial sponsorship from Adidas. Run DMC were genuinely singing about the emotions, the politics etc that defined their culture. By chance Run DMC had enabled a brand to get very close to the hearts of a particular community. Conventional marketing practice will rarely generate that kind of passion.

Connected generation can kill brand success

In the previous chapter we already showed that communities have dominating power in smart mob behaviour, and isolated examples already of community power overwhelming the advertising spend. The examples included the downfall of the Philippines government, the Kryptonite lock disaster, and the power of smart mobs to ruin Hollywood movie success. During 2005 we will see ever more of these kinds of examples, as communities learn to wield their new-found power.

Change has vested interests lined up against it

The problem we face is that the change we discuss in this book is so profound there a great many vested interests who would rather the whole problem would just go away. Machiavelli had a view on this centuries ago when he explained: "There is nothing more difficult to take in hand, more perilous to conduct, more uncertain in its success, than to take the lead in introducing a new order of things; because the innovator will have for enemies all who have done well under the old conditions and only lukewarm defenders in those who may do well under the new."

So what are you going to do as a business or a brand, play out your 30-second TV commercial and hope for the best? Or are you going to roll your sleeves and really think about how your are going to engage your customers and stakeholders, how you are going to co-create *value*, facilitate greater more valuable experiences, become the conduit to communities who are passionate about whatever floats their boat?

Tomi T Ahonen & Alan Moore

And celebrate that fact that businesses, marketing, creativity, technology and people can come together in ways today which were not imaginable five years ago. Or is that too hard for you to think about as you watch the minnows eat the big fish as they understand the new dynamics of communities and business in the 21st century? In our next chapter we will examine ways of how to do it, in what we call "engagement marketing".

Customer evangelists

Customer evangelism is the ultimate goal of marketing. We do not want us as the brand to convince our target audience. We want some of our first customers to fall in love with our offering, so much so that they become evangelists. As we have seen, our customers believe the community members more than they do our messages. So evangelists are the ideal method to spread the word. Rob Scoble, who works for Microsoft and authors a popular blog, writes about a visit to various wineries in 2004, where he encounters what he describes as a customer evangelist. Our blogger describes how a wine evangelist stopped on her way out to say hello and explain why she thought Christopher Creek was such a great winery:

> And she sold us on the lifestyle of wine. It gives her great joy, she told the eight people sitting at the tasting room bar. I'd never met a wine evangelist quite like Amy before. But she convinced us that we should try more wine in our lives, and that Christopher Creek is a great place to start.
> http://radio.weblogs.com/0001011/2004/04/17.html#a7223

Naturally there are always two sides to the argument, but if people are passionate about your product, service, brand, celebrate and reward them. These people can help and enable you because they are motivated. Like Run DMC's 20,000 fans who all wore Adidas as a display of loyalty to their iconic hip hoppers.

120,000 volunteers have joined Boeing Design Team

Yet what today makes this so much more powerful is the eco-system of the connected society. The speed of interaction in the blogosphere alone is enormous. Rob Scoble may have been talking about an intimate experience and in many ways it is, but no doubt many who read his blog and visit Sonoma will consider paying Christopher Creek a visit.

The new customer

Brands need to rethink how they creates value that "pulls" rather than "drives" customers to their services, products and even retail stores. Brands need to also understand the notion of the connected society. Connected communities of interest, business communities, social networks and digital networks are all active and in dialogue with each other.

All this means that in many ways we have moved from a culture that was passive, that found the process of learning unexciting and was focused on image, to one that is self-actualising, that seeks experiences, finds learning exciting and is based upon content and knowledge. It's new world vs old world.

Therefore brands of the 21st century will need to be about engaging their audiences by being enabling, life-simplifying navigation partners; procreators of greater and more valuable experiences. Brands need to embrace the interactive age to break with traditional, ineffective interruptive marketing, using engagement marketing to change customer behaviour through involvement. Brands have to become immersive, sensorial and multi-dimensional.

Dominate!

We have shown that advertising and branding is in trouble. We have proven that communities are emerging as a new force in business. And we have clearly illustrated that there are interested communities that take it upon themselves to position against brands. Very soon there will be communities aligned on behalf of their members against any brand. As communities have the numbers, the power to directly influence buying behaviour, and are trusted more than your marketing messages, their word will overpower yours. The only way to win is to join. To dominate you must join the communities. Treat the community as the most important of your VIP customers, you cannot afford to lose their good will. As Baltasar Gracian said: "Friends provoked become the bitterest of enemies."

Tomi T Ahonen & Alan Moore

Case Study 12

Twins Mobile Music Service

Hong Kong is a mobile telecoms market with incredibly high penetration rates (120% at the end of 2004 and still growing). While advanced in penetration rates, Hong Kong is not seen as advanced in the portfolio of mobile services in contrast with other leading markets such as Japan, Korea and Finland. However, a radical mobile service offering was pioneered in Hong Kong with the introduction of Twins Mobile. In contrast to Japan, where the whole industry is bustling with activity centered around the attractive services available, the Hong Kong mobile phone market, with its strong emphasis on technological advances and price competition, and relative lack of innovative content, fell victim to a vicious cycle causing a business slowdown.

New World Mobility, a mobile operator in Hong Kong, turned to the highly innovative Japanese mobile internet company Cybird to find a solution to rapidly move it from the price battleground, to a marketspace built on value creation for the consumer. After two months of market research Cybird proposed "reconstructing the value chain by creating services that would engage users, providing value for both the telecommunications company the information providers and a passionate fan base." In Hong Kong, mobile phones must first be activated with an IC card called a SIM. Cybirds proposal involved the addition of a new surprise to the SIM. This idea led to the branded SIM cards called "Twins Mobile", based on the ultra popular Hong Kong pop music idol Twins, and turned an ordinary mobile phone into a portal with the power to bring Twins closer to their fans.

The service is based upon the intense passion fans have for their favourite pop idol. The service provided the latest news from Twins, concert info and direct advertising of upcoming live performances; Twins Ringtones, logo, screensaver, e-card and website with a fan chat area. Chat rooms are very successful, and this enabled the Twins mobile service to continually connect its fans and therefore link a community together who could all share information, swap stories, gossip and discuss and even discover there are more Twins fans in my street or close by. The Twins Mobile was also, of course, a traditional mobile phone service with voice and text messaging services, a phone number etc. So users would not need to switch SIM cards to access "regular" telecoms services. This boosted revenues to the Twins Mobile service portfolio.

Members can use loyalty points to enjoy more premium services. Twins was launched via a PR campaign drawing in fans for a consumer event. This was followed by an advertising campaign from New World Mobile where the "Twins Mobile" logo was applied to Twins albums and concerts. There was an email collection campaign for limited edition goods through SMS fan mail and finally acquisition through a chance to win concert tickets

Twins Mobile demonstrates how much a community will commit if their interest and attention is continually rewarded. Twins Mobile was making a healthy profit for both customer (the Twins pop duo) and the operator New World Mobility. Twins was smart because it was designed as a community service. The ability to discuss at length your intense obsession with others who equally share the same degree of passion is priceless. Twins was able to create a community where one could belong, participate in and share one's passion for Twins.

Twins was, and is, bleeding edge in terms of marketing strategy. Designing such marketing initiatives requires that everyone wins, an understanding of social networks, a belief that there is a different way of doing things. Also that the marketing cycle is ongoing as it does not cease at the point of purchase. The chat rooms, email and text updates makes the whole experience dynamic. Twins also lived in the real world and the virtual world for the operators and for Twins this expanded exponentially their ability to generate revenue and profits, for the Twins fans it enabled them to leave the concert (physical space) and moved into the virtual world via their mobile to continue to pursue their unsatiated passion.

The Twins experience had viral, social contagion and buzz built in to fit. One might argue that it was acquisition, CRM and brand all rolled into one.

New World Mobility began the sales of Twins Mobile in August of 2002. The phenomenal success of the branded Twins SIM card has provided evidence of the possibilities of mobile multi-platform branding. Creating communities, extending the brand and driving sales. Now the lessons are being applied in America where rap artist Nelly and glam rockers Kiss have announced similar plans, including several cuts of music pre-stored onto the mobile phone.

Tomi T Ahonen & Alan Moore

*"What I admire in Columbus is not his having discovered a world, but his
having gone to search for it on the faith of an opinion."*

A Robert Turgot

XIV
From Disruption To Engagement
Capitalising on Communities

"I hear you knockin' but you can't come in" is something as customers we say to
brands on a daily basis, consciously or unconsciously. Yet businesses need to grow,
revenues and profits increased. This book is ultimately about how you do that in a
changing world. This is not the time for nostalgia or for the board to sing "just keep
swimming, swimming, swimming". So the question we presented ourselves with is
how do you overcome the problems caused by technological change in society and in
business? We have explored how customers change and how a new Generation-C is
emerging. We explained how communities act as a counterbalancing force to branding and advertising power. Now it remains for us to expose the way to capitalise on
the dramatic change in business. We call it engagement. Now, some people may say
that, yes, but all communications is about engagement. We don't think it is.

A END OF INTERRUPTION

We are witnessing the unprecedented convergence of a number of global industries
– eg telecom, entertainment, computing and electronics – alongside the fragmentation and diminishing effectiveness of traditional media. We know that consumers
are looking for relationships with brands and for them to provide complementary,
meaningful and relevant experiences to enhance their lives and earn their loyalty.
We also know that brand owners are increasingly recognising the importance of

integrated, relationship marketing and concluding that conventional brand communication is no longer the answer. And in Claus von Clausewitz's terms, the era of *set-piece* competition is over. We have entered the era of *total competition*. No matter what your industry, there is a company somewhere working on how to enter your industry; how to steal your revenues, your customers, your future cashflows, your profits, your existence.

Revolution will not be on TV

The marketing communication landscape has changed more in the past five years than in the previous 50. Traditional marketing delivers a fraction of the Return on Investment (ROI) it did only two years ago.

Previously marketers could define their brands for consumers. They could make one TV commercial and run it in some top-rated TV show, where millions of consumers would see it and the job was done! Today, consumers are defining brands, even redefining them. And because consumers experience brands multi-dimensionally these days it is no longer good enough to produce a wonderful TV commercial or any other marketing communication for that matter – extolling the virtues of a brand – if the brand's claims do not match up to the actual brand experience. Especially in this age of the connected and informed consumer, they will share good and bad experiences with their friends. Consumers have far more control. They must be shown enormous respect as people if marketers are to have any hope of them respecting their brands.

Communication channels are exploding and fragmenting. The term "mass media" is on the verge of becoming an oxymoron. Audiences are diminishing as they are given ever more media choices. They have more distractions than ever before. Against this scenario we find many conventional advertising agencies and marketing service companies struggling with the change. It is not that advertising does not work; it is more that with an over-proliferation of interruptive communications, combined with a fragmenting media environment, only the very best interruptive marketing can work when combined with huge spending on media.

Communities cannot be ignored

Communities have started to become self-aware, enlightened. They are testing the extent of their power. The early signs are that the power of communities is enormous and will completely overwhelm any opposing advertising and marketing communications. The only way to prevent communities from harming your brand, goods or service, is to engage them.

Communities are in many ways self-selecting. Businesses are waking up to

Tomi T Ahonen & Alan Moore

communities and the consumers' interests in becoming involved. Roger Adams of General Motors, for example, says: "The consumer wants to be in control and we want to put them in control."

2% of your customers are Alpha Users

For the rest of this decade at least, probably much longer, the *power of communities will continue to grow*. Communities of the future will be tremendously more powerful than the first ones emerging today. Bear that in mind as you plan your actions and you learn from your first attempts at engagement.

We can build it

Communities can be identified. Their leaders can be identified. Community behaviour has patterns. The patterns can be learned, they can be understood and exploited in win-win scenarios. A marketing organisation can become involved with communities and, if done intelligently, a brand's influence through its related communities will always be more potent than attempting to work around communities – or, worse, against them.

Communities can be influenced but a community will react with increasing hostility to traditional invasive mass media advertising. Communities require an intelligent dialogue with the brands, goods and services they are interested in.

At least initially over the next years there will be a vast difference between the most astute marketing organisations that will adjust to the new communities-based marketing environment and those that attempt to ignore the change. Thus early community engagement need not be a traumatic catastrophic reorganisation of all of the business. It is a competitive world. A leader in engagement marketing will need to keep an eye on the competition and ensure it is doing its engagement noticeably better than its competitors. The beauty of communities is that they are brutally honest and immediate in their evaluation and feedback. eBay's earliest message boards are testament to this. If you are better at engagement than your competitors your connected customers will know and openly acknowledge it.

Death of interruptive advertising

Up until now advertising has always relied on *interruption*. Whether travelling to work, reading their favourite newspaper, watching TV or just generally going about their daily business, consumers are constantly *interrupted* by advertising messages.

But the power of these *interruptive* messages is eroding simply because there are so many of them around us and they cost so much to do. More TV channels, more magazines, more billboards, more doordrops, more email spam means more and more ads; *interruptive* advertising is beginning to become as much of a headache for marketers as it is for the suffering consumer. Customers are increasingly retraining their brains to actively ignore all interruptions and especially those containing marketing messages.

B   ENTER ENGAGEMENT

What corporations need to do today is to acknowledge the new preferences of their audiences of interest, be they customers, suppliers, shareholder-owners etc. Corporations need to create the context, appreciate the mood of their audience, and to identify their passions and interests. Then corporations must build community structures to serve these interests. The most difficult part – but the one that early on will bring the biggest rewards, and later will have to be done simply to keep up with competition – is *engagement*. The brands must find methods to activate the communities and to build bi-directional communications.

Create new marketspaces

The spread of connectivity is redefining the distribution channels linking business with customers, suppliers and employees, and therefore the pace of innovation, digitalisation and convergence can be either life-threatening or life-enhancing. To lead, companies need to understand the opportunity to create new marketspace using combinations of digital platforms and new channels.

The changing of customers' habits and behaviours wrought by technology means the old ways just do not work anymore. The crisis of many businesses is the crisis of meaning. Leadership for brands and businesses will be through the creation and management of meaning. Brands have to co-create value and experience to deliver an added value, a "value plus" (value+) if you will, to customers. Why is that? Because our ideas of shopping, having relationships, being a parent, having a job etc are being modified from the old models of the past. A job is no longer for life, shopping can now be done far more easily on eBay, Amazon, or a host of other internet sites.

Invite the customer to participate

Companies must learn to move from interruption to inviting participation. For all marketing initiatives this no longer means communicating by *interruption*, but by *engagement*. Engagement marketing is about brands becoming part of the fabric of

Tomi T Ahonen & Alan Moore

peoples lives – enhancing life, not interrupting it. Put simply, it is about getting out of the ad break and understanding that marketing can become so much richer and more powerful than it is today, by understanding the Four Cs, by understanding that embedded value is vital for success. Forget what you have learned, because where you are going you are going to need very different skills.

With the explosion of new technologies – in particular digital TV, out of home TV, the internet and mobile phones – there is an ever increasing array of new tools with which marketers can attract their consumers with new types of engaging content. But do not think *engagement* is purely about lowest common denominator entertainment, far from it.

Some Engagement Marketing Tools include:

- **Entertainment, Info-tainment, Edu-tainment intiatives**
- **Information Service brands for edited choice**
- **Audience activation via SMS text messaging, IM Instant messaging etc**
- **Participation in discussion threads via blogs, chat etc**
- **Gaming including sponsored gaming and adver-games**
- **Real-time community information**
- **Previews offered to the community**
- **Embedded sponsorship rather than passive sponsorship**
- **Managing multiple communications channels, so that each target member is reached by his/her preferred channel**
- **Activate through influencers and "Alpha Users"**
- **Good will through volunteer evangelists**
- **Word-of-mouth, viral marketing and "buzz" to promote**

These tools are new and consequently not well defined at present. The list is by no means definitive but these tools have been found to function in building engagement. There is a growing list of real-life case-studies that are already showing how brands can "get out of the ad space" and into the fabric of customers' lives – giving them new and compelling multi-media content, services, or experiences that they enjoy, value and thus welcome. And why is all this of value? Because these properties as "assets" can be assessed by metrics such as revenue, share and margins. Interruptive communications, one could argue, is about "buying" revenue.

A philosophy of acceptance

The marketing communications philosophy needs to unlearn its prejudices and re-learn a new attitude. Only by embracing the philosophies of *accepting a plurality of opinions*, *promoting alternate views* and *not extinguishing dissenting views*, can an engagement marketing philosophy hold onto the trust of the community. The communications channel is no longer controlled only at the sending end. The receiving end is equally – if not more – in control. The community cannot be forced to join, they can only be enticed to join in a dialogue. To use a cooking analogy; use honey, not vinegar, to attract the crowd.

In practical terms, this means that your engaged community will also talk about your brand weaknesses. You cannot hide from those, they are reality, and the community knowledge will be based on truth, not your propaganda. Resist the temptation to attempt to control the dialogue. You cannot. You either maintain the trust of the community or you do not. To maintain the trust, you must allow dissenting opinions and even harsh criticism. Living in an open feedback environment is very different from one where you did not have to listen to active real-time feedback.

It is absolutely vital to bear in mind that digitally aware communities of the Connected Age will disappear from the sponsored sites and reorganise on rogue sites incredibly fast if the community feels the supporting brands are not being trustworthy.

Continuous improvement

Adam Singer, ex-CEO of Flextech Telewest and founder of the consultancy Cordelia, talks about broadcast, his speciality, of aggregating audiences over time. This turns conventional broadcast on its head, because traditional broadcasting was based on trying to get as many people to watch the same programme *at the same time.* We were struck by this thought and wondered, what if corporations could invite people in when they are ready to come and not at a predefined date and time. eBay's Senior Vice President of Technology was quoted in *eWeek* as saying:

> *We're in a continual improvement process, where our community tells us in real-time what's working and what isn't. We've got 114 million people working in our behalf, telling us what to do. We're the heart, the brain, the soul. The greatest thing about this place is that we get real-time feedback from everyone. That's why we have the community boards and our engineers go out and talk to the community.*

eWeek 30 August 2004

This is one of the powers of the community, and the gains from engagement. If you engage your community, bring their contributions to your brand, you will be

Tomi T Ahonen & Alan Moore

immensely more powerful. Your customers as a group are a powerful contributor to improvement ideas. Their ideas can easily be measured and tested, and often will bring more immediate results than some plans by the R&D department or outside design consultants.

Survival of the fastest

Communities continously self-improve. A good example comes from the professional experts community on the fixed internet, **Ecademy**. All Ecademy members were invited to submit digital photos to their personal biography pages. Then one of the members suggested it would help personalise the service if for every discussion stream, the system would automatically display the image of the Ecademy member. It would seem more real, when you saw the face of who was posting a comment. The idea was trialed and deployed in a week. The community loved the innovation and the sudden appearance of the face images acted as a catalyst for those who had not yet posted their image to do so.

Because they exist solely in a virtual space, and on digital platforms, communities can evolve at far faster speeds than any real business entity can ever hope to match. The contrast would be like comparing the acceleration ability of a bicycle to a jet fighter. For the first few seconds the bicycle might seem like it might stay in the contest of accelerating, but the jet can keep on accelerating long past the absolute top speed of the fastest conceivable bicycle. No business, brand, good or service can "outwit" or "defeat" a community. There can be no victory in a battle against a community, the only way to win is to join the community. Or more precisely to participate and engage *each* community that is relevant to the brand.

Ever wanted to design airplanes?

One of the most dramatic early engagement marketing examples comes from something as incredibly removed from "consumer influence" as aerospace design. Engineers at Boeing are as close to being literally rocket scientists as most professionals can hope to become. One would think that this community would be the most actively exclusive, eliminating "common man ideas" on behalf of the "better wisdom" of their advanced science and decades of training and knowhow. Yet Boeing has created the **Boeing Design Team** which has already attracted 120,000 participants, to advise Boeing on the design of their next new aircraft. This global resource aggregates its information. This is what the website says:

Would you like to help design the new Boeing Airplane?
Be a part of the first airplane design of the twenty-first century. Boeing is
transforming air travel with the 7E7 Dreamliner, an innovative airplane that
will be efficient, fast, environmentally friendly and unsurpassed in passenger
comfort. And, we'd like your help in making our dream airplane a reality.
Become part of the Boeing new airplane World Design Team – flyers and
aviation enthusiasts from around the world sharing the excitement of creating
the airplane of the future. We'll send you regular updates and newsletters that
will help you track the progress of the new Boeing airplane. You'll also have
the opportunity to tell us what you like and don't like about air travel today,
as well as the features you'd like to see in your dream airplane. Please join
the World Design Team and help us determine what features we should build
into your new airplane. Anyone 18 or older can join the World Design Team.
                                                 www.newairplane.com/en-US/WDT.html

Not only has the corporation created a context for people to want to engage in a
particular activity, it has done this to build better aircraft because in the end nobody
is as clever as everybody. If one of the world's largest engineering companies, with
decades of leadership in the extremely demanding field of aeronautics – keeping
metal planes in the air with hundreds of people in them, safely – can use common
people inputs for their design, surely so can any less-demanding industry.

Of course Boeing is not alone. We have seen many early examples. Such as the
Philips Streamium Café where owners of Philips's new WiFi TV sets and hifi systems tell Philips where they think Streamium is going and what Streamium should
be able to do. Current discussions involve everything from the time format on the
appliances' displays to "Support for Real Player RadioPass + Real Rhapsody". How
long before the discussion turns to the question of which *other* Philips appliances
should become WiFi enabled?

Then there is internet darling Google: Google's social networking site **Orkut**
includes two communities with over 1,000 subscribers: "What Should Google Do?"
and "What Should Orkut Do?". Google seeks the opinion of its own community,
its users, to find ways how to grow and evolve. These are all examples of engaging
customers. It can be done and, as Philips and Boeing illustrate, engagement is not
limited to "dot-com" companies.

Won't cost much

If you think of business-to-business communication tools of the 1980s and compare
them to today 20 years later, nobody will argue that email is dramatically faster,
more efficient and most of all cheaper at immense orders of magnitude than the pre-

Tomi T Ahonen & Alan Moore

vious ways of communication using regular mail, express delivery parcel services and fax. The cost of sending an official communication from a business to another business is a tiny fraction today of what it was 20 years ago.

We are now on the verge of a similar revolution in the costs of marketing. Up to now there was no viable and cost-effective means to identify individual user communities, isolate the influencing members of each such social network and engage those directly in proactive two-way communications. The best possible effects marketing could do was to attempt to target by viewer demographics of TV shows, readership demographics of print media etc, and through the cumbersome "personalisation" in junk mail and spam type email. These kinds of marketing communications cost literally *hundreds of billions* of dollars globally.

Alpha Users reach directly over half of your total customer base

Five years ago it would have been impossible to do otherwise. Today, we can identify our user communities. Many are already spontaneously forming on the fixed internet, on blogging sites, via mobile phone swarms, etc. What would have previously cost millions to run and taken months to generate using traditional marketing research methods can now in many cases be found with a simple Google search.

Plain grass-roots contacts

Some of the emerging examples are so simple and elegant. In the US, Canada, New Zealand and Australia, NAMM (National Association of Music Merchants) has embarked on what it terms "**Weekend Warriors**". Weekend Warriors appeals to lapsed musicians; Mums and Dads that used to play music when they were younger, etc.

Weekend Warriors is a grassroots market-building programme designed to get non-active musicians back into making music. The programme provides an ongoing activity that creates new long-term customers, rather than a one-time event to boost sales among existing customers. Weekend Warriors targets adults who for one reason or another have stopped playing music and now have significantly more disposable income to spend on their recreational interests.

Via its participating dealerships, NAMM puts people together by musical ability and capability (recruits the community). The dealership then provides rehearsal space and a mentor to coach them (supports the community space) to performance level of a song they all agree they like (builds loyalty and feeds passion). The Weekend Warriors perform and record their own music. The outcome is a great customer experience which is likely to lead those involved to decide to start playing again, to buy some equipment. The word of mouth will spread to other lapsed musicians.

The cost to the dealerships is minimal compared to any mass-market ad campaign. The campaign is brilliant in its simplicity. It is grass roots and local. By reconnecting these consumers with music products and the social interaction and fun of being in a rock band again, music products retailers can create loyal customers and steady revenue streams.

Activate with digital communication channels

We can activate, cultivate and motivate such communities through games, interactivity and feedback systems using new tools like SMS text messaging, IM Instant messaging, blogging and the new "MMS" multimedia or picture messaging. Receiving feedback through the most efficient digital communication channels is vast, rich and rapid.

For example, Vodafone Omnitel in Italy introduced the game of **show us your dream** via picture messaging. Any customer could snap a picture with a camera-phone of what that person's dream was and send it to Vodafone. Maybe a mountain bike, maybe a leather sofa, maybe a new music entertainment system, etc. Vodafone would show many of the more interesting entries and award the best dreams to those who sent them. The game had a limit of 15,000 Euros in value. This kind of campaign strikes at the heart of the community, activating early adopter-type of evangelist users to play with the new service, allowing the company to promote it and getting the *community active in sharing experiences* with it.

Because they are part of the real-time connected society, communities instinctively share experiences. Armed with members who are very capable information-hunters, communities will discover what works elsewhere. Whether by accident or design, communities will learn by association and copy what works elsewhere. The contagion effect of one successful community action in one part of the world will rapidly spread to the rest of the world.

C RECRUIT YOUR EVANGELISTS

Once you have found the major communities that are involved with your brand, the next stage is to establish the dialogue with them. You could try to talk to the whole group but group behaviour science has brought us a much more cost-efficient way. If you can identify those who influence any given group and establish a constructive dialogue with them, you have in fact harnessed the most potent evangelists your brand can ever hope to find.

Tomi T Ahonen & Alan Moore

2% are your influencers

As we saw in the Community chapter only last year the marketing world has discovered the Alpha User; the single key member in any community who is the most powerful influencer for that community, the ultimate candidate to become your evangelist. From 2004 these Alpha Users could be identified and now the first series of analysis has been done. About 2% of your potential customer base are Alpha Users. And those Alpha Users can reach anywhere from 52% to 86% of all of the community directly on one call from their phones, as reported by customer analytics specialist firm Xtract Ltd.

Never before was targeted marketing this precise. We can not only identify our communities by their communication patterns, we can identify the 2% which are the true influencers. By identify we mean that you can on some technologies actually know the name and other details of each of the 2% of the Alpha Users of that given community. Rather than attempt to flood the mass media channels where we hope our community's attention may lie, we can now spot the exact influencers and talk to them directly.

Any brand, goods or service that can spot the 2% of its most loyal and passionate supporters can do better than any marketing before. Spending millions in shotgun interruptive advertising mostly reaches audiences totally uninterested in your campaign, with the aim of hitting a few of the intended target audience. This is expensive, imprecise, inefficient and incomplete and slow. If the targeted engagement campaign is precisely aimed only for those 2% of the influencers and delivered on their media of choice, the success rate is incomparably better. This way brands can increase the marketing success in every possible measure. Better word of mouth, faster adoption, less complaints, faster revenues, more profits, better market share, less churn and more loyalty, more satisfaction, return business. Whatever the measure, shifting the spend from interruptive advertising to engagement marketing will bring immense rewards, *immediately and into the future.*

Many proxies for Alpha Users

As we saw, no other networks can truly spot Alpha Users as on all other network technologies there are too many potential multiple users on any given contact point such as a fixed wireline telephone or an internet computer etc. Only mobile operators are even in a position to accurately spot Alpha Users for any community. Note that mobile operators will be able to identify Alpha Users for most communities, not only those involved with telecoms services. Car owners, football fans, mountain bikers all use mobile phones and thus their communities can be identified.

We need to caution marketing managers from rushing to the nearest mobile operator to run an Alpha identification project. Most mobile operators are still learning the fundamentals of marketing and are mostly still involved in the basics of customer segmentation. Only selected pioneering operators are equipped to run Alpha User projects today and these tend to be the established ones in Scandinavia etc. This will change but since the very concept is technically less than two years old it may take years in many markets for the operators to achieve this ability.

The key for the mobile operators is to learn to understand their customers in a new way. No longer is it enough to identify segments of user types, now the real power is discovering what are the communities we interact with. As Jouko Ahvenainen, the Chairman of Xtract Ltd, says: "It is not enough for mobile operators to analyse individual customer's behaviour, they must now learn to isolate the social networks among the customer base and start to market to the most influential of the groups."

This does not mean that the Early Adopter, Communicator, Influencer, Evangelist etc type of profile is beyond current discovery. For very many products and services such groups can be more than adequately discovered using many proxy methods.

Bloggers are influencers

For example, today in 2005 any bloggers involved with the brand tend to be typical infuencers. So the first and fastest way for any brand, goods and service to get in touch with its most passionate brand evangelists is to find the related blog sites. You can do that today. You do not need to commission a lengthy market research project. Today! The active bloggers should be identified and an intelligent dialogue established with them.

Audi for example, jumped into blogging via sponsoring the jalopnik.com site dedicated to automobiles that amongst other things links to other car-related blogs. Audi's argument is that 85% of its buyers do research online. Jim Taubitz, online marketing manager for Audi, was asked about risk. He replied in an article on Business Week Online, saying: "There's always that risk, but that same risk exists in any other media outlet in which Audi advertises."

It is absolutely crucial to keep in mind the new marketing philosophy that is vital for winning the confidence and long-term trust of these people. The brand must allow for plurality of opinions, dissent and criticism. If these influencers feel they are being stifled or any so-called "marketing bullshit" is being thrust upon them, they will *turn on your brand* and become your *staunchest enemies*. Remember, anyone who is already blogging in 2005 is very familiar with the power of this communication technology, they can do much bigger damage to you than you can hope to try to recover with an advertising budget. Do not offend these early influencers. Listen to them and tread with the utmost caution and respect.

Tomi T Ahonen & Alan Moore

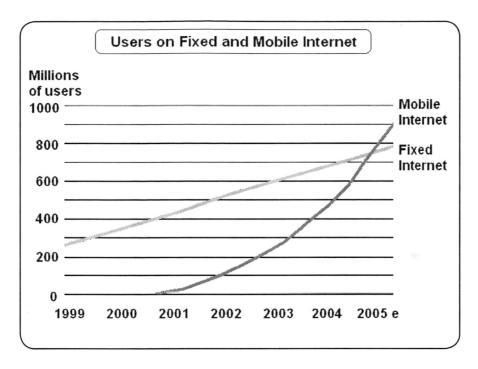

Users on Fixed and Mobile Internet

Millions of users

Mobile Internet

Fixed Internet

1000 — 800 — 600 — 400 — 200 — 0

1999   2000   2001   2002   2003   2004   2005 e

Fan club members are influencers

Many brands have formal or informal fan clubs of some kind. Pop music bands and movie stars and other such celebrities have very formal fan clubs but many brands have passionate user groups ranging from Harley Davidson motorcycle riders to VW Beetle owners, new Beetle and old, etc. Depending on the size of the fan clubs these may be much larger than the actual influencer type of personalities but many of the true Alpha Users are also part of the fan club. By harvesting eager communicators from fan clubs using such tools as games, feedback methods and searches for "beta testers" etc., the influencers can be identified.

Follow the Twins

We showed the example of the Hong Kong pop music duo **Twins**, who engaged their fans via the mobile phone. Twins released their own line of branded mobile phones, subscriptions, phone covers, ring tones, logos etc in 2002 and built vast fan activity around the services. Now music artists from rap artist Nelly to heavy hetal rockers Kiss have embraced this powerful way to connect with their fans. By selling mobile phones and subscriptions in their name, with pre-installed music, custom games, a fan letter, chat and special offers on upcoming music releases and concerts, musicians are laying their stake on the most powerful communication tool in the pockets of their fans.

Spotting the influencers and establishing a dialogue with them is hard work. In almost every industry today it requires considerable marketing effort; it is not just a matter of pressing a button on a database. But these influencers will have a *disproportionate* effect on the success of your goods, service or brand. And contacting them directly and engaging them will cost a tiny fraction of any mass-market advertising campaign. Most of all, after the dialogue has been established, influencers will maintain the dialogue with you, taking much of the responsibility of the communication activity. You do not have to "convince them" but rather *they will come to you*. In effect, you will be "preaching to the choir". These are your most passionate fans and if you engage them, they will become your evangelists and spread the word.

The biggest single difference between interruptive advertising and engagement marketing is that the target audience will *believe and trust the message* they receive through the influencers, while they would distrust that message coming directly from you.

85% of Audi buyers do research online

Find your most passionate fans

Most products and services have some truly dedicated, fanatical advocates. These may well do alone, on their own time and budget, better quality promotion work than the best professional agencies. Because they are so in love with your product. Consider George Masters, a regular school teacher, who loves his iPod so much he created a homemade ad for it. *Wired* magazine explains:

> *Masters' 60-second animated ad features flying iPods, pulsing hearts and swirling 70s psychedelia. It's set to the beat of "Tiny Machine" by 80s pop band the Darling Buds. Masters quietly posted the spot to his site a few weeks ago. It received moderate traffic until it was picked up by several blogs last week. In a matter of days, the ad has been watched more than 37,000 times and is making the rounds on blogs and email.*
>
> Wired December 13 2004

Tomi T Ahonen & Alan Moore

Such fans are more precious than gold. You should find them, recruit them to work with you, never try to "brainwash" them, but let them be themselves and use their own creativity and passion to promote your product or service. Find gentle but supportive means to promote them and their work. *Pay them* for their intellectual property, *at least as well* as you would reward a star-performing advertising agency. Celebrate this kind of passion – you will ignite *other such sleeping giants* from amidst your fan base.

D ENGAGEMENT IS INEVITABLE

We have already seen the emergence of the community. As we have proven this is a development which cannot be undone. Where before there was no way for specialist brand-oriented communities to form and act together, today they exist and are growing increasingly powerful. Uni-directional market communications will at best be ignored, at worst will ignite the community to revolt. As some competitors are already taking the steps to engage the brand-oriented communities, this strategy will be soon copied all over. The dawn of engagement marketing is now, the era of engagement marketing is inevitable.

Intellectually mature

Whether you are talking to the top 1% of income earners in the country or first-time mothers, engagement requires sophistication and maturity that is missing from mainstream marketing initiatives today. Mass-market advertising speaks to the lowest common denominator of any ad campaign. The campaign cannot be too sophisticated or demanding, as the mainstream audience member will not be able to concentrate or hold interest enough. Thus almost all mass-market ad campaigns are "dumb", talking to what seems like a stupid audience.

The potential evangelists for your brand mostly already know about you and your offering. They want to be treated as intelligent, influential and important customers. They want *intelligent* dialogue, not dumb advertising. Engagement is about creating win-win situations for the brand and its multiple stakeholders. For example, each company will have a satellite of stakeholders that surround it. These include employees, suppliers, outsourcing relationships, consultants, the media and customers. Understanding how to engage different stakeholders around a central philosophy, theme, idea or concept can deliver massively for any business.

E   A PROFESSION DISINTERMEDIATED

So far we have made the case that the very fundamentals of marketing and especially marketing communications will change. The change is total, comprehensive, absolute. The skills that today's professionals in marketing have tend to be poorly suited for the new world of engagement and specific skills now needed. The newly critical skills are completely different from what was listed on the job advertisements before. Most successful marketing professionals were not recruited based on these new attributes. What worked before is irrelevant to success in the future.

A revolution in marketing skills

What does it take to succeed in interruptive advertising? To be visible and heard, loud, eccentric, creative, brave, to crowd out the competition, gain the attention of the audience, even annoy. This breeds an arrogance of "we know what is best, we won the awards, we have the training, we have the track record". This means many rogue marketers break rules, live by their own rules, force their opinions upon others.

What does it take to succeed in engagement marketing? To be humble, to listen, to empathise, to care, to be innovative, to be flexible and adaptive, to *live by other people's standards and rules*. Subjecting one's own ego and ideas to the opinions and desires of the community: *"They know best"*. To repeatedly readjust the existing and "own" ideas to the feedback of the community. My idea was not perfect, of course it should be revised again and again until my contribution disappears.

These attributes are not diametrically opposed. However, the skills of most highly successful professionals involved in traditional marketing communications professionals – in advertising, PR and branding – are skills that do not assist in building community engagement. Scott Donaton made the point very clearly that new skills are needed when he wrote in *Advertising Age*:

> *That means recruiting talent with new skill sets and retraining existing work forces. It means redefining metrics around behaviour and engagement rather than distribution and impressions. It means reconfiguring organisations, redirecting spending and confronting the operational challenges of the marketing revolution. Make no mistake, it's nothing short of a revolution. Those who don't embrace it – and resistance to change remains disappointingly strong – will be crushed by it.*
>
> *Advertising Age* 21 October 2004

Tomi T Ahonen & Alan Moore

The revolution of engagement is built upon the power of the meritocracy of ideas, and the strategic combinations of different media to propel that idea into the world. It is about connecting large or small communities with engaging content to a commercial or social agenda. Rather than boiling everything down to a unique selling proposition, engagement marketing is able to create bigger ideas that emotionally engage its audience. Rather than focus on the single proposition that would result in a manufactured communication strategy, engagement marketing is built upon the fundamental notion of shared and co-created experience, something which interruptive communications cannot do.

Focus shift from individual to society

Underneath this transition is a shift in the focus of insight and knowhow. Up to now, marketing research focused on the preferences on the individuals. These preferences were analysed for patterns of behaviour and based on those customers were grouped into segments.

All of that is good and well. But now it is obvious that in the future our customers will form opinions and preferences based on what social communities think, want and prefer. This requires a shift in skills from analysing the individual (marketing pyschology) to understanding behaviour of communities (social anthropology and ethnography). Again, not mutually exclusive in the educational background and interests of marketing professionals, but a distinct shift in where noticeable performance gains can be achieved.

Most marketing managers and directors need at least to be retrained. Many will want to shift careers, where they will find that engagement marketing is not rewarding in the traditional sense as they have expected of their careers. But equally, a new generation of marketing professionals, especially those of Generation-C, will thrive and succeed in the new frontier of engagement marketing. The legends and careers of this generation will all be made through bold deployment of methods of engagement marketing.

New management tools and metrics

What is also needed in the new world of engagement marketing is a whole new range of training methods, case studies, management processes, measurements and metrics and, of course, incentives. For these we can only point the industry into the new direction and let creativity and innovation lead the way. Perhaps in a few years we will start to have best practices to share, discuss and evaluate. That, of course, will by necessity need to be another book...

Three shifts in the marketing paradigms

Linda Wolf, chairman and CEO of Leo Burnett Worldwide, offered her own assess-
ment of the paradigm shift (in marketing communications), which she says involves
exposure giving way to engagement, interruption giving way to permission and
broadcasting giving way to customisation. We do agree that these shifts are happening, but while customisation and permission are relevant trends, the true seismic
shift is to engagement. Customisation and permission can still be part of a controlled marketing communication that is mostly uni-directional, ignoring the community. But only engagement truly allows community influence. Thus we would
take Linda's thoughts a step further and say exposure, interruption and broadcasting
all give way to engagement. And engagement by definition will include permission
and customisation.

There are many early examples of success when brands engage their communities. Shoe designer John Fluevog has a section on his site entitled **Open Source
Footwear** to invite his customers to submit ideas for shoe design. Winning designs
are put into production. The Mini forum **MINI2** is an independent site for the new
Mini car. The visitors to the Mini forum have created the busiest Mini discussion
area on the internet. The **Lonely Planet Thorn Tree** is an an online bulletin board
with over 5,000 posts a day. Lonely Planet uses users' feedback to constantly fine-
tune their content.

You will be assimilated

So what are you going to do as a business or a brand? Return to your ad agency,
spend millions more to run out your 30-second TV commercials at the next big
sports championship and hope for the best? The community power is inevitable and
companies that ignore communities will wither and disappear from the free marketplace, to be taken over by the new players who understand the relevance of this
new customer power. Just like those engineering companies that embraced electricity-based dispersed machinery over the steam-engine-based centralised machinery
system.

Or are you going to roll your sleeves and really think about how you are going
to engage your customers and stakeholders, how you are going to invite customers
to join to co-create value, facilitate greater more valuable experiences, become the
conduit to communities who are passionate about whatever floats their boat.

And celebrate the fact that businesses, marketing, creativity, technology and
people can come together in ways today which were not imaginable five years ago.
Or is that too hard for you to think about as you watch the minnows eat the big fish,
as they understand the new dynamics of communities engagement and business

Tomi T Ahonen & Alan Moore

in the 21st century. Engagement marketing will be the creative leap of the human imagination that will drive sales and business success in the 21st century.

Final thoughts

In a digitally connected world the old ways of advertising, branding and marketing do not work. Communities from gamers to bloggers to the youth of Generation-C are discovering their power. They will counter any coercive marketing. So ask yourself this question, does my business and marketing strategy rely on spending large sums of money interrupting consumers with commercial messages? Could I spend far less money – and yet achieve greater results – by engaging rather than interrupting? Could engagement deliver stronger customer relationships, greater advocacy and deeper loyalty? Am I siloed in my silo?

Remember, the 21st century consumer is too busy, and faces too many choices, to respond to conventional marketing tactics. It is time to abandon interruptive advertising and embrace engagement marketing. It requires a total revision of how marketing is conducted and very likely needs new holistic skills. There is a broader definition of creativity that includes and understands the business needs and objectives, strategy and cross-platform media selection. Winners at the end of this decade will be companies that mastered engagement early. And as a guide for all those instances when you have a colleague whose resolve is faltering, use our book as your principle. Do not act against the interests of communities, as "communities dominate brands".

Case Study 13

Orange Bicycles

A most interesting development happened in the Netherlands. It is a highly advanced Western country, but because it is relatively small in size and extremely flat in topography, it also has a remarkable bicycle population – more bikes than people actually – and bicycle routes are everywhere.

Also typical of Northern European cultures, the Dutch have a relatively high proportion of younger people who support "green" values: nature, conservation, recycling etc.

Orange the mobile phone network decided to launch a promotion for bicycle users, as a hands-free mobile phone kit, so bikers could safely talk

---

on the phone while holding both hands on the handlebars of the bicycle. Perhaps by accident or design, Orange also included a gimmick that got lots of publicity and headlines. It included a mobile phone recharger that ran on peddling power; as the biker moved, the mobile phone could be recharged.

To top it off, for a two-year contract, Orange threw in the phone, hands-free kit, recharger and new bicycle – all, of course, branded with the little Orange square logo.

For most who heard this story, it seemed like a quaint gimmicky marketing ploy. Yes, but if everybody in Holland already has a bike anyway, how many could this campaign really attract?

The amazing thing was that for those with a "green" value system, suddenly these clearly labelled Orange bikes became instantly visible, loud symbols promoting their commitment to ecological values. Of course I want one of those bikes, I want *everybody* to use peddling power to recharge their phones, rather than wasting natural resources to generate that electricity. That kind of philosophy had the bikes and Orange phone bundles moving at much higher than anticipated rates.

It is worth pointing out, that anyone of phone-using age, even if "green" by philosophy, will understand that in the big picture, the total amount of electricity wasted by recharging a mobile phone from the national electrical grid is truly insignificant in the overall scheme of things.

But it is the principle, both in activism – I want to lead by example, no matter how small the gesture, it still helps – and in promoting the philosophy of eco-friendly values. I want everybody to see this bike and know they too can do this.

The key point about bicycles and mobile phone subscriptions is that on the surface of it these two have nothing in common. Yet Orange has tapped into a distinct community and activated it to identify with Orange, to promote the community and steer the group to select the Orange network as their communication provider of choice.

By discovering a pent-up demand for the ecologically responsible Dutch consumers to show their colours and profess their value systems, Orange was able to connect with a community at its values. This is the very essense of engagement marketing.

Tomi T Ahonen & Alan Moore

"Don't be afraid to take a big step if one is indicated.
You can't cross a chasm in two small jumps."
David Lloyd George

XV
What Next?
Time to go to work

In our book we have shown how all the major trends in digitalisation, convergence, disruption etc are drastically altering our society and the very core of business and industry. We have shown the emergence of new types of customers, a whole new Generation-C, and the power of the community. We have illustrated community examples from blogging to digital gaming and swarms activated by mobile phone. We have also shown how advertising and branding are diminishing in their efficiency. Finally we propose our hypothesis that communities dominate brands, and we provide the way forward in the form of engagement marketing.

Which community wins

We have devoted a chapter each to three types of new communities. We had one on Gen-C, the mobile phone "community" generation, another on blogging and bloggers, and a third on virtual worlds and their stars and influencers. We have also talked about the evangelists and Alpha Users. Which community is the most relevant?

That is really not the point. The point is that your brand will interact with communities – plural. Many communities. Very likely there is a blogging community already, perhaps several, that have an influence on your brand. There may be a fan club or other dedicated and more formal groups. Certainly, no matter what, there will be spontaneous communities that emerge that communicate with the mobile phone. And all distinct communities will have one Alpha User (each). And in most cases it is possible to seek evangelists to promote your story, your success, your brand and its message. Ideally the Alpha User could become an evangelist, but evangelists are likely to be found more often from among the interested community in general and may be far removed from the Alpha User.

We do not want to say one community is more important than another, but rather, like we say in the title of the book, it is *communities* – plural – that dominate brands. You must discover the communities that are most relevant to you and then try to isolate the most influential members of those communities to channel your marketing communications.

Certainly currently a small part of the total population is the blogger community. At four million users they are a mere 0.5% of fixed internet users. However, bloggers are naturally very opinionated, and have considerable experience using digital communication methods to spread their word. They are extremely widely followed and others rely on bloggers as those who know. These are remarkably powerful and potent as a group.

At the other extreme, way larger than any internet or email community, is the user base of mobile phones. As we said, with the cellular phone population at over 1.6bn at the end of 2004, nearly 30% of the human population can be reached via mobile phone. Practically the whole economically viable portion of mankind can be reached by mobile phone. And the vast majority of that population already uses SMS text messaging. So if you think of the biggest community, invariably that will be on mobile phones.

Tomi T Ahonen & Alan Moore

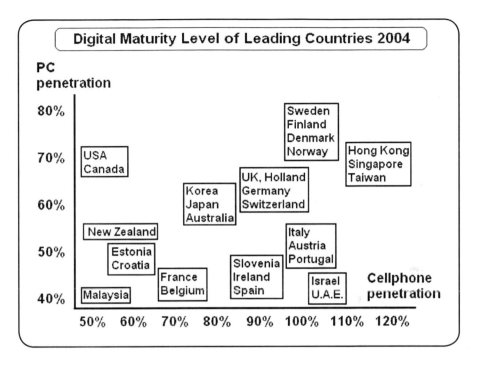

Digital Maturity Level of Leading Countries 2004

PC penetration

(Y-axis: 80%, 70%, 60%, 50%, 40%)

Sweden / Finland / Denmark / Norway

Hong Kong / Singapore / Taiwan

USA / Canada

UK, Holland / Germany / Switzerland

Korea / Japan / Australia

New Zealand

Estonia / Croatia

Italy / Austria / Portugal

Slovenia / Ireland / Spain

France / Belgium

Israel / U.A.E.

Malaysia

Cellphone penetration

(X-axis: 50% 60% 70% 80% 90% 100% 110% 120%)

Can I see the future?

We can see the future. It is happening in some countries already. If you want to see where broadband internet, 3G mobile telecoms, mobile blogging and MMOG virtual worlds are the most advanced, make a pilgrimage every year to South Korea. They are a year ahead of Japan on these fronts, and many years ahead of the rest of the world.

If you want to see what blogging and the business on the fixed internet is like in the future, visit the USA. To see the future of videogaming, electronics, mobile commerce and convergence, the obvious country where that future already exists is Japan. If you want to see how society changes with the adoption of the mobile phone, the leading country is still Finland by a wide margin, because they got to that situation first. Finland is no longer the country with the most advanced mobile technology, but there grandparents send SMS text messages on a regular basis to their 10-year-old grandkids and nobody thinks twice about it.

Very useful countries also to keep a close eye on with mobile phone related phenomena are Israel, Hong Kong, Singapore, Italy, Norway, Denmark, the UK, Austria and Portugal. On the internet remember also Canada and Sweden.

We had chapters on blogging, advertising and virtual economies. You might have expected us to cover TV, the internet and music, and we did. But we have listed examples from so varied industries as airlines, sports, movies, automobiles, politics, soft drinks, retail, libraries, art, education, restaurants, wineries, cosmetics, fashion, lockmaking and shoemaking. Communities are simultaneously appearing everywhere, globally, in all walks of business.

We also gave 13 real case studies of how communities dominate. We gave dozens more examples of real instances of businesses embracing communities. We presented Engagement Marketing as the way forward and showed solid theoretical proofs for Reachability, Generation-C, the Four Cs, and the new Communication Model. But you do not have to accept the theories. We listed real companies doing real engagement marketing, successfully, already today. Not just companies in the digital economy like eBay, Google, Ecademy, or companies close to it like Apple, Nokia, Sony, Vodafone and Orange. We gave examples from many of the globally leading brands that are not primarily known for contributions in the digital area. We showed engagement marketing by such stalwarts as Coca-Cola, Boeing, Ford, Audi, Guinness, Thomas Cook, Adidas. We also gave many examples of the dangers of ignoring community power, from the Kryptonite case study to Nokia N-Gage, Hutchison Three, Verizon, and of Hollywood movies flopping due to bad "text-of-mouth". Your company cannot afford to anger the community. Always, always the community will dominate the brand.

Engage to dominate

If 20th century marketing was about interruption, then 21st century marketing will be about Engagement. The previous century was about brand control: you will think what we want you to think. This new century is about humility with empowered customers. Engagement shifts the control to the communities, and brands become servants to communities, seeking their voluntary involvement.

Hong Kong cellphone penetration 120%

Every brand will be facing communities. These communities communicate in two dimensions, to and from the brand and *amidst themselves*. They cannot be stopped or coralled. Most importantly, communities are self-learning, thus they improve themselves continuously.

The communities are autonomous. They are digitally connected and will be faster, more powerful and more nimble than any marketing communication department,

Tomi T Ahonen & Alan Moore

unit or agency can hope to be. If challenged, the communities will rise against the brands. However, communities can be harnessed and they can be identified. For communities there are rules of behaviour and all communities are strongly influenced by a few key members. If recruited to become evangelists, these key decision-makers will help the community work with you, even for you.

The company and brand must honestly recruit the good will of the community. The brand must approach the community with humility, openness and tolerance. The brand must entice the community to allow the brand to work with it; a community cannot be captured or coerced.

The method to achieve community cooperation is engagement. The next 10 years will see the emergence of engagement marketing which will graduate marketing professionals from the interruptive, one-way communications of the past, to the intelligent, caring and involving dialogue of the future. Seeking voluntary involvement from the customer communities – that is the heart of engagement. Marketing will never be the same. When done sincerely and thoroughly, engagement marketing addresses the greatest needs and concerns of your customers. Then you will fulfill what Hugo Paulson intended when he said: "Good firms worry about competition. Great firms worry about clients."

"Is there another word for synonym?"

George Carlin

Abbreviations

2G	Second Generation (current digital) mobile telephony, first launched 1991
2.5G	Second Generation (current digital) mobile telephony enhanced beyond 2G but that are not 3G, first launched 1999
3G	Third Generation (new generation) mobile telephony, first launched 2001
3.5G	Third Generation (new generation) mobile telephony enhanced beyond 3G but that are not 4G, expected to be launched 2005/2006
4Cs	Four Cs – Commerce, Culture, Community and Connectivity
4G	Fourth Generation (next generation) mobile telephony, also known as "Systems Beyond IMT 2000" expected to be launched 2012
5Ms	Five Ms – Movement, Moment, Me, Money and Machines
802.11	IEEE standard for wireless connectivity, see W-LAN and WiFi
802.16	IEEE standard for broadband wireless, see WiMax
802.20	IEEE standard for broadband wireless
A&R	Artist Representation
ABC	American Broadcasting Company
ADSL	Asynchronous Digital Subscriber Line
AOL	America On-Line
ATM	Automated Teller Machine
B2B	Business to Business
B2C	Business to Consumer
BBC	British Broadcasting Corporation
BBS	Bulletin Board System
bcc	blind carbon copy
Blog	weB log
BT	British Telecom
CAN	Closed Audience Network
CBS	Colombia Broadcasting Service
cc	carbon copy
CD	Compact Disc
CEO	Chief Executive Officer
CMO	Chief Marketing Officer
COO	Chief Operating Officer
CRM	Customer Relationship Management
DIY	Do It Yourself
DJ	Disc Jockey
DR	Direct Response
DVD	Digital Video Disc
EA	Entertainment Arts
ERP	Enterprise Resource Planning

FT	Financial Times
HBO	Home Box Office
GDP	Gross Domestic Product
Gen-C	Generation-C (Community)
GIGO	Garbage In Garbage Out
IM	Instant Messaging
IMC	Integrated Marketing Communication
IP	internet Protocol, also Intellectual Property
IPv6	internet Protocol version 6
ISDN	Integrated Services Digital Number
ISP	internet Service Provider
IT	Information Technology
ITC	Independent Television Commission
LP	Long Play record
M&S	Marks & Spencer
MIT	Massachussetts Institute of Technology
Moblogging	Mobile web logging
MMOG	Massively Multiplayer Online Game
MMS	Multimedia Messaging Service
MP3	MPEG-2 Layer 3 (Motion Picture Experts Group)
MTV	Music TV
MVNO	Mobile Virtual Network Operator
NAMM	National Association of Music Merchants
NBC	National Broadcasting Company
P&G	Procter & Gamble
P&L	Profit & Loss
P2P	Person to Person
PBS	Public Broadcasting Service
PC	Personal Computer
PDA	Personal Digital Assistant
PR	Public Relations
PVR	Personal Video Recorder
RCA	Radio Corporation of America
REM	Rapid Eye Movement
RFID	Radio Frequency IDentification
RSS	Really Simple Syndication
RTS	Royal Television Society
SIM	Subscriber Identity Module
SMS	Short Message Service
SUV	Sports Utility Vehicle
TCP/IP	Transmission Control Protocol/internet Protocol
TIM	Telecom Italia Mobile
UKP	United Kingdom Pounds
URL	Uniform Resource Locator
USB	Universal Serial Bus
VCR	Video Cassetter Recorder
vlogging	Video Logging
VOD	Video On Demand

WAP	Wireless Application Protocol
WiFi	Wireless Fidelity (see also 802.11 or W-LAN)
WiMax	Worldwide Interoperability for Microwave Access (see also 802.16)
W-LAN	Wireless Local Area Network (see also WiFi and 802.11)
WWW	WorldWide Web
xDSL	(various versions of) Digital Subscriber Line

Tomi T Ahonen & Alan Moore

"Never judge a book by its movie."

J.W. Eagan

Bibliography

Ahonen Tomi. m-Profits: Making Money from 3G, Wiley, 2002, 360 pp

Ahonen Tomi, Barrett Joe. Services for UMTS: Creating Killer Applications in 3G, Wiley, 2002, 373 pp

Ahonen Tomi, Kasper Timo, Melkko Sara. 3G Marketing: Communities and Strategic Partnerships, Wiley, 2004, 333 pp

Bayler Michael, Stoughton David. Promiscuous Customers, Capstone, 2001, 256 pp

Beck John, Wade Mitchell. Got Game, Harvard Business School Press, 2004, 208 pp

Christiansen Clayton. The Innovator's Dilemma, Harper Business, 2003, 320 pp

Curtis Mark. Distraction, Futuretext London 2005, 222 pp

Cohen Adam. The Perfect Store. Inside eBay Piatkus 2002, 332 pp

Evans Phillip, Wurster Thomas. Blown to Bits, Harvard Business School Press, 1999, 261 pp

Florida, Richard. The Rise of the Creative Class and How it's Transforming Work, Leisure, Community and Everyday Life, Basic Books, 2002, 404 pp

Foster Richard, Kaplan Sarah. Creative Destruction: Why companies that are built to last underperform the market, Currency, 2001, 384 pp

Frank Thomas. One Market Under God, Anchor, 2001, 464 pp

Frengle Nick. i-Mode, A Primer, M&T Books, 2002, 485 pp

Gladwell Malcolm. The Tipping Point: How little things can make a big difference, Back Bay Books, 2002, 304 pp

Golding Paul. Next Generation Wireless Applications, Wiley, 2004, 588 pp

Grant John. After Image. Mind Altering Marketing, Profile, 2002, 270 pp

Hannula Ilkka, Linturi Risto. 100 Phenomena, Yritysmikrot 1998, 212 pp

Hughes Thomas P. Human Built World, University of Chicago Press, 2004, 240 pp

Jaokar Ajit, Fish Tony. Open Gardens: Innovator's Guide to the Mobile Industry, Futuretext, 2004, 176 pp

Klein Naomi. No Logo: No Space No Choice No Jobs, Picador, 2000, 528 pp

Kopomaa, Timo. City in your Pocket, the birth of the information society, Helsinki: Gaudeamus, 2000, 143 pp

Mau Bruce. Life Style, Phaidon, 2000, 626 pp

May Paul. Mobile Commerce, Cambridge University Press, 2001, 302 pp

May Paul. The Business of E-Commerce, Cambridge University Press, 2000, 288 pp

McLelland Stephen. Ultimate Telecom Futures, Horizon House, 2002, 232 pp

Mitchell Alan. Right Side Up: Building Brands in the Age of the Organised Customer, Harper Collins 2002, 256 pp

Mitchell Alan, Bauer W. Andreas, Hausruckinger. The New Bottom Line. Bridging the value gaps that are undermining your business, Capstone 2003, 253 pp

Monbiot George. Captive State, Pan, 2000, 430 pp

Moore, Geoffrey. Crossing the Chasm, revised edition, Capstone Publishing, 2002, 256 pp

Moore, Geoffrey. Inside the Tornado, Capstone Publishing, 1999, 272 pp

Morgan Adam. Eating the Big Fish: How challenger brands can compete against brand leaders, 1999, 304 pp

Pachter Marc, Landry Charles. Culture at the Crossroads, Comedia 2001

Peppers Don, Rogers Martha. One to One Future, Currency, 1996, 464 pp

Polhemus Ted. Style Surfing, Thames & Hudson, 1996, 144 pp

Raymond Martin. The Tomorrow People, Financial Times Management, 2003, 279 pp

Rheingold Howard. Smart Mobs: The next social revolution, Basic, 2002, 288 pp

Rifkin Jeremy. Age of Access, Tarcher, 2001, 320 pp

Rogers Everett. Communication of Innovations, Free Press, 1971, 476 pp

Searls Doc, Weinberger David. Cluetrain Manifesto: End of business as usual, Perseus, 2001, 190 pp

Stiglitz Joseph. Globalization and its Discontents, W.W. Norton, 2003, 304 pp

Willmott Michael, William Nelson. Complicated Lives Sophisticated Consumers; intricate lifestyles simple solutions, Wiley, 2003, 260 pp

"In a connected age, sharing information is power."
Tomi T. Ahonen

Recommended Websites
(In semi-random order)

Adage
www.adage.com

American Association of National Advertisers
www.ana.net

American Marketing Association
www.marketingpower.com

The Institute of Practitioners in Advertising
www.ipa.co.uk

Marketing Society UK
www.marketing-society.org.uk

World Association of Newspapers
www.wan-press.org

Mobile Data Association   **MDA**
www.mda-mobiledata.org

Mobile Computer Users Group   **MCUG**
www.mcug.org.uk

SMS Association   **160Characters**
www.160characters.org

Ethnograhic research and insight   **Everyday Lives**
www.edlglobal.net

Building Challenger Brands   **Eatbigfish**
www.eatbigfish.com

Customer analytics   **Xtract**
www.xtract.info

Mobile/3G news and data   **the3Gportal.com**
www.the3gportal.com

User Interfaces **Fjord**
www.fjord.co.uk

Engagement marketing, Marketing strategy **SMLXL**
www.smlxtralarge.com

Qualitative research **2cv**
www.2cv.co.uk

University short courses **Oxford University**
www.conted.ox.ac.uk

Writing guru **Ann Wylie**
www.wyliecomm.com

Mobile consultancy **TomiAhonen Consulting**
www.tomiahonen.com

Executive coaching **Marcia Reynolds**
www.covisioning.com

Executive seminars and research **Frost & Sullivan**
www.frost.com

Interactive Marketing Communications **Lateral**
www.dmc.co.uk

Media training and consulting **HBL Media**
www.hblmedia.com

Strategy Consultancy **Decipher**
www.decipher.co.uk

Strategic Leadership and Organisation **Hilderbrand Hamill**
www.hildebrandhamill.com

Corporate mobile solutions **Verista**
www.verista.com

Viral marketing **Digital Media Communications**
www.dmc.co.uk

And best business humour **Dilbert**
www.dilbert.com

Tomi T Ahonen & Alan Moore

"For every action, there is an equal and opposite criticism."
Steven Wright

Recommended Blogsites

Bag and Baggage	http://bgbg.blogspot.com/
Blog for America	http://www.blogforamerica.com/
Bloggerme	http://www.bloggerme.co.uk/
the Big Blog Company	www.thebigblogcompany.net
Complexity, Innovation and Knowledge	http://euromed.blogs.com/baets/
Cinecultist	http://www.cinecultist.com/
Couchpundit	http://babelogue.citypages.com:8080/amadzine/
Defense Tech	http://www.defensetech.org/
Doc Searls' blog	http://doc.weblogs.com/
Gary Hart's Blog	http://www.garyhartnews.com/hart/
Gigaom	http://gigaom.com/
Guardian News Blog	http://blogs.guardian.co.uk/news/
Guardian Blog online	http://blogs.guardian.co.uk/online/
Indymedia	http://indymedia.org
Joho the blog	http://www.hyperorg.com/blogger/
Living Without Microsoft	http://www.livingwithoutmicrosoft.org/
Lessig blog	http://www.changethis.com/
MBA League of Bloggers	http://mbaleague.blogspot.com/

Overstated	http://overstated.net/
Plastic	http://www.plastic.com/
Poynter online	http://www.poynter.org/
Radio Free Blogistan	http://radiofreeblogistan.com/

Commercial Blogs

800 CEO Read	http://www.800ceoread.com/blog/
Buzz Machine	http://www.buzzmachine.com/
Fast Company Magazine	http://blog.fastcompany.com/
Jonathan Schwartz (COO Sun Microsystems)	http://blogs.sun.com/jonathan
Jupiter Research	http://weblogs.jupiterresearch.com/
Hewlett Packard	http://devresource.hp.com/blogs/index.jsp
General Motors	http://smallblock.gmblogs.com/
Online Business Networks	http://www.onlinebusinessnetworks.com/blog/
Social Customer Manifesto	http://socialcustomer.typepad.com/
Tom Peters	http://www.tompeters.com/

Marketing, Advertising and PR

Adbusters	http://adbusters.org/home/
Adrants	http://www.adrants.com/
Ad Freak	http://adweek.blogs.com/
Association of National American Advertising	http://ana.blogs.com/liodice/
Boing Boing	http://www.boingboing.net/
BL Ochman	http://www.whatsnextblog.com/

Tomi T Ahonen & Alan Moore

Brand Central Station	http://brandcentralstation.blogspot.com/
Change this	http://www.changethis.com/
Chen PR	http://www.chenpr.com/index.php
Fusion Brand	http://fusionbrand.blogs.com/fusionbrand/
Influx Insights	http://www.influx.bsands.com/
Johnnie Moore weblog	http://www.johnniemoore.com/blog/
Kraneland	http://www.kraneland.com/
Marketing Wonk	http://www.marketingwonk.com/
Media Insider	http://mediainsider.prnewswire.com/blog
Modern Marketing	http://www.collaboratemarketing.com/
Moores Lore	http://www.corantc.com
Pop PR	http://pop-pr.blogspot.com/
PR Communications	http://pr.typepad.com/pr_communications/
PSFK Trend watching	http://www.psfk.com/
Seth Godin	http://sethgodin.typepad.com/
SMLXL	http://www.smlxtralarge.com/
Spin Bunny	http://spin_bunny.typepad.com/spin_bunny/
The Good Seed	http://goodseed.blogspot.com/
The View from Object Towers	http://www.bloglines.com/blog/andismit
Urban Intelligence	http://www.urbanadvertising.com/intelligence/
Z+partners trends	http://www.zpluspartners.com/zblog/

Political and Economic Blogs

The Angry Economist	http://angry-economist.russnelson.com/

Big Blunkett	http://big-blunkett.blogspot.com/
Global Growth	http://www.global-growth.org/
Global Trade Watch	http://citizen.org/trade
The Globalisation Institute	http://www.globalizationinstitute.org/blog/
The EZLN	http://ezln.org
New Economics Foundation	http://neweconomics.org
Privacy Digest	http://privacydigest.com/
Reclaim Democracy	http://reclaimdemocracy.org/
Samizdata	http://www.samizdata.net/blog/
Vigilant TV	http://vigilant.tv/
White Rose	http://whiterose.samizdata.net/

Index

Tomi T Ahonen & Alan Moore

About the Authors

Tomi T Ahonen is an independent consultant based in London and considered the global guru on the business of next generation mobile telecoms, so-called 3G and 4G. He authored the three pioneering books on the business, services and marketing of next generation mobile, each a bestseller. He lectures at Oxford University on 3G telecoms. Tomi has delivered keynote addresses on six continents and been quoted in over 120 press stories. Tomi's client list reads like the who's who of 3G, starting with Ericsson, Orange, Nokia, NTT DoComo, Siemens, Teliasonera and Vodafone. Tomi has also provided consultancy to non-telecoms customers including Aller Group, Bank of Finland, DHL, Economist Group, HSBC, Kemira, Pohjola, United Nations Security Council, etc. Tomi was earlier employed by Nokia as Head of 3G Consulting and end-user 3G Research Centre; at Elisa Group where he created the world's first fixed-mobile service bundle, and set the world record for taking market share from the incumbent;  and at Manhattan internet provider, OCSNY. Tomi holds an MBA from St John's University NY and a bachelor's in marketing from Clarion University. His books are *m-Profits*, *3G Marketing* (with Timo Kasper and Sara Melkko) and *Services for UMTS* (with Joe Barrett). For more see www.tomiahonen.com

Alan Moore is the CEO of SMLXL (Small Medium Large Xtralarge), the marketing specialist firm based in Cambridge and London UK. Alan has 16 years' experience as a creative brand strategist, representing global brands at leading international marketing agencies including: Publicis London, DDB Needham Vienna, Hasan & Partners Finland, HHCL & Partners in London and Lowe & Partners Worldwide, Stockholm. Alan's notable projects include the brand strategy and integrated communications program for a Pan-Nordic 3G mobile service; Saab's global brand communication strategy; H&M's store-opening strategies in the US; several projects for Coca-Cola against considerable business challenges. His company has worked extensively in the areas of; news media, broadcast, mobile telecoms, and fast moving consumer goods. Alan's company is increasingly rec-  ognised as the most forward-thinking in how innovative marketing strategy can deliver significant business success for its clients. Alan delivers speeches and lectures on marketing, brand strategy and advertising in London, the Nordics and the US. Published in the Financial Times, Market Leader – the official journal of the Marketing Society UK – and by the Magnus University Business School India. Alan released research in 2003 "From interruption to Engagement. New Models of Marketing Communication". Alan writes a daily blog at www. smlxtralarge.com.

Tomi T Ahonen & Alan Moore

Other books by Tomi T Ahonen:

M-Profits: Making Money from 3G Services
By Tomi T Ahonen (360 pages, hardcover, John Wiley & Sons, 2002)
ISBN 0-470-84775-1

World's first business book on next generation wireless became world's bestselling 3G book October and December 2003. Covers revenues, revenue sharing, pricing, profits, mobile services. m-Profits includes 170 service ideas including 50 real services in use around the world. Written with a clear money focus, m-Profits includes mobile industry issues as Money Migration, Hockey Sticks, and the 5 Ms theory. The book covers service creation, revenue sharing, content partnerships, telecoms economics, contrasts major wireless technologies.

"Only book to give comprehensive view of the issues of marketing and revenue."
Sophie Ghnassia, France Telecom.
"Good read for industry professionals, operators, bankers and analysts."
Voytek Siewierski, NTT DoCoMo

3G Markting: Communities and Strategic Partnerships
By Tomi T Ahonen, Timo Kasper and Sara Melkko (333 pages, hardcover, John Wiley & Sons, 2004)
ISBN 0-470 -85100-7

World's first book on marketing for next generation mobile, and only book on winning in marketshare wars, became world's bestselling book on telecoms in October 2004. Covered all major issues of marketing including promotion, pricing, sales, branding, distribution channel, and service creation and management, with a telecoms focus including handsets, subsidies, portals, billing. Introduces Alpha Users, Reachability, Murfing, Omega customers, and Reachability.

"Insightful look into how wireless carriers capitalize customer data."
Jan-Anders Dalenstam, Ericsson.
"Extensive menu of marketing techniques introduced."
Mike Short, O2.

Services for UMTS: Creating Killer Applications in 3G
Edited by Tomi T Ahonen and Joe Barrett (373 pages, hardcover, John Wiley & Sons, 2002)
ISBN 0471 485500

World's first book on 3G services was also the world's bestselling 3G book in October 2002. Covers 212 service ideas with lots of illustrations, statistics, charts and forecasts. Written by 14 leading 3G experts, for the non-technical reader. Includes the 5 Ms theory, service creation, content partnerships, revenue sharing, marketing and competition in 3G. Covers all major service groupings such as SMS, MMS, m-commerce, video, music, gaming, mobile advertising, infotainment, B2B, B2C, B2E, etc etc

"Significant revenue opportunities to bring value to mobile operators."
Dr Stanley Chia, Vodafone.
"Explains some of the compelling services the industry will be able to deploy."
Jeff Lawrence Intel

Other books by Futuretext:

OpenGardens : The innovator's guide to the Mobile data industry By Ajit Jaokar and Tony Fish

OpenGardens is all about creating and marketing innovative mobile data applications. Specifically, it is about how innovative companies can create and deploy new services through the mobile operators. It covers strategy, technology, partnership models and marketing strategies for new services launched in partnership with the operators.

OpenGardens is a book for the innovator – ie, the person with an idea who wants to create a commercially successful service within the mobile data industry. While the mobile data industry holds considerable promise in future, the existing ecosystem is challenging for the 'grassroots entrepreneur'. This book acts as a guide by offering a two-stage roadmap. Firstly – how to work within the existing ecosystem and then how to prepare for a more complex ecosystem of the future. We believe that without an 'innovative component', new services will not succeed in this industry (especially when they are not backed by strong brands, extensive funding etc). Thus, innovation is necessary – both for the new entrant but also for the industry as a whole to thrive. Further, we believe that opportunities exist 'on the fringe' by combining one or more elements to create a new service. Hence, the book takes a holistic view and acts as a catalyst and mentor to innovators. It prepares them to exploit opportunities in an industry estimated to earn a trillion dollars ($1,000 billion) in revenues worldwide by 2010.

You can buy OpenGardens at www.opengardens.net

Distraction by Mark Curtis

Summary

Only 10 years ago we had hardly heard of the internet and were only just starting to use mobile phones. Now they are part of everyday life, embedded in what we do. It's time to look at the effect these new technologies are having on us. It is not all positive. We are distracted by their potential to summon us. All kinds of behaviour are changing as a result, and individuals, families and businesses need to work out how to handle this, or we risk a social crash. This book gives the evidence, discusses what we might keep, what lose and what to build which is new.

The book has two halves: in part one – The Social Price of New Technology – chapters one to seven examine the impact of new communications on society. In the second half – The Social Potential of New Technology – it explores what opportunities we can grasp to make our lives better.

We start by looking at the unfortunate tendency of the digital era to strip out context. An essential problem with the digitisation of things is that context has a tendency to go awol and subtleties of meaning and connection are lost. I'll give examples of this and explore why it happens, if it is important and what could be done about it. Context gives meaning, reward, focus, helps us make decisions. In the age of 10,000 songs in your pocket, why are sales of old-fashioned records booming? Yet we run the risk of believing that data is everything, and confusing information with knowledge.

We then look at how our sense of time and space may be changing radically, and not for the first time in human history. Digital space is upon us but what will it look like?

The importance of this question now becomes apparent when we consider that the widespread adoption of mobile technology over the last five years is a social tipping point of no return: for we are becoming 'always on'. Not only connected to the network, but distributing ourselves through it. Mobile opens up radical new communications possibilities still barely tapped. Expect before too long to see graffiti sprayed in thin air, messages you view through a phone, like invisible sticky Post-its in all kinds of unexpected places.

The risk is that this is all just used as a distraction. Is it possible for individual humans to deal elegantly with the abundant communication possibilities of the modern world? There is a plenty of evidence that we are in real danger of paying more attention to the potential of a text message than the here and now around us. Looking at our emerging behaviour as we seek to find ways to incorporate email and mobile into our lives, it is clear that the boundaries between private and public space are breaking down. Perhaps it is not so much the famous 'death of distance' that we are witnessing, but the fatal wounding of closeness.

At this stage it is worth asking a question – can media have a distracting effect? Is their influence overrated? We look at dramatic evidence from the most powerful country in the world, and one of the smallest, that television alone has changed societies, and not always for the better. Now we are adding many more channels of all kinds to our lives.

In fact, communication may just be reaching the stage where we cannot deal with the volume, and some kind of radical response will be required at all levels of society simply to cope. Spam is an early warning signal: surprisingly it appears that organisations are having just as many problems with sustainable communication as private citizens. We are also destabilised by some of the uses we put the technology to: current social norms may not be able deal with the explosion of dating, flirting and sex made so easily available.

These are good examples of how we use new communications possibilities to feed the culture of immediacy that pervades Western life. We want gratification now. However, at this point the revenge effect steps in with a vengeance: in feeding the short-term pleasure principle, new technology often ends up making life more complicated. Lack of time is the most frequent complaint of harassed adults in the early 21st century, but we are working no more hours per week than previous generations. So where has all the time gone? We look at how a simple act like buying and using a digital camera can eat up time unexpectedly in consumption work.

So what can we do to make the best of new technology? Firstly I argue that it is time to push the new media and make them work better for us: I suggest guidelines and challenges for improving the quality of what we use and consume. These include a call for greater storytelling and beauty in these often very functional environments. We have to drag context back to the surface from where it is too often hidden in the depths, and explore how we can invigorate digital conversation with body language.

Next we examine how our sense of self, maybe the most precious thing we have, is changing and how technology can both threaten this and be used to build it up. What can we learn from a virtual hotel run by teenagers? Digital gives us an opportunity to map out and fashion new expressions of identity. New kinds of trust will be required and, at the same time, privacy may become a thing of the past but we will be prepared to trade it for security.

Digital connects us together more than ever before. We have only just started to explore the ramifications of this. New thinking in science, partly catalysed by questions of how the internet works, shows that networks underpin much of the way the universe works. We can and should embrace the wonderful ability of communications to build and reinforce new social networks and structures in order to reach towards a more interdependent world.

At the same time we look at how we need to change many of our habits, and take control not of the technology (not usually the problem), but of ourselves. Only by doing so can we hope to fight off distraction and build long-lasting value in society. Indeed we could do with a new determination to construct for the future, to think long-term.

Perhaps we can do this first at a personal level; for the final hopeful sign of digital technology is that it is enabling normal people to find new levels of creativity for themselves. We are all going to become media owners, in the process reducing our reliance on traditional content suppliers and evolving more multi-faceted identities. We will also leave a clearer sense of the complex beings we are for our children's children. If we can use new technology to be creative and celebrate us, we can leave a vibrant legacy for the future.

You can buy the book Distraction at www.futuretext.com

Printed in the United States
54914LVS00001B/2